National Contract Management Association
21740 Beaumeade Circle, Suite 125
Ashburn, Virginia 20147
www.ncmahq.org
(800) 344-8096

ISBN 978-0-9828385-2-5

Certified Professional Contracts Manager
Study Guide
SECOND EDITION

National Contract Management Association

Margaret G. Rumbaugh, CPCM, Fellow
John W. Wilkinson, EdD, CPCM, Fellow

Contents

Preface

Certification is a mark of distinction and serves to reflect professionalism attained through experience, education, training, and knowledge. A Certified Professional Contracts Manager (CPCM) certification demonstrates that you are knowledgeable about all facets of contracts management, both within the government and the commercial arenas. The CPCM implies a level of deep and broad contracting expertise.

Certification is a reflection of your professional strength. The NCMA Salary Surveys have consistently shown that those with the CPCM earn substantially more per year than those with no certification. However, those with a CPCM and higher salary realize professionalism does not rest solely on certification. Employers want people who can make quick and accurate decisions, and who can solve problems with less than perfect information. The professional contracts manager must be proficient at solving complex problems and providing sound business advice. In addition, they must know how to influence multi-functional teams to achieve organizational goals (whether in charge of the team or not), and must be able to establish long-term partnerships with those inside and outside the organization. Whether you are a buyer or seller, you are expected to perform at a high standard—and certification can serve as evidence of your professional progression. Certification is not the culmination of professional development—it is the beginning.

The CPCM Study Guide is designed to serve as a foundation for CPCM candidates to use in preparation for the examination. Though it's not intended to be a sole-source resource manual, it should provide the candidate with a strong roadmap toward achieving the CPCM certification.

The guide is divided into the same five foundational competencies as the Contract Management Body of Knowledge (CMBOK):

1. Pre-Award
2. Acquisition Planning and Strategy
3. Post-Award
4. Specialized Knowledge Areas
5. Business

For study purposes, all of these foundational competencies are explored in multiple ways in this study guide. First, a narrative section describes each foundational competency and its subject matter competencies. Second, each subject matter competency is presented with its own lexicon. Third, following the narrative sections and lexicons is a 10-question quiz to test your knowledge of the foundational competency. The questions are in the same multiple-choice format you will expect to see on the CPCM examination. Fourth, the next section provides the correct answers to the questions and explanations for the incorrect responses. Finally, a list of recommended readings is provided to further develop your knowledge and comprehension of the competencies described in the associated section. All of these recommended readings are from *Contract Management* magazine and the *Journal of Contract Management*, and they can all be found on the NCMA website.

To assist you in rapidly finding terms and phrases, a comprehensive index is provided. This will also be beneficial in locating terms and phrases common to multiple competencies.

A mastery of these foundational contract management competencies should provide a strong knowledge base and help the candidate to be very well prepared for the examination, and ultimately, earn NCMA's Certified Professional Contracts Manager designation.

NCMA Certifications

NCMA awards the following certifications:

- **Certified Federal Contracts Manager (CFCM):**
  A CFCM certification validates your education, training, experience, and your knowledge of the *Federal Acquisition Regulation*.

- **Certified Commercial Contracts Manager (CCCM):**
  A CCCM certification validates your education, training, experience, and your knowledge of the Uniform Commercial Code.

- **Certified Professional Contracts Manager (CPCM):**
  A CPCM certification demonstrates that you have met NCMA's highest standards for education, training, and experience, and have demonstrated your knowledge of the contract management competencies in the Contract Management Body of Knowledge (CMBOK).

The CPCM, CFCM, and CCCM are certifications awarded to candidates who meet rigorous standards, including experience, education, training, and knowledge. NCMA certifications are competency-based, legally defensible, and are based on psychometrically sound, objective examination of knowledge. The NCMA professional certification program is designed to elevate professional standards, enhance individual performance, and distinguish those who demonstrate knowledge essential to the practice of contract management.

Preparing for the CPCM Examination

The CPCM examination is based on the third edition of the CMBOK (published July 2011) and contains scenario questions in addition to the standard multiple-choice questions. The scenario questions will be presented with a scenario based upon actual events (i.e., GAO decisions) with 3–5 applicable multiple-choice questions to test your contract management knowledge.

The multiple-choice questions on the CPCM examination are psychometrically sound. This means that every test question has undergone the full rigor of educational and statistical testing necessary to ensure that it elicits the exact response desired, that it is unambiguous, and that it has only one correct answer. However, three other plausible responses will separate those who know and understand the material from those who do not. Furthermore, multiple-choice testing can test more than simple recall of facts and recognition of words. It can test for understanding of content and for responses indicating the ability to apply principles to a situation.

The benefits of multiple-choice examination lie in the objective assessment of question answers. There is no scope for alternative interpretation of results. That is not to say that every question is perfect. Rather, the multiple-choice format has the flexibility that allows NCMA, working in conjunction with psychometricians, or test developers, to change the examination and make every question fair, valid, and reliable.

The number of items or questions devoted to a task or topic is determined by the relative importance of a task or topic. The exam is also subject to change over time, and the current focus of the market may also influence the number or questions or their specific focus.

Multiple-choice questions allow for a wider sampling of the body of knowledge. On one hand, this means candidates are bound to find areas with which they are familiar. On the other hand, it means candidates may be unsure exactly where to concentrate their study. However, candidates should feel confident that the examination will ask only those questions that determine whether a contract manager has the knowledge to be a good practitioner. NCMA will not be testing on extraneous or trivial matter.

The Anatomy of a Multiple-Choice Question

A multiple-choice question has its own terminology. The question itself is called the *stem*. The stem should contain all the information needed to provide the correct answer. The stem should be phrased in clear, unambiguous language that will leave no doubt as to what is being asked. A knowledgeable candidate should be able to discern the correct answer upon reading only the stem. The answers also have specific terminology. The correct answer is the *key* and the other possible answers are the *distracters*. The *key* is the only correct answer; the distracters are plausible answers only to those who don't know the correct answer.

How to Study

Given that the examination samples a wide slice of the body of knowledge, how should a candidate prepare? First of all, candidates should relax—examinations do not include "everything but the kitchen sink." Rather, the examinations will reflect the sum of the eligibility requirements and current contract management practice.

Self-assessment is the first step to a study program. Does the candidate work better alone or in a group? Are there areas of the CMBOK about which the candidate has little or no knowledge? Are there areas the candidate is confident enough to teach others? In a review program, the areas where the candidate is confident would be areas of less intense study.

Even working alone, it is good to have a study plan. For example, candidates might plan to study one hour on a weekend for the next eight weeks, or three hours per weekday for the next six weeks. Even as little as half an hour of study can help candidates gain knowledge and increase comprehension. It is not recommended that candidates sit for the exam without preparation.

An alternative study method would be to join a group—for example, a group of office colleagues or a study group at the chapter level. NCMA chapters have provided study groups for hundreds of examination candidates. Study groups successfully allow for multiple points of view, as well as for sharing information and resources. Furthermore, chapter study group sessions are often led by experts in the field. In terms of time spent, expert information beats informal research almost any day. Candidates should contact their local chapters for study group information. Visit the NCMA website for chapter contact information.

How to Approach the Examinations

For the mental side of examinations, here are a few good test-taking techniques:

1. Relax. The examination is based on your profession.

2. Read the questions carefully, focusing first on those you can easily and quickly answer. It is usually a good idea to go with your first impression when answering a question; second-guessing can cause you to change a correct answer to an incorrect one.

3. Skip over or flag questions that appear too difficult and return to them later.

4. Don't stop. Keep going. Keep reading questions until you find one you can answer. The questions you've read will be in the back of your mind; when you return to them, you'll have a fresh perspective.

5. Avoid overanalyzing and second-guessing the question. Choose the correct answer for the question as it is written. Do not make assumptions about what the question means. Don't regard questions as being "trick questions" or concentrate on the exceptions to normal practice.

6. Keep an eye on the clock. Judge the time you have so you don't spend a lot of time puzzling over one question to the detriment of being able to answer several others. Flag questions you are having trouble with and move on (see numbers 3 and 4).

7. Don't try to "game" the system by choosing answers to ensure that an equal number of As, Bs, Cs, and so on are selected. In the long run (over a lifetime), this may be a good technique, but in the short run (for one examination), the statistical underpinning for this method has not been proven.

8. Try to answer the question in your mind before you read the choices. Good test questions are constructed to allow the knowledgeable examination candidate to do this.

9. If you can't readily identify the correct answer, make an educated guess. Eliminate the choices you know to be false and select from those remaining. There is no penalty for wrong answers.

10. Look over your answers, if time permits. However, avoid trying to second-guess your answers (see number 5).

11. Don't worry about the examination. You may feel wrung out and exhausted at the end of the exam, but that is not an indication of how well or how poorly you may have performed (see number 1).

About the National Contract Management Association

NCMA was formed in 1959 to foster the professional growth and educational advancement of its members. NCMA is a membership-based professional society whose leadership is composed of volunteer officers.

NCMA is devoted to education and training, to research and study, and to a certification program that reflects the highest standards of professional achievement. Guided by a code of ethics, the association is committed to developing and providing programs, products, and services that nurture and enhance contract management competencies through leadership and business management partnering.

Thousands of professionals enhance their knowledge and leverage opportunities in purchasing, procurement, project management, and contract management with NCMA. Comprising individual members and professional groups from the nonprofit world, industry, and government, NCMA provides unique resources for the contracting community.

For more than 50 years, members have taken advantage of NCMA membership benefits to advance their careers. Practical, proven survival techniques and industry news help members stay informed about current contract management events. NCMA continues to provide vital information about the career field through the association's prestigious publications, educational materials, and professional resources.

NCMA is located at 21740 Beaumeade Circle, Suite 125, Ashburn, Virginia 20147. The NCMA office is open between the hours of 8:30am and 5:00pm ET, Monday through Friday. Please visit our website at www.ncmahq.org.

The NCMA Vision, Mission, and Values

I. Our Vision

NCMA will lead and represent the contract management profession. Our vision is that enterprises will succeed through improved buyer–seller relationships based on common values, practices, and professional standards.

II. Our Mission

NCMA's mission is to improve organizational performance through effective contract management.

III. Our Value Propositions

- NCMA provides the tools, resources, and leadership opportunities to enhance each member of the profession's performance, career, and accomplishments.

- NCMA provides structure, name recognition, and products directly and through chapters to contracting professionals worldwide.

- NCMA provides employers ready access to skilled human capital, learning resources, best practices, standards, and metrics of the profession.

- NCMA enables other entities such as researchers, consultants, trainers, recruiters, advertisers, and universities to gain broad access to defined segments of our community of practice and our Body of Knowledge for the purpose of advancing the profession and fulfilling their individual goals.

IV. Our Values

We are committed to

- Principled professional conduct and achievement, as dictated by the Contract Management Code of Ethics;

- An open exchange of ideas in a neutral forum;

- A culturally and professionally diverse membership;

- Excellence in everything we do, especially in our service to our members and the contract management community;

- Continuing education, training, and leadership opportunities through a network of local chapters;

- Remaining the preeminent source of professional development for contract professionals;

- Recognizing and rewarding professional excellence and superior individual achievement in support of the contract management profession;

- Demonstrated professional achievement through certification;

- Quality volunteer leadership; and

- Members' highly principled freedom of action and responsibility to the people and organizations they serve.

Contract Management Code of Ethics

Each member of the contract management profession ("the profession") accepts the obligation to continuously improve one's professional knowledge and job performance in the field of contract management, and to abide by the letter and spirit of the ethical standards set forth below.

Each member of NCMA shall:

1. Strive to attain the highest professional standard of job performance, to exercise diligence in carrying out one's professional duties, and to serve the profession to the best of one's ability.

2. Conduct oneself in such a manner as to bring credit upon the profession, as well as to maintain trust and confidence in the integrity of the contract management process.

3. Avoid engagement in any transaction that might conflict or appear to conflict with the proper discharge of one's professional duties by reason of a financial interest, family relationship, or any other circumstances.

4. Comply with all laws and regulations that govern the contract management process in the jurisdictions in which one conducts business, including protection of competition-sensitive and proprietary information from inappropriate disclosure.

5. Keep informed of developments in the contract management field, utilizing both formal training and ad hoc means, to continuously increase knowledge, skill, and professional competence.

6. Share one's knowledge and experience openly to contribute to the development of other professionals, improve performance quality, and enhance public perception of the profession.

7. Not knowingly influence others to commit any act that would constitute a violation of this code.

Competency

1.0:

Pre-Award

Pre-award activities include actions intended to state the buyer's needs, identify potential sources, and determine the techniques to be used to satisfy those needs. A well-planned procurement will be structured to comply with the numerous acquisition laws and regulations as well as to obtain, most effectively, the goods or services needed by the buyer.

1.1 Laws and Regulations

At its core, the contracting profession is about the knowledge and application of laws and regulations. Contracts are legal documents of agreement whose terms and conditions are legally binding and enforceable in various courts of law and other administrative bodies. These sources of law and guidance include:

- The Uniform Commercial Code (UCC),

- The *Federal Acquisition Regulation* (*FAR*),

- Laws related to international contracting, and

- Case law.

Commercial Contract Law: The states, not the federal government, are the primary source of law on commercial transactions in the United States; this includes state statutory and common (judge-made) law and private law. Private law principally includes the terms of the agreement between the parties who have exchanged promises for consideration. Statutory law may require some contracts be put in writing and executed using specific procedures.

Government Contract Law: The origin of the government's authority to enter into a contract comes from the *U.S. Constitution* and is subject to various statutes and regulations. Although the *U.S. Constitution* does not specifically refer to government contracts, the government has the implied

1

power to use contracts to fulfill its responsibilities. The government contracting process involves all three branches of the United States Government: legislative, executive, and judicial. Congress, as the legislative branch, enacts laws that impact the contracting process and provides funding. The agencies, as part of the executive branch, draft regulations implementing the laws, solicit offers, and award and administer contracts. The federal courts, representing the judicial branch, interpret legislation and sometimes resolve disputes. These three branches thus work together to preserve the system of checks and balances necessary for the U.S. government. Each has an integral function in the procurement process.

Laws Related to International Contracting: When contracting beyond the geographic limits of the United States, whether with foreign governments or foreign corporations, contracting professionals must be careful to ensure a complete understanding of the legal, regulatory, political, and social consequences of their actions. Some of the more significant issues regarding international contracting include (see lexicon for each):

- Anti-boycott regulations,

- Export regulations,

- The Foreign Corrupt Practices Act (FCPA),

- Foreign laws and customs, and

- *International Traffic in Arms Regulations (ITAR)*.

LEXICON FOR LAWS AND REGULATIONS:

Acceptance: The act of an authorized buyer, by which the buyer assents to ownership of existing and identified supplies, or approves specific services rendered, as partial or complete performance of a contract. It must be communicated and (in common law) must be the mirror image of the offer.

Agency: A relationship whereby the principal authorizes another (the agent) to act for and on behalf of the principal and to bind the principal in contract.

Anti-Boycott Regulations: The U.S. Department of Commerce and the U.S. Department of Treasury both enforce regulatory requirements to prevent U.S. companies from entering into foreign transactions that could be construed as supporting a foreign boycott against a country that is friendly to the United States. Violations can result in fines, imprisonment and loss of their privilege to export.

As is: A contract phrase referring to the condition of property to be sold or leased, and generally pertains to a disclaimer of liability.

Bilateral and unilateral contracts: A bilateral contract is one in which both parties make promises. A unilateral contract is one in which only one party (promissory) makes a promise.

Breach of contract: The failure, without legal excuse, to perform any promise that forms the whole or part of a contract.

Common law: A body of law common to the whole population, produced primarily by the efforts of the judiciary to harmonize their decisions with precedent decisions and changes in law or regulation.

Compensable delay: A delay for which the buyer is contractually responsible that excuses the seller's failure to perform and is compensable.

Condition precedent: A condition that activates a term in a contract.

Condition subsequent: A condition that suspends a term in a contract.

Contract: A contract is an agreement between two or more parties, especially one that is written and enforceable by law. For a contract to be valid, both parties must indicate that they agree to the terms. This is accomplished when one party submits an offer that the other accepts within a reasonable time or a stipulated period. If the terms of the acceptance vary from those of the offer, that acceptance legally constitutes a counteroffer; the original offering party may then accept it or reject it. At any time prior to acceptance, the offer may be rescinded on notice unless the offering party is bound by a separate option contract not to withdraw. Only those terms expressed in the contract can be enforced; secret intentions are not recognized. For a contract to be binding, it must not have an immoral or criminal purpose or intent or be contrary to public policy. Since a contract is an agreement, it may be made only by parties with the capacity to reach an understanding.

A legally binding contract must contain the following elements:

- Must involve two or more parties that have the capacity to contract;

- Must show agreement, including offer, acceptance, and mutual assent;

- Must show something of value changing hands between the parties to a contract, or other inducement that leads a person to make a promise;

- Must be for a legal purpose; and

- Must be in the correct form.

A contract is executed when all the parties have fully performed their contractual duties. (It can also refer to both parties signing (executing) the contract document before performance.)

Commercial contracting refers to a contract between two or more commercial (non-governmental) entities. Government contracting refers to a contract between two or more entities, at least one being a government entity.

Contract formation: The elements of offer, acceptance, mutuality of consideration, competent parties, legal subject matter, and mutuality agreement.

Discharge of a contract: Results when the obligations incurred by the parties when they entered the agreement are excused, and the parties are no longer bound to perform as promised.

Export regulations: The Bureau of Export Administration (BXA), a federal bureau in the Department of Commerce, is charged with enforcing the *Export Administration Regulation* (*EAR*). The *EAR* governs the export of commercial goods and data, and the BXA controls such exports by issuing general and specific export licenses. Violations of these regulations can result in civil and criminal penalties for the entire organization, and loss of the organization's exporting privileges in the future. It can also result in debarment from government contracting. It is important to be aware of the applicable EAR requirements when entering into a contract.

Express contract: An express contract is one in which the terms of the contract are stated in words, either written or spoken.

Federal Acquisition Regulation (*FAR*): The *FAR* is the principal source of contracting guidance within the federal government and has been in place since April 1, 1984. The *FAR* is prepared, issued, and maintained jointly by the Secretary of Defense and the administrators of the General Services Administration (GSA) and the National Aeronautics and Space Administration (NASA) via two councils, who must agree to all revisions proposed by either council. The *Defense Acquisition Regulations* Council chair is appointed by the Secretary of Defense. Remaining council membership includes representatives from the military departments, the Defense Logistics Agency, and the National Aeronautics and Space Administration.

The Civilian Agency Acquisition Council chair is appointed by the Administrator of General Services. Remaining council membership includes representatives from the Departments of Agriculture, Commerce, Energy, Health and Human Services, Homeland Security, Interior, Labor, State, Transportation, and Treasury; and from the Environmental Protection Agency, Social Security Administration, Small Business Administration, and the Department of Veterans Affairs.

The *FAR* is printed, published, and distributed by the *FAR* Secretariat, which is controlled by the General Services Administration.

Federal Acquisition Regulation system: Consists of the *FAR* and various agency acquisition regulations that supplement the *FAR*.

Federal regulations: Applicable directives and instructions issued by the several departments and agencies that establish and implement acquisition policies. Examples include the *FAR*, agency *FAR* supplements, and Office of Management and Budget (OMB) circulars.

Federal statutes: Applicable laws enacted by the legislative branch and signed by the president that affect acquisition. Examples include the Armed Services Procurement Act (1947), the Federal Property and Administrative Services Act (1949), the Competition in Contracting Act (1984), and the Federal Acquisition Streamlining Act (1994).

Forbearance: An intentional failure of a party to enforce a contract requirement, usually done for an act of immediate or future consideration from the other party. It is sometimes referred to as a nonwaiver or one-time waiver, but not as a relinquishment of rights.

Foreign Corrupt Practices Act (FCPA): The FCPA is primarily concerned with the issues of bribery and other corrupt payments, as well as record-keeping and accounting provisions to facilitate the review or audit of international transactions. The FCPA prohibits the payment or promise of payment of money or other items of value to foreign officials to influence or attempt to influence obtaining business, retaining business, or directing business to anyone. The record-keeping and accounting provisions require that reasonable record systems and accounting controls be present to ensure that all transactions and the disposition of assets are reflected. These requirements apply to domestic as well as foreign operations.

Foreign laws and customs: In addition to ensuring compliance with applicable U.S. laws and regulations, U.S. firms pursuing or contemplating international contracting need to become knowledgeable regarding the myriad foreign laws, regulations, customs, and practices that may impact their ability or desire to conduct business in foreign countries. Particular care is required when dealing with or in foreign countries whose legal, political, business, and social systems are vastly different from our own.

Implied contract: An implied contract (sometimes called "implied in fact") is one in which the terms of the contract are wholly or partly inferred from conduct or surrounding circumstance.

International Traffic in Arms Regulations (ITAR): The State Department's Office of Defense Trade Controls (DTC) controls all exports of defense articles, related technical data, and services by issuing licenses and approvals. The U.S. Munitions List, located in Part 121 of the *ITAR*, details the items subject to DTC control. The *ITAR* also provides instructions on the procedures and types of licenses required. Violations of the *ITAR* can result in substantial civil fines; willful violations can result in criminal penalties including up to 10 years of imprisonment and fines up to $1 million. U.S. exporters need to be aware of the *ITAR* status before entering into a contract.

Novation agreement: A legal instrument executed by the seller (transferor), the successor in interest (transferee), and the buyer, by which the transferor guarantees performance of the contract, the transferee guarantees performance of the contract, and the buyer recognizes the transfer of the contract and related assets.

Offer: A legally binding promise, made by one party to another, to enter into a contractual agreement.

Quasi contract: Quasi contracts (sometimes called "implied in law") are obligations imposed by law to prevent the unjust enrichment of one person at another's expense.

Sarbanes-Oxley Act (SOX): SOX was signed into law on July 30, 2002. The substance of the law is to create requirements to prevent companies from accounting for profits not realized in an effort to portray value where none exists. SOX has had a significant impact on the accounting practices of nearly all public companies doing business in the United States. Indirectly, SOX has had a significant impact on the contract management functions as well. A sales contract is typically the primary record underlying a revenue transaction. Before SOX, many companies (even very large companies) did not have standard practices for contract creation or management. Under SOX, firms could no longer be *laissez faire* in how they created, recorded, and managed contracts. Since SOX was passed into law, a mini-industry for creation and implementation of contract management software systems has boomed. Many firms have devoted more attention to the contract management function than ever before in order to ensure SOX compliance.

SOX has had a disproportionate impact on commercial companies versus those that do business principally with the U.S. federal government. This is because companies who did substantial business with the federal government were already required to maintain a higher standard of contract management and cost accounting systems in order to comply with the *FAR* and associated laws and regulations.

Trade: Law in the United States, including the Robinson-Patman Act, unfair-trade laws, fair-trade laws, and other legal and regulatory restrictions on the conduct of business, especially with respect to pricing.

Uniform Commercial Code: Uniform law governing commercial transactions, developed by the National Conference of Commissioners on Uniform State Laws and the American Law Institute, which has been adopted by all states in the United States except Louisiana and is sometimes used to aid in the interpretation and enforcement of government subcontracts.

In regard to contracts, the UCC has several underlying concepts: (1) Merchants are professionals in their field and should be held to higher standards than a casual buyer; (2) Every contract imposes an obligation of good faith in its performance or enforcement; and (3) A reasonable time for taking any action depends on the nature, purpose, and circumstances of such action.

Contract principles are fundamentals of acquisition that all contracting professionals must comprehend. These fundamentals often are a part of a larger contract framework.

Contract: An agreement between two or more parties to perform or to refrain from some act now or in the future. A legally enforceable agreement. (See section 1.1 for an expanded definition of a contract.)

Unilateral and bilateral contracts: Every contract involves at least two parties— the offeror/promisor, who makes the offer/promise to perform; and the offeree/promisee, to whom the offer/promise is made. *Unilateral contract*: A unilateral contract arises when an offer can be accepted only by the offeree's performance (e.g., X offers Y $15 to mow X's yard). *Bilateral contract*: A bilateral contract arises when a promise is given in exchange for a promise in return (e.g., X promises to deliver a car to Y, and Y promises to pay X an agreed price).

Express contract: A contract in which the terms of the agreement are fully and explicitly stated orally or in writing.

Implied-in-fact contract: A contract formed in whole or in part by the conduct (as opposed to the words) of the parties. In order to establish an implied-in-fact contract,

The seller must have furnished some service or property to the buyer,

The seller must have reasonably expected to be paid and the buyer knew or should have known that a reasonable person in the seller's shoes would have expected to be paid for the service or property rendered by the seller, and

The buyer must have had the opportunity to reject the services or property and failed to do so.

Quasi or implied-in-law contract: A fictional contract imposed on parties by a court in the interests of fairness and justice, typically to prevent the unjust enrichment of one party at the expense of the other.

Formal and Informal Contracts:

Formal contract: A contract that requires a special form or method of formation (creation) in order to be enforceable.

- **Contract under seal**: A formalized writing with a special seal attached.

- **Recognizance**: An acknowledgment in court by a person that he or she will perform some specified obligation or pay a certain sum if he or she fails to perform (e.g., personal recognizance bond).

- **Negotiable instrument**: A check, note, draft, or certificate of deposit—each of which requires certain formalities.

- **Letter of credit**: An agreement to pay that is contingent upon the receipt of documents (e.g., invoices and bills of lading) evidencing receipt of and title to goods shipped.

Informal contract: A contract that does not require a specified form or method of formation in order to be valid.

Execution and Validity of Contracts:

Executed contract: A contract that has been signed by both parties; can also be a contract that has been completely performed by both (or all) parties. By contrast, an **executory contract** is a contract that has not yet been fully performed by one or more parties.

Valid contract: A contract satisfying all of the requisites discussed earlier—agreement, consideration, capacity, legal purpose, assent, and form. By contrast,

- A **void contract** is a contract having no legal force or binding effect (e.g., a contract entered into for an illegal purpose);

- A **voidable contract** is an otherwise valid contract that may be legally avoided, cancelled, or annulled at the option of one of the parties (e.g., a contract entered into under duress or under false pretenses); and,

- An **unenforceable contract** is an otherwise valid contract rendered unenforceable by some statute or law (e.g., an oral contract that, due to the passage of time, must be in writing to be enforceable).

Contract Interpretation:

The key to contract interpretation is to give effect to the intent of the parties as expressed in their agreement.

Intent is generally to be ascertained objectively, by looking at

- The words used by the parties in the agreement,

- The actions of the parties pursuant to the agreement, and

- The circumstances surrounding the agreement

as they would be interpreted by a reasonable person, rather than the parties' *subjective* intentions (usually expressed after the fact).

The Plain Meaning Rule: When a contract is clear and unequivocal, a court will enforce it according to its plain terms, set forth on the face of the instrument, and there is no need for the court either to consider extrinsic evidence or to interpret the language of the contract.

Rules of Interpretation: When a contract contains ambiguous or unclear terms, a court will resort to one or more of the following rules in order to determine and give effect to the parties' intent.

- Insofar as possible, the contract's terms will be given a reasonable, lawful, and effective meaning.

- The contract will be interpreted as a whole and its various provisions will be "harmonized" to yield consistent expression of intent.

- Negotiated terms will be given greater consideration than standard-form, or "boilerplate," terms.

- A non-technical term will be given its ordinary, commonly accepted meaning, and a technical term will be given its technical meaning, unless the parties clearly intended something else.

- Specific terms will prevail over general terms.

- Handwritten terms prevail over typewritten terms, which in turn prevail over printed terms.

- When the language used in a contract has more than one meaning, any ambiguity is construed against the drafting party.

- An ambiguous contract should be interpreted in light of pertinent usages of trade in the locale and/or industry, the course of prior dealing between the parties, and the parties' course of prior performance of the contract.

- Express terms are given preference over course of prior performance, which is given preference over course of dealing, which is given preference over usage of trade.

- Words are given preference over numbers or symbols.

Transactions: The major categories of transactions using contractual agreements are:

- Procurement of goods and services;

- Purchase of real property;

- Sale of real or personal property;

- Grants, cooperative agreements, cooperative research and development agreements, and "other agreements"; and

- Employment of personnel.

Ordinarily, each of these transactions can be readily distinguished from the others. However, there can be a significant overlap between procurement transactions and other types of contractual arrangements.

Procurement: Also known as "acquisition," involves contracting for goods and services. The major categories of procurement are:

- **Supplies**: All property except land or interest in land. It includes (but is not limited to) public works, buildings, and facilities; ships, floating equipment, and vessels of every type, character, and description, together with parts and accessories; aircrafts and aircraft parts, accessories, and equipment; machine tools; and the alteration or installation of any of the foregoing.

- **Construction**: Construction, alteration, or repair (including dredging, excavating, and painting) of buildings, structures, or other real property. Construction does not include the manufacture, production, furnishing, construction, alteration, repair, processing, or assembling of vessels, aircraft, or other kinds of personal property.

- **Service contract**: A contract that directly engages the time and efforts of a contractor whose primary purpose is to perform an identifiable task rather than to furnish an end item of supply. A service contract may be either a personal or nonpersonal contract. It can also cover services performed by either professional or nonprofessional personnel whether on an individual or organizational basis. Some of the areas in which service contracts are found include the following:

  - Maintenance, overhaul, repair, servicing, rehabilitation, salvage, modernization, or modification of supplies, systems, or equipment;

  - Routine recurring maintenance of real property;

  - Housekeeping and base services;

  - Advisory and assistance services;

  - Operation of government-owned equipment, facilities, and systems;

  - Communications services;

  - Architect-Engineering;

  - Transportation and related services; and

  - Research and development.

- **Research and development**: The primary purpose of contracted R&D programs is to advance scientific and technical knowledge to the extent necessary to achieve agency and national goals. Unlike contracts for supplies and services, most R&D contracts are directed toward objectives for which the work or methods cannot be precisely described in advance. It is difficult to judge the probabilities of success or required effort for technical approaches, some of which offer little or no early assurance of full success. The contracting process is used to encourage the best sources from the scientific and industrial community to become involved in the program and must provide an environment in which the work can be pursued with reasonable flexibility and minimum administrative burden.

- **Rental of real property**: General authority for leasing real property for the federal government is vested in the General services Administration (GSA). The GSA has in turn delegated authority for leasing certain types of property and location to other agencies.

Other contractual arrangements: There are numerous other types of contractual relationships the federal government engages in.

- **Purchase of real property**: The purchase of real property is not covered by procurement statutes. Per 41 U.S.C. § 14, "[n]o land shall be purchased on account of the United States, except under a law authorizing such purchase."

- **Sale of property**: Article IV, Section 3, Clause 2 of the *U.S. Constitution* gives Congress the exclusive authority to dispose of federal government property. This authority is granted to the GSA administrator, who may delegate this authority to other agencies.

- **Grants and cooperative agreements**: These are used when the federal government intends to provide assistance or support to private organizations or to state and local governments. A grant without contractual obligations on the part of the recipient may be characterized as a gift. Most grants require the recipient to use the funds or property only for specified purposes. Such grants are contractual agreements but are not procurement contracts.

- **Employment contracts**: The employment of individuals by the federal government is accomplished pursuant to civil service laws. However, services may be acquired under a procurement contract, either from an individual or an organization, as long as an employer–employee relationship is not established between the government and the person performing the services.

Standards of conduct refers to the ethical conduct of personnel involved in the purchase or sale of goods and services. It includes personal conduct and compliance with laws, regulations, and corporate standards. There are many federal, state, and local laws, regulations, and ordinances that provide the legal framework in which many activities, including the operation of government and business in general, as well as the contracting profession in particular, are conducted. In addition to the legal framework, there are other procedural or policy documents that exist to formalize basic concepts and guide employers and employees in the performance of their functions. These documents are commonly referred to as standards of conduct, codes of ethics, statements of professional responsibility, standards of ethical conduct, and similar terms. Regardless of the title used to identify them, these documents normally reflect all or some of the following characteristics:

- They are formal, written statements that act as a guide for how people in the organization should act in order to make ethical decisions.

- They can be issued by government agencies at various levels, individual business entities, business associations, professional organizations, and similar groups.

- They typically address issues related to:

  o Conflict of interest,

  o Behavior toward competitors and suppliers,

  o Privacy of information,

  o Gift giving and receiving,

  o Making and receiving political contributions,

  o Levels of dedication and work effort required,

  o Encouraged behavior, and

  o Discouraged or prohibited behavior.

Though standards of conduct can sometimes be codified as law when issued by a government agency, and can sometimes be issued by corporations as a requirement of the law, they are also sometimes issued as a matter of policy or preference or to promote an organization's values to the general public.

LEXICON FOR STANDARDS OF CONDUCT:

Apparent authority: The right of an agent for a principal to exercise power where the principal knowingly permits the agent to exercise authority, though not actually granted; differs from actual, implied, or expressed authority.

Conflict of interest: Term used in connection with public officials and fiduciaries and their relationships to matters of private interest or gain to them. Ethical problems connected therewith are covered by statutes in most jurisdictions and by federal statutes on the federal level. A conflict of interest arises when an employee's personal or financial interest conflicts or appears to conflict with his or her official responsibility.

Corporate responsibility and personal conduct: Laws and standards governing both corporate and individual behavior, including standards of ethics and conduct, social responsibility, law, regulation, and public policy.

Defective specifications: Mistakes and omissions in the requirements set forth are generally identified in this way. This area is frequently the basis for claims and litigation between contracting parties.

Delegation of authority: The conferring of authority, from one government agency or representative to another, to accomplish contract administrative tasks. Such authority may be shared or recalled.

Ethics: Of or relating to moral action, conduct, motive, or character, as ethical emotion; professionally right or benefitting; conforming to professional standards of conduct. Though ethical conduct can be viewed as both the means and the end, there is also a practical application and benefit associated with high ethical standards and conduct; ethics is good for business and government. Business flourishes in an environment of profitability and sustainability. Government functions best in an environment of efficiency, trust, and service to the governed. Ethics is a critical component to both business and government models.

Fraud: Fraud is more than unethical, it is illegal. An intentional perversion of truth for the purpose of inducing another in reliance upon it to part with something of value belonging to him or her or to surrender a legal right. A false representation of a matter of fact, whether by words or conduct, by false or misleading allegations, or by concealment of that which should have been disclosed, which deceives and is intended to deceive another so that he or she shall act upon it to his or her legal injury. Anything calculated to deceive. Includes offer and acceptance: conduct that communicates a promise on the part of one party and a manifestation to the terms of the offer by the other party. Conduct of both parties represents capacity to contract, good faith dealings (honesty in fact and reasonable standard of fair dealing), and legality of purpose. Includes apparent authority: the authority that, although not actually granted, the principal knowingly permits an agent to exercise or the principal holds the agent out as possessing.

Kickback: The process of the seller providing a portion of the purchase price to the buyer to induce purchase or to influence future purchases. A federal statute makes kickbacks a criminal offense in connection with a contract for construction or repair of a public building or a building financed by loans from the government.

1.4 Socioeconomic Programs

Socioeconomic programs are designed to benefit particular groups. They represent a multitude of program interests and objectives unrelated to procurement objectives. Some examples of these are preferences for small business and for American products, required sources for specific items, and minimum labor pay levels mandated for contractors.

LEXICON FOR SOCIOECONOMIC PROGRAMS:

Accessibility: The availability of public conveyances, facilities, utilities, technologies, and other designated resources to all persons.

In the United States, accessibility considerations are the purview of the Access Board, an independent federal agency devoted to accessibility for people with disabilities. The Access Board develops and maintains accessibility requirements for the built environment, transit vehicles, telecommunications equipment, and electronic and information technology; provides technical assistance and training on these guidelines and standards; and enforces accessibility standards for federally funded facilities.

Domestic end product: A type of product considered to be manufactured in the United States if the cost of components mined, produced, or manufactured exceeds 50 percent of the cost of all its components.

Employment: Legal requirements addressing Equal Employment Opportunity (EEO), discrimination, and others aspects of the employer–employee relationship.

Environmental issues: Policies and procedures supporting the government's program for protecting and improving the quality of the environment through pollution control, energy conservation, identification of hazardous material, and use of recovered materials.

Labor Surplus Area: A geographical area identified by the Department of Labor as an area of concentrated unemployment or underemployment, or an area of labor surplus.

Labor laws: These laws are frequently a matter of concern for contracting professionals, particularly as they relate to service contracts. As a matter of policy, the government seeks to maintain sound relations with both industry and labor and usually remains impartial concerning disputes between labor and contractor management. Some of the significant issues and policies related to the application of labor laws include:

- Restrictions on the use of convict labor;

- The requirement to pay at least the prevailing wage rate for construction contracts subject to the **Davis-Bacon Act**;

- The Anti-Kickback provisions of the **Copeland Act**, which make it illegal to require, induce, intimidate, or otherwise force employees on construction contracts to give up any part of their compensation;

- The requirement to pay overtime for work in excess of 40 hours per week as governed by the **Contract Work Hours and Safety Standards Act**;

- The provisions of the **Walsh-Healy Public Contracts Act**, which require various stipulations regarding minimum wages, maximum hours, child labor, convict labor, and safe and sanitary working conditions for certain types of supply contracts;

- The provisions of the **Service Contract Act of 1965** regarding minimum wages and fringe benefits, safe and sanitary working conditions, and notification to employees of the minimum allowable compensation for contracts covered by the act; and

- Various laws, executive orders, and policies that deal with equal employment opportunity, age discrimination, veteran's preference, providing employment opportunities for the disabled, and other related matters.

Privacy and Freedom of Information: The Privacy Act of 1974 and the Freedom of Information Act have implications that sometimes affect government contracts. When a contract requires a contractor to design, develop, or operate a system of records on individuals, the contracting agency is required to apply the requirements of the Privacy Act to the contractor and its employees. The Freedom of Information Act generally provides that information contained in government records be made available to the public. There are some exceptions to the general rule that apply to acquisitions. For example, proposals submitted in response to a competitive solicitation may not be released under the Freedom of Information Act. Also, there are exceptions that relate to classified information, trade secrets, confidential commercial or financial information, and other matters.

Small business: A small business is one that is independently owned and operated and is not dominant in its field; a business concern that meets government size standards for its particular industry type. Types of small businesses include:

- **Small business 8(a)**: A small business operating in conjunction with the SBA's Business Development (BD) Program, authorized by Section 8(a) of the Small Business Act. Fundamentally, the SBA acts as a prime contractor for other government agencies and issues subcontracts to 8(a) firms. The SBA sometimes delegates contract execution authority to the requiring agency. 8(a) contracts may be awarded competitively or noncompetitively.

- **Small disadvantaged business**: A small business that is owned (at least 51 percent) by members of socially and economically disadvantaged groups (i.e., groups that have been subjected to racial or ethnic prejudice or cultural bias).

- **HUBZone small business**: A small business that operates in a Historically Underutilized Business (HUB) zone in an area located within one or more qualified census tracts, qualified nonmetropolitan counties, or lands within the external boundaries of an Indian reservation. The business must also appear on the List of Qualified HUBZone Small Business concerns maintained by the SBA.

- **Women-owned small business**: A small business that is at least 51 percent owned by a woman or multiple women, or in the case of a publicly owned business, at least 51 percent of the stock of which is owned by one woman or multiple women; and whose management and daily business operations are controlled by one woman or multiple women.

- **Veteran-owned small business**: A small business not less than 51 percent of which is owned by one veteran or multiple veterans, or in the case of publicly owned businesses, not less than 51 percent of the stock of which is owned by one veteran or multiple veterans; and the management and daily business operations of which are controlled by one veteran or multiple veterans.

- **Service-disabled veteran–owned small business**: A veteran-owned small business in which the 51 percent veteran criteria refers to veterans with a disability that is service-connected.

Small Business Administration (SBA): The SBA mission statement is, "The U.S. Small Business Administration (SBA) was created in 1953 as an independent agency of the federal government to aid, counsel, assist, and protect the interests of small business concerns; to preserve free competitive enterprise; and to maintain and strengthen the overall economy of our nation. We recognize that small business is critical to our economic recovery and strength, to building America's future, and to helping the United States compete in today's global marketplace. Although SBA has grown and evolved in the years since it was established in 1953, the bottom-line mission remains the same. The SBA helps Americans start, build and grow businesses. Through an extensive network of field offices and partnerships with public and private organizations, SBA delivers its services to people throughout the United States, Puerto Rico, the U.S. Virgin Islands, and Guam."

Small business set-aside: A small business set-aside reserves an acquisition exclusively for small businesses. A small business set-aside may be open to all small businesses. A small business set-aside may relate to a single acquisition or a class of acquisitions and may be total or partial. For federal government contracts, all acquisitions within a certain dollar range are automatically set aside for small business. Small business set-asides may be withdrawn by the contracting officer if award would be detrimental to the public interest (e.g., paying more than a fair market price).

Socioeconomic programs (other): Federal contracting professionals need to be aware of and comply with federal laws and policies that have some form of socioeconomic implication. Commercial contracting professionals whose organizations perform under federal contracts are also often bound by these laws and policies, which are normally included as terms and conditions in government contracts. Some of the significant socioeconomic programs include:

- **Indian Incentive Program**: Government policy states that Indian organizations and Indian-owned economic enterprises, including Alaskan Natives, shall have the maximum practicable opportunity to participate in performing contracts awarded by federal agencies. The policy also provides for incentive payments to Indian-owned economic enterprises that perform as subcontractors.

- **Disaster or emergency assistance activities**: When contracting for disaster or emergency assistance services following a major disaster or emergency, the government provides a preference to organizations, firms, or individuals residing or doing business in the area affected by the disaster or emergency. Such services can include debris clearance, distribution of supplies, or reconstruction.

- **Historically black colleges and universities and minority institutions**: The government promotes the participation of historically black colleges and universities and minority institutions in federal procurement, in compliance with Executive Order 12928, particularly for the types of services normally acquired from higher educational institutions.

- **Diversity**: Programs designed to encourage a diverse workforce or education and training group, such as programs that prohibit employment or workplace discrimination based on race, color, religion, sex, national origin, age, or disability.

Workplace and environmental considerations: The government implements various workplace and environmental policies through the acquisition process. These policies include:

- **Drug-free workplace**: Contractors are sometimes required to agree to take specified steps, including establishing an on-going drug awareness program; providing published statements to its employees prohibiting the manufacture, distribution, dispensing, possession, or use of controlled substances; and taking appropriate action against employees who violate the policies.

- **Energy conservation**: Some contracts contain clauses that help implement government policies to acquire goods and services that promote energy and water efficiency, advance the use of renewable energy products, and help foster markets for emerging technology.

- **Hazardous materials**: Sometimes contractors are required to provide information to the government regarding hazardous materials that may be introduced into the workplace as a result of performance on a government contract.

- **Recovered materials**: The government seeks to acquire products that meet performance requirements and are composed of the highest percentage of recovered materials practicable.

- **Ozone-depleting substances**: Government policy strives to minimize the procurement of materials and substances that contribute to the depletion of stratospheric ozone, and gives preference to the procurement of alternative products that reduce overall risk to human health and the environment.

1.5 Contract Structures

Contract structures are specific pricing arrangements employed for the performance of work under contract. They are specific business arrangements that govern the buyer–seller relationship. Also, they are types of promises or sets of promises that courts will enforce.

LEXICON FOR CONTRACT STRUCTURES:

Fixed price: A type (family) of contract providing for a firm pricing arrangement established by the parties at the time of contracting. This family of contracts includes firm fixed price, fixed price with economic price adjustment, fixed price incentive, fixed price redetermination (prospective and retroactive), firm fixed price level of effort, and fixed price award fee.

- **Firm-fixed-price contract**: Provides for a price that is not subject to any adjustment on the basis of the contractor's cost experience in performing the contract. This contract type places on the contractor maximum risk and full responsibility for all costs and resulting profit or loss. It provides maximum incentives for the contractor to control costs and perform effectively and imposes a minimum administrative burden on the contract parties.

- **Fixed-price contract with economic price adjustment**: Provides for upward and downward revision of the stated contract price on the occurrence of specified contingencies. There are three general types of economic price adjustments: (1) Adjustments based on established prices where price adjustments are based on increases or decreases from an agreed-upon level in published or otherwise established prices of specific items or the contract end items. (2) Adjustments based on actual costs of labor or material where price adjustments are based on increases or decreases in specified costs of labor or material that the contractor actually experiences during contract performance. (3) Adjustments based on cost indexes of labor or material where price adjustments are based on increases or decreases in labor or material costs standards or indexes that are specifically identified in the contract.

- **Fixed-price incentive contract**: Provides for adjusting profit and establishing the final contract price by a formula based on the relationship of final negotiated total cost to total target cost.

- **Fixed-price contract with prospective price redetermination**: Provides for (1) a firm fixed price for an initial period of contract deliveries or performance, and (2) prospective redetermination at a stated time (or times) during performance of the price for subsequent periods of performance.

- **Fixed-price contract with retroactive price redetermination**: Provides for (1) fixed ceiling price and (2) retroactive price determination within the ceiling after completion of the contract.

- **Firm-fixed-price, level-of-effort contract**: Requires the contractor to provide a specified level of effort, over a stated period of time on work that can be stated only in general terms; requires the buyer to pay the contractor a fixed dollar amount.

- **Fixed-price award-fee contract**: Award-fee provisions may be used in fixed-price contracts when the government wishes to motivate a contractor and other incentives cannot be used because contractor performance cannot be measured objectively. Such contracts shall establish a fixed price (including normal profit) for the effort. This price will be paid for satisfactory contract performance. Award fee earned (if any) will be paid in addition to that fixed price.

Cost reimbursement: A form of pricing arrangement that provides for payment of allowable, allocable, and reasonable costs incurred in the performance of a contract to the extent that such costs are prescribed or permitted by the contract. This family of contracts includes cost plus award fee (CPAF), cost plus fixed fee (CPFF), cost plus incentive fee, and cost sharing.

- **Cost contract**: Cost-reimbursement contract in which the contractor receives no fee. This is the least complicated type of cost-reimbursement contract.

- **Cost-sharing contract**: Cost-reimbursement contract in which the contractor receives no fee and is reimbursed only for an agreed-upon portion of its allowable costs.

- **Cost-plus-incentive-fee contract**: Cost-reimbursement contract that provides for an initially negotiated fee to be adjusted later by a formula based on the relationship of total allowable costs to total target costs.

- **Cost-plus-award-fee contract**: Cost-reimbursement contract that provides for a fee consisting of (1) a base amount (which may be zero) fixed at inception of the contract; and (2) an award amount, based on a judgmental evaluation by the government, sufficient to provide motivation for excellence in contract performance.

- **Cost-plus-fixed-fee contract**: Cost-reimbursement contract that provides for payment to the contractor of a negotiated fee that is fixed at the inception of the contract. The fixed fee does not vary with actual cost but may be adjusted as a result of changes in the work to be performed under the contract. This contract type permits contracting for efforts that might otherwise present too great a risk to contractors, but it provides the contractor only a minimum incentive to control costs.

Agreements:

- **Basic agreement**: A written instrument of understanding, negotiated between a buyer and seller, that contains contract clauses applying to future contracts between the parties during its term and contemplates separate future contracts that will incorporate, by reference or attachment, the required and applicable clauses agreed on in the basic agreement. A basic agreement is not a contract.

- **Basic ordering agreement**: A written instrument of understanding, negotiated between a buyer and seller, that contains terms and clauses applying to future contracts (orders) between the parties during its term; a description, as specified as practicable, of supplies or services to be provided; and methods for pricing, issuing, and delivering future orders under the basic ordering agreement. A basic ordering agreement is not a contract.

Other types: Miscellaneous contracts that use a form of pricing arrangement (such as time-and-materials, labor hour, and letter contracts) or are described by the terms governing ordering (indefinite delivery contracts).

- **Definite quantity contract**: Provides for delivery of a definite quantity of specific supplies or services for a fixed period, with deliveries or performance to be scheduled at designated locations upon order.

- **Delivery order contract**: Contract for supplies that does not procure or specify a firm quantity of supplies (other than a minimum or maximum quantity) and that provides for the issuance of orders for the delivery of supplies during the period of the contract.

- **Indefinite delivery/indefinite quality contract** (IDIQ)/Government-wide agency contract (GWAC): Contracts that provide for an indefinite quantity within stated limits of supplies or services to be furnished within a fixed period with deliveries or performance to be scheduled by placing orders with the contractor. Examples of these contracts are delivery order, task order, definite quality, requirements, and indefinite quantity. GWACs are government-wide acquisition contracts available to multiple buyers.

- **Indefinite quantity contract**: Provides for an indefinite quantity, within stated limits, of supplies or services during a fixed period. The buyer places orders for individual requirements. Quantity may be stated as number of units or as dollar values.

- **Labor hour contract**: Variation of the time-and-materials contract, differing only in that materials are not supplied by the contractor.

- **Letter contract**: A written preliminary contractual instrument that authorizes the contractor to begin immediately manufacturing supplies or performing services.

- **Requirements contract**: Provides for filling all actual purchase requirements of designated government activities for supplies or services during a specified contract period, with deliveries or performance to be scheduled by placing orders with the contractor.

- **Task order contract**: A services contract that does not procure or specify a firm quantity of services (other than a minimum or maximum quantity) and that provides for the issuance of orders for the performance of tasks during the period of the contract.

- **Time-and-materials contract**: Provides for acquiring supplies or services on the basis of direct labor hours at specified fixed hourly rates that include wages, overhead, general and administrative expenses, profit, and materials at cost, including, if appropriate, material handling costs as part of material costs.

Incentive contracts: Incentive contracts are appropriate when a firm-fixed-price contract is not appropriate and the required supplies or services can be acquired for lower costs and, in certain instances, with improved delivery or technical performance, by relating the amount of profit or fee payable under the contract to the contractor's performance. Incentive contracts are designed to obtain specific acquisition objectives by (1) establishing reasonable and attainable targets that are clearly communicated to the contractor efforts that might not otherwise be emphasized, and (2) discouraging contractor inefficiency and waste.

- **Cost incentives**: Most incentive contracts include only cost incentives, which take the form of a profit or fee adjustment formula and are intended to motivate the contractor to effectively manage costs. No incentive contract may provide for other incentives without also providing a cost incentive (or constraint). Incentive contracts typically include a target cost, a target profit or fee, and a profit or fee adjustment formula. These targets and the formula provide that (within the constraints of a price ceiling or minimum and maximum fee) (1) the actual cost that meets the target will result in the target profit or fee, (2) the actual cost that exceeds the target will result in downward adjustment of target profit or fee, and (3) the actual cost that is below the target will result in upward adjustment of target profit or fee.

- **Delivery incentives**: Should be considered when improvement from a required delivery schedule is a significant government objective. It is important to determine the buyer's primary objectives in a given contract (e.g., earliest possible delivery or earliest quantity production).

- **Performance incentives**: May be considered in connection with specific product characteristics (e.g., a missile range, an aircraft speed, an engine thrust, or vehicle maneuverability) or other specific elements of the contractor's performance. These incentives should be designed to relate profit or fee to results achieved by the contractor compared with specified targets.

- **Multiple-incentive contract**: Such contracts should motivate the contractor to strive for outstanding results in all incentives areas and compel trade-off decisions among the incentive areas consistent with the buyer's overall objectives for the acquisition.

Fixed-price incentive contract: Provides for adjusting profit and establishing the final contract price by application of a formula based on the relationship of total final negotiated cost to total target cost. The final price is subject to a price ceiling, negotiated at the outset. There are two forms of fixed-price incentive contracts—firm target and successive target.

- **Fixed-price incentive (firm target) contract**: Specifies a target cost, a target profit, a price ceiling (but not a profit ceiling or floor), and a profit adjustment formula. These elements are all negotiated at the outset.

- **Fixed-price incentive (successive targets) contract**: Specifies the following elements, all of which are negotiated at the outset: an initial target cost, an initial target profit, and an initial profit adjustment formula. These targets and formula are used to establish (1) the firm target profit, including a ceiling and floor for the firm target profit; (2) the production point at which the firm target cost and firm target profit will be negotiated (usually before delivery or shop completion of the first item); and (3) a ceiling price that is the maximum that may be paid to the contractor, except for any adjustment under other contract clauses providing for equitable adjustment or other revision of the contract price under stated circumstances.

Fixed-price contract with award fees: Used when the buyer wishes to motivate a seller and other incentives cannot be used because contractor performance cannot be measured objectively. Such contracts shall establish a fixed price (including normal profit) for the effort that will be paid for satisfactory contract performance. Such contracts shall establish that the award fee earned (if any) will be paid in addition to that fixed price and provide for periodic evaluation of the contractor's performance against an award-fee plan.

Cost-plus-incentive-fee contract: A cost-reimbursement contract that provides for the initial negotiated fee to be adjusted later by a formula based on the relationship of total allowable costs to total target costs.

Cost-plus-award-fee contract: Provides for a fee consisting of (1) a base amount fixed at inception of the contract; and (2) an award amount that the contractor may earn in whole or in part during performance and that is sufficient to provide motivation for excellence in such areas as quality, timeliness, technical ingenuity, and cost-effective management.

Cost-plus-a-percentage-of-cost contract: This type of contract is not used in federal contracting.

1.6 Contracting Methods

Contracting methods are the processes employed for soliciting offers, evaluating offers, and awarding a contract.

LEXICON FOR CONTRACTING METHODS:

Auction: A sale in which property, services, or merchandise are sold to the highest bidder. Reverse auctions are purchases in which property, services, or merchandise are purchases from the lowest bidder. In these two applications of bidding, the buy-side (reverse auction) supports the procurement function while the sell-side supports asset management and surplus disposition.

Competitive negotiation: A method of contracting involving a request for proposal that states the buyer's requirements and criteria for evaluation; submission of timely proposals by a maximum number of offerors; discussions with those offerors found to be within the competitive range; and award of a contract to the one offeror whose offer, price, and other consideration factors are most advantageous to the buyer.

Competitive range: The range of prospective offers as determined by the buyer, which is based upon cost or price and other factors that were stated in the solicitation. The goal is to include all proposals that have a "reasonable chance of being selected for award." However, the comptroller general has described its standard of review for the determination of competitive range as "a matter primarily within the discretion of the procuring agency, and we will not overturn that determination in the absence of clear evidence that it had no reasonable basis or is in violation of federal procurement laws or regulations."

Electronic commerce: A group of automated processes that can be used to accomplish business transactions. Electronic commerce includes such processes as electronic mail or messaging, Internet technology, electronic bulletin boards, electronic funds transfer, electronic data interchange, and similar tools. In the federal sector, the contracting officer must make available through the GPE (Governmentwide Point of Entry, commonly FedBizOpps; see FAR 5.003) solicitations synopsized through the GPE, including specifications and other pertinent information determined necessary by the contracting officer. Transmissions to the GPE must be in accordance with the interface description available through the internet at www.fbo.gov.

Federal Supply Schedules (FSS): A program directed and managed by the General Services Administration (GSA). The FSS program provides federal agencies, as well as some state and local governmental agencies, with a streamlined process for obtaining commonly used commercial goods and services. Fundamentally, the supply schedules are a series of pre-negotiated, awarded contracts that can be used by authorized sources to issue orders for required goods or services.

Framework pricing arrangement: A contract that is definitive in all respects except pricing. The agreement or contract specifies a predetermined index, formula, or algorithm (i.e., the "framework") for the calculation of price at the point of sale.

Gap fillers: Interim agreements that define the rights and obligations of the parties, and establishes the basis for the conduct of business prior to the establishment of a long-term contractual relationship. Includes memorandums of understanding (MOUs), letter contracts, teaming agreements, and other short-term agreements.

Government purchase card: Authorized for use in making and/or paying for purchases of supplies, services, or construction. The card may be used by contracting officers and other designated individuals. The card may be used only for purchases that are otherwise authorized by law or regulation. The card may be used to

- Make micro-purchases;

- Place a task or delivery order (if authorized in the basic contract, basic ordering agreement, or blanket purchase agreement); or

- Make payments, when the contractor agrees to accept payment by the card.

Invitation for bid (IFB): The method of solicitation for the sealed bid process. The IFB must describe the requirements of the government clearly, accurately, and completely. Unnecessarily restrictive specifications or requirements that might unduly limit the number of bidders are prohibited. The IFB includes all documents (whether attached or incorporated by reference) furnished prospective bidders for the purpose of bidding.

Master agreements: Business arrangements in which the parties determine the underlying commercial arrangement governing the relationship (e.g., terms and conditions), but defer specific negotiation of elements of the contract to specific events or transactions (e.g., price).

Modular contracting: The use of at least one (but usually more than one) contract to acquire major information technology (IT) systems in successive, interoperable increments. The intent of modular contracting is to divide the acquisition of complex, major IT systems into a series of smaller, related contracts that are easier to issue and manage than a single all-inclusive contract would be.

Negotiations: A method of contracting that uses either competitive or other-than-competitive proposals and (usually) discussions. It is a flexible process that includes the receipt of proposals from offerors, permits bargaining, and usually affords offerors an opportunity to revise their offers before award of a contract.

Performance-based contract: A contract that is structured around the purpose of the work to be performed as opposed to either the manner in which the work is to be performed or a broad statement of work (SOW). Typically, a performance work statement (PWS) is used to describe the requirement.

Point-of-sale transactions: Business arrangements in which the entire business arrangement between the parties is executed in a single event.

Prequalification: A buyer's announcement of interest, including criteria for selecting proposals, and selecting offerors capable of meeting the requirements.

Request for information (RFI): Tool used for gathering information from independent vendors for the purchase of determining availability of products and services and gathering market information on capabilities to perform.

Request for proposal (RFP): The major form of solicitation in negotiated procurement. The RFP, like the IFB, requests the proposer to submit an offer. In competitive negotiation, if acceptance without negotiation is not possible or desirable, the government conducts oral or written negotiations with all offerors within the competitive range.

Request for quotation (RFQ): A solicitation document used in negotiated procurements to request information and quotes. The RFQ differs from the RFP in that an RFQ is fundamentally a request for information. Quotations received in response to an RFQ are not offers. The resulting purchase order is either an offer or a counter offer.

Reverse auctions: Purchase transactions in which goods and services are purchased from the lowest bidder.

Sales contract: A business arrangement in which all elements of the transaction are determined and defined between the parties at the time of contract formation, including mutual assent, exchange of consideration, capacity to contract, and legal purpose.

Sealed bidding: An acquisition method in which the government issues an invitation for bid (IFB). The IFB is publicized by distributing it to prospective bidders, posting it in public places, and posting it on the FedBizOpps website. Sufficient time must be allowed between the time the IFB is publicized and bids are opened publicly to enable prospective bidders to prepare and submit bids. An IFB should describe the government's requirements clearly, accurately, and completely. Unnecessarily restrictive specifications or requirements that might unduly limit the number of bidders are prohibited. The invitation includes all documents (whether attached or incorporated by reference) furnished to prospective bidders for bidding purposes. Agencies must use a fixed-price contract for sealed bidding.

Simplified acquisition: A less rigorous method for entering into relatively low-dollar threshold contracts. Simplified acquisition usually occurs without the elaborate and formal solicitation techniques required by sealed bidding and negotiation. Very small purchases must be made using simplified acquisition tools such as charge cards.

Single-source negotiation: Negotiation with a single provider, because either (1) the provider is the sole supplier of the product or service, or (2) the relationship with the provider is of strategic importance, based on long-term relationships and built on mutual trust.

Two-step sealed bidding: A combination of competitive procedures designed to obtain the benefits of sealed bidding when adequate specifications are not available. Step one consists of the request for the submission of technical proposals, evaluation, and discussion without pricing. Step two involves the submission of sealed-price bids by those who submitted acceptable technical proposals in step one.

Undefinitized contract actions: Any contract action for which the contract terms, specifications, or price are not agreed upon before performance is begun under the action. Examples are letter contracts, orders under basic ordering agreements, and provisioned item orders, for which the price has not been agreed upon before performance has begun.

Unsolicited proposal: A research or developmental proposal that is made by a prospective contractor without prior formal or informal solicitation from a purchasing activity.

1.7 Contract Financing

Contract financing is the means of obtaining the funds necessary for performing the contract, including payment methods, loan guarantees, advanced payments, progress payments, and contract funding. Contract financing issues are important in both the commercial and government contracting environments.

LEXICON FOR CONTRACT FINANCING:

Absorption of costing: A method of determining the actual cost of a unit of production (either at various stages of completion or when service is provided) which treats fixed indirect costs as product costs.

Accrual accounting: This type of accounting recognizes important concepts, such as receivables due from customers, payables due to vendors, interest due from investments, and other matching concepts, as a means of providing an accurate picture of a company's financial position.

Acquisition cost: Includes all costs associated with generating and processing an order and its related paperwork. It is the sum of the ordering, transporting, handling, and all inventory handling costs associated with the acquisition of material.

Audit: The systematic examination of records and documents and/or the securing of other evidence by confirmation, physical inspection, or otherwise for one or more of the following purposes: determining the propriety or legality of proposed or completed transactions; ascertaining whether all transactions have been recorded and are reflected accurately in accounts; determining the existence of recorded assets and the inclusiveness of recorded liabilities; determining the accuracy of financial or statistical statements or reports and the fairness of the facts they represent; determining the degree for compliance with established policies and procedures in terms of financial transactions and business management; and appraising an account system and making recommendations concerning it.

Contract financing (commercial): Financing in commercial contracting may include obtaining loans and lines of credit and from financial institutions; obtaining advance funding of accounts receivable or funding of purchase orders from private firms; or obtaining funds from venture capitalists. It may include negotiating favorable payment clauses such as a sizable down payment or milestone payments as the work progresses.

Commercial contract financing could also include such methods as commercial advance payments made before performance has begun, commercial interim payments made after some work has been done, and delivery payments made after receiving and accepting a portion of the total work to be performed.

Contract financing (government): In some cases, successfully completing a government contract may require the government's assistance with some form of contract financing. For example, contract financing might be appropriate in a multi-million dollar contract for goods that require the contractor to make substantial initial investments in labor, materials, and production costs. In cases where the government determines that some type of contract financing is appropriate, it usually takes one of two forms, private or government.

When a contractor requests financing, the government contracting officer is to consider the following order of preference for methods of contract financing: private financing, customary contract financing other than loan guarantees, loan guarantees, unusual contract financing, and advance payments.

- **Private financing** without government guarantee includes loans from financial institutions, sale of bonds or stocks, and loans from family members or other private sources. However, the contractor should not be required to obtain private financing at unreasonable terms or from other agencies. In addition, under assignment of claims provisions, a financing institution can receive payments directly from the government in consideration for making a private loan to a contractor.

- **Progress payments** based on incurred costs at customary progress payment rates can be made on the basis of costs incurred by the contractor as work progresses under a fixed-price contract.

- **Loan guarantee:** If a contractor applies for a conventional loan to finance a government contract, the private financial institution involved may submit an application for a loan guarantee to the Federal Reserve Bank in its district. The Federal Reserve Bank acts as a fiscal agent and transmits the application to the guaranteeing agency. The president has designated seven agencies as guaranteeing agencies: Department of Defense, Department of Energy, Department of Commerce, Department of the Interior, Department of Agriculture, General Services Administration, and National Aeronautics and Space Administration. The guaranteeing agency makes a determination of eligibility in accordance with the applicable *FAR* provisions. If the loan guarantee is approved, the private financial institution makes the loan and collects interest from the contractor, the guaranteeing agency guarantees the loan, and the Federal Reserve Bank acts as the "intermediary," or fiscal agent that processes the paperwork between the private financial institution and the contractor.

- **Unusual contract financing**: FAR Subpart 32 provides guidance for customary progress payments (i.e., liquidation rates). Any progress payments that do not comply with this guidance for "customary" progress payments are considered "unusual." As such, unusual progress payments require advance agency approval.

- **Advance payments** are advances of money by the government to a contractor. They are not measured by performance; they are made in anticipation of performance. Advance payments are the least preferred method of contract financing and generally should not be authorized if other types of financing are reasonably available to the contractor in adequate amounts. Loans and credit at excessive interest rates or other exorbitant charges, or loans from other government agencies, are not considered reasonably available financing. Contractors may apply for advance payments before or after the award of a contract. If advance payments are approved, a special bank account may be required. Interest is usually charged on the advance payments, and any interest earned is refundable to the government.

Cost principles: The regulations that establish rules and policies relating to the general treatment of costs in government contracting, particularly the allowability of costs.

- **Allocable cost**: A cost that can be assigned or charged to one or more activities or items (cost objects) on the basis of benefits received or other such equitable or logical association, although a direct (causal) relationship may not be established.

- **Allowable cost**: A cost that is reasonable, allocable, and within accepted standards, or otherwise conforms to generally accepted accounting principles, specific limitations or exclusions, or agreed-upon terms between contractual parties.

Cost Accounting Standards (CAS): Federal standards designed to provide consistency and coherency in defense and other government contract accounting.

Direct costs: The costs specifically identifiable with a contract requirement, including but not restricted to costs of material and/or labor directly incorporated into an end item.

Direct labor: All work that is obviously related and specifically and conveniently traceable to specific products.

Fair value: Examines product or service features that enhance profits for the final product and the ability of a commercial firm to maintain a competitive advantage in the marketplace.

Generally Accepted Accounting Principles (GAAP): A term encompassing conventions, rules, and procedures of accounting that are "generally accepted" and have "substantial authoritative support." The GAAP have been developed by agreement on the basis of experience, reason, custom, usage, and to a certain extent, practical necessity, rather than being derived from a formal set of theories.

Market price: The exchange value of a good or service, calculated with due consideration to market conditions, legal constraints, competitive pressures, and change in market factor.

Payment bond: A bond that secures the appropriate payment of subcontracts for their completed and acceptable goods and/or services.

Payments: The amount payable under the contract supporting data required to be submitted with invoices, and other payment terms such as time for payment and retention.

Profit: The term used to describe the net proceeds from selling a product or service when costs are subtracted from revenues.

Risk management: The methodical process used to enhance opportunities and reduce risks by identifying potential opportunities and risks, assessing associated probabilities of occurrence and impacts, and determining courses of action.

1.8 Intellectual Property

Intellectual property is the kind of property that results from the fruits of mental labor. Intellectual property rights include patents, trademarks, copyrights, trade secrets, trade names, service marks, and the like.

LEXICON FOR INTELLECTUAL PROPERTY:

Copyright: Royalty-free, nonexclusive, and irrevocable license to reproduce, translate, publish, use, and dispose of written or recorded material and to authorize others to do so.

Data: Recorded information, regardless of form or the media on which it may be recorded. Rights to use technical data developed by the contractor may vary depending on the source of funds used to develop the item, component, process, software, or software documentation.

Data rights: Rights of ownership of data under any contract. In any contract that may involve the production of scientific or technical data, the rights to those data must be clearly ascribed. Generally, a rights in data clause will protect the government's right to use and distribute—without limitation, free from payment or royalties, and with immunity against lawsuits for copyright infringement or misuse of data—any data produces under a contract funded by the government.

Employee agreement: A contract by which one person (the employee) is to do something for the benefit of the employer or a third person for which the employee receives compensation. The contract may be oral or written.

Licensing: A license permits the usage of software, patents, trademarks, or technology by another entity without transferring ownership rights. The sale of a license permitting the use of patents, trademarks, or other technology to another firm. A license covering a patent, technical or proprietary data, technical assistance, know-how, or any combination of these—granted by a U.S. firm to a foreign firm or government—to produce, coproduce, or sell a defense article or service within a given sales territory. An exclusive license grants this right without competition from any other licensees or from the licensor. For a nonexclusive license, competition may be permitted with other licensees and/ or the licensor. Licensing involves the many procedures administrative agencies perform in conjunction with issuance of various types of licenses.

Nondisclosure agreement: A legally binding document setting forth the conditions under which proprietary information is offered and received between the parties.

Ownership, royalties, escrow agreement: Legal title or right to something. Mere possession is not ownership. With ownership comes the potential of royalties for use. Royalties are rights delegated (as to an individual or corporation) by a sovereign party, including a share of the profit or product reserved by the grantor. Also includes payments made to an author or composer for each copy of a work sold or to an inventor for each article sold under a patent. Owners may also escrow assets, creating an instrument and especially a deed of money or property held by a third party to be turned over to the grantee and to become effective only upon the fulfillment of some condition; a fund or deposit designed to serve as an escrow. Includes source code under certain circumstance, as when the licensor goes out of business or fails to make required modifications to the software.

Patent: Government grant of exclusive rights to an inventor that prohibits others from making, using, or selling an invention.

Royalties: Any costs or charges in the nature of royalties, license fees, patent or license amortization costs, or the like that are paid for the use of or for rights in patents and patent applications in connection with performing a contract or subcontract.

Shop rights: The right of an employer to use without payment of royalties, an invention conceived by an employee in the course of employment, or through the use of the employer's facilities, in which the employee was not hired to perform such work.

Trademark: Distinctive mark of authenticity. Words, symbols, devices, or designs affixed to or placed on an article or its container to identify an article offered for sale. Also includes "services marks," which designate particular manners or modes of service delivery protected as intellectual property.

Trade secrets: Any information, process, or procedure used in business that may give the owner some advantage over its competitors.

1. In the federal government, contracting without providing for full and open competition shall not be justified on the basis of

   a. inadequate staffing to conduct a competition.
   b. a lack of training in competitive source selection.
   c. a lack of advance planning by the requiring activity.
   d. customer preference for a specific contractor.

2. The Truth in Negotiations Act requires

   a. that all parties participating in a negotiation must execute non-disclosure agreements.
   b. executive agencies to get certified cost or pricing data in certain circumstances.
   c. prime contractors to disclose executive salaries for upper management.
   d. executive agencies to use negotiated acquisition as the preferred method for contracts over $1 million.

3. Which act requires federal agencies to conduct market research and acquisition planning?

   a. Truth in Negotiations Act
   b. Procurement Integrity Act
   c. Federal Acquisition Streamlining Act
   d. Competition in Contracting Act

4. The Federal Acquisition Streamlining Act

   a. expanded the definitions of commercial and non-developmental items.
   b. requires executive agencies to report how long it takes to purchase supplies and services.
   c. established a new acquisition method—streamlined acquisition for simplified purchases.
   d. requires agencies to develop specifications in a succinct and streamlined fashion.

5. Submitting an offer below anticipated costs expecting to increase the contract amount after award through change orders is called

   a. buying in.
   b. a value engineering change proposal.
   c. a kickback.
   d. a contingent fee.

6. Which federal law prohibits federal agency procurement officials from knowingly soliciting or accepting any promise of future employment or business opportunity from any competing contractor or consultant?

   a. Federal Ethics Law
   b. Competition in Contracting Act
   c. Federal Acquisition Reform Act
   d. Procurement Integrity Act

The following scenario and associated questions is a new, additional style of CPCM exam question. The questions appear after the scenario.

Use the information provided in the following scenario to answer questions 7–10. The questions ask you to apply your knowledge of contract management to the given scenario. These questions require candidates to understand the concepts and terminology and apply that knowledge to answer the question correctly.

Scenario

The agency issued an RFP for technical services that included phase-in tasks, project management, engineering design, emergency on-call engineering support, inspection services, and data compilation/recordkeeping. Award was based on an integrated assessment of technical and price factors, with price being less important than technical merit. The agency received proposals from two firms: Jack of All Trades (JAT) and Creative Management Technology (CMT).

After the agency awarded the contract to JAT, CMT protested the contract award because JAT used a government employee as a key person in their proposal.

Jack of All Trades (JAT) proposed Jean Green as their project manager. Jean Green was a contracting officer's technical representative (COTR) on the predecessor contract with this agency until she retired, one day after JAT won the protested contract.

In their protest, Creative Management Technology (CMT) contends that JAT's proposed employment of the former COTR constitutes a prohibited conflict of interest. CMT also contends that Jean Green assisted the agency in drafting the RFP to favor JAT's capabilities and used inside source selection information to assist JAT in writing the winning proposal.

The agency acknowledges that Jean Green served as the COTR for the predecessor contract. The agency asserts, however, no procurement integrity or conflict of interest regulations were violated by JAT's proposed use of Jean Green as the project manager.

The agency reports that JAT approached Jean Green and offered her a job as the project manager for the upcoming competition. Jean Green accepted the employment offer provided that doing so would not constitute an improper conflict of interest. In accordance with agency procedures, Jean Green reported the employment contact to the agency, and by memorandum formally requested an ethics advisory opinion. The agency determined that employment with JAT was permissible since Jean Green was not involved in any aspect of the current procurement.

Scenario Questions

7. Someone who is in a position to materially influence an agency's recommendations and/or decisions and, because of their personal activities, relationships, or financial interests, may lack or appear to lack objectivity or appear to be unduly influenced by personal financial interest may have a(n)

   a. personal conflict of interest.
   b. organizational conflict of interest.
   c. conflict of employment.
   d. procurement integrity conflict.

8. A contractor that has present or planned interests that either directly or indirectly relate to the work to be performed under a contract and may result in an unfair competitive advantage may have a(n)

   a. personal conflict of interest.
   b. organizational conflict of interest.
   c. conflict of employment.
   d. procurement integrity conflict.

9. The Procurement Integrity Act applies to government employees who

   a. request an agency ethics determination after receiving a job offer from a contractor.
   b. plan to leave government service within one year of contract award.
   c. participate efficiently and effectively in a federal agency procurement.
   d. participate personally and substantially in a federal agency procurement.

10. Sue Blue, the contracting officer, is considering a job offer from Creative

Management Technology (CMT). What should she do when she finds out that CMT submitted a proposal?

a. Exclude CMT from the competitive range to avoid the appearance of a conflict of interest.
b. Notify the Source Selection Authority of the issue and disqualify herself from participating in the source selection.
c. Obtain a ruling from the agency ethics official after awarding the contract to CMT.
d. Notify the agency head that she needs to resign from the agency immediately.

1. In the federal government, contracting without providing for full and open competition shall not be justified on the basis of

   a. inadequate staffing to conduct a competition. *Lack of staffing is not an acceptable exception to providing full and open competition.*
   b. a lack of training in competitive source selection. *Insufficient training is not an acceptable exception to providing full and open competition.*
   c. **(Correct) a lack of advance planning by the requiring activity.**
   d. customer preference for a specific contractor.

(Source: FAR 6.301)

2. The Truth in Negotiations Act requires

   a. that all parties participating in a negotiation must execute non-disclosure agreements.
   b. **(Correct) executive agencies to get certified cost or pricing data in certain circumstances.**
   c. prime contractors to disclose executive salaries for upper management.
   d. executive agencies to use negotiated acquisition as the preferred method for contracts over $1 million.

(Source: Rumbaugh, Margaret G. *Understanding Government Contract Source Selection.* (Vienna, VA: Management Concepts, Inc.) 2010.)

3. Which act requires federal agencies to conduct market research and acquisition planning?

   a. Truth in Negotiations Act. *TINA requires certified cost or pricing data.*
   b. Procurement Integrity Act. *The Procurement Integrity Act prohibits the government from releasing source selection information before contract award.*
   c. Federal Acquisition Streamlining Act. *FASA establishes a preference for commercial item acquisition.*
   d. **(Correct) Competition in Contracting Act.**

(Source: Rumbaugh, Margaret G. *Understanding Government Contract Source Selection.* (Vienna, VA: Management Concepts, Inc.) 2010.)

4. The Federal Acquisition Streamlining Act

   a. **(Correct) expanded the definitions of commercial and non-developmental items.**
   b. requires executive agencies to report how long it takes to purchase supplies and services.
   c. established a new acquisition method: streamlined acquisition for simplified purchases.
   d. requires agencies to develop specifications in a succinct and streamlined fashion.

(Source: Rumbaugh, Margaret G. *Understanding Government Contract Source Selection.* (Vienna, VA: Management Concepts, Inc.) 2010.)

5. Submitting an offer below anticipated costs expecting to increase the contract amount after award through change orders is also called

   a. **(Correct) buying in.**
   b. a value engineering change proposal.
   c. a kickback. *A kickback is any money, fee, commission, gratuity, or thing of value provided to a prime contractor or subcontractor for the purpose of improperly obtaining or rewarding favorable treatment in connection with a prime contract or subcontract.*

d. a contingent fee. *A contingent fee is any commission, percentage, brokerage, or other fee that is contingent upon the success that a person or concern has in securing a government contract.*

(Source: FAR 3.501)

6. Which federal law prohibits federal agency procurement officials from knowingly soliciting or accepting any promise of future employment or business opportunity from any competing contractor or consultant?

   a. Federal Ethics Law
   b. Competition in Contracting Act
   c. Federal Acquisition Reform Act
   d. **(Correct) Procurement Integrity Act**

(Source: Rumbaugh, Margaret G. *Understanding Government Contract Source Selection.* (Vienna, VA: Management Concepts, Inc.) 2010.)

7. Someone who is in a position to materially influence an agency's recommendations and/or decisions, and because of their personal activities, relationships, or financial interests may lack or appear to lack objectivity or appear to be unduly influenced by personal financial interest may have a(n)

   a. **(Correct) personal conflict of interest.**
   b. organizational conflict of interest.
   c. conflict of employment.
   d. procurement integrity conflict.

8. A contractor that has present or planned interests that either directly or indirectly relate to the work to be performed under a contract and may result in an unfair competitive advantage may have a(n)

   a. personal conflict of interest.
   b. **(Correct) organizational conflict of interest.**

   c. conflict of employment.
   d. procurement integrity conflict.

9. The Procurement Integrity Act applies to government employees who

   a. request an agency ethics determination after receiving a job offer from a contractor.
   b. plan to leave government service within one year of contract award.
   c. participate efficiently and effectively in a federal agency procurement.
   d. **(Correct) participate personally and substantially in a federal agency procurement.**

10. Sue Blue, the contracting officer, is considering a job offer from Creative Management Technology (CMT). What should she do when she finds out that CMT submitted a proposal?

    a. Exclude CMT from the competitive range to avoid the appearance of a conflict of interest.
    b. **(Correct) Notify the Source Selection Authority of the issue and disqualify herself from participating in the source selection.**
    c. Obtain a ruling from the agency ethics official after awarding the contract to CMT.
    d. Notify the agency head that she needs to resign from the agency immediately.

Use the full text of the Comptroller General Decision for a better understanding of the correct answers for the scenario questions.

MATTER OF: CREATIVE MANAGEMENT TECHNOLOGY, INC. B-266299, 96-1 CPD ¶ 61

Creative Management Technology, Inc. (CMT) protests the award of a contract to AJT and Associates under request for proposals (RFP) No. F08650-95-R-A078, issued by the Department of the Air Force for technical engineering and spacelift services (TESS) to support the agency's 45th Space Wing Eastern Launch Range Space Program. CMT contends that the Air Force failed to apprise the firm of informational deficiencies in its proposal, thereby depriving the protester of the opportunity to improve its moderate risk proposal rating. CMT contends that it should have received the award since the agency's risk concerns were unreasonable, and it offered a lower price than the awardee. CMT also argues that the technical evaluation and subsequent award to AJT were tainted by a conflict of interest.

We deny the protest.

The TESS services are critical engineering support necessary to ensure scheduled space program launches and missions including Titan IV, Atlas II, Delta II and III, Trident D-5, and various commercial satellite programs. The procured services include phase-in tasks; project management; engineering design; emergency on-call engineering support; inspection services; and data compilation/recordkeeping. The RFP was issued on May 15, 1995 and contemplated the award of a 1-year contract with 4 option years based on an integrated assessment of technical and price factors, with price less important than technical merit. The RFP required each offeror to submit a technical/management proposal, which was to be evaluated under seven criteria of equal importance. The RFP further provided that risk analysis of each proposal would be performed and considered as part of the overall evaluation.

By the June 21 closing date, four offers were received, including offers from CMT and AJT. During the next 2 months, numerous "Clarification Requests/Deficiency Reports" (CR/DR) were issued to each of the four offerors.

On September 7, after reviewing and concurring in the SSET's finding, the source selection authority (SSA) awarded the contract to AJT. Although CMT's price was lower than AJT's, the SSA determined that AJT's lower performance risk warranted paying an approximately 12-percent price premium. Specifically, the SSA noted that any interruption in the required TESS services—including delays in providing emergency on-call engineering services—could potentially cause launch delays that would cost the agency approximately $1 million per day. On September 26, after attending the agency's debriefing, CMT filed this protest.

Discussion

The record shows that AJT's proposed project manager was a contracting officer's technical representative (COTR) who served on the predecessor contract until he retired, 1 day after the current contract was awarded to AJT. CMT contends that AJT's proposed employment of the project manager constituted a personal conflict of interest prohibited by the procurement integrity provisions of FAR subpart 3.104. Alternatively, CMT contends that AJT's proposed project manager must have used inside source selection information to assist the awardee in drafting the winning proposal; CMT also maintains that the project manager similarly must have assisted the agency in drafting the current RFP to favor AJT's capabilities, resulting in an improper organizational conflict prohibited by FAR subpart 9.5.

The Air Force acknowledges that AJT's proposed project manager served as the COTR for the predecessor contract; however, the agency asserts that contrary to the protester's contentions, no procurement integrity or organizational conflict of interest regulations were violated by AJT's proposed use of the COTR.

The Air Force reports that AJT approached the COTR on April 18, 1995, and offered him an employment position as project manager for the upcoming procurement. The COTR accepted the employment offer with an effective start date of October 1, but conditioned his acceptance of AJT's employment offer on the Air Force's determination that such employment would not constitute an improper conflict of interest. The COTR then reported the employment contact to the agency and, by memorandum dated May 8, formally requested an ethics advisory opinion regarding his potential post-government employment by AJT. The Air Force determined that employment with AJT was permissible since the COTR was not involved in any aspect of the current TESS procurement.

The interpretation and enforcement of post-employment conflict of interest restrictions are primarily matters for the procuring agency and the Department of Justice. Our general interest, within the confines of a bid protest, is to determine whether any action of the former government employee may have resulted in prejudice for, or on behalf of, the awardee during the award selection process. Cleveland Telecommunications Corp., B-257294, Sep. 19, 1994, 94-2 CPD p 105; Technology Concepts and Design, Inc., B-241727, Feb. 6, 1991, 91-1 CPD p 132.

Here, we find nothing improper in either the COTR's conditional acceptance of employment while still an Air Force employee, or in AJT's proposed use of the COTR in its proposal. Although procurement officials are prohibited from engaging in employment negotiations during the conduct of a procurement, FAR 3.104-3(b), the COTR was not a procurement official as defined within these regulations: the COTR had no involvement with drafting, reviewing or approving the RFP specifications; evaluating proposals; selecting sources; conducting negotiations; or approving the award to AJT. FAR 3.104-4(h). Further, while any government employee is prohibited from

"participating personally and substantially" in any matter that would "affect the financial interests of any person with whom the employee is negotiating employment," FAR 3.104-1(b)(2), there is no evidence that the COTR participated in any way in the procurement on behalf of the Air Force or AJT. See Cleveland Telecommunications Corp., supra. Nor did the COTR participate in the drafting or negotiation process for the predecessor solicitation, known as the Ground Systems Associate Contract (GSAC). In this regard, the Air Force reports that the GSAC requirements underwent substantial changes, rewriting, and restructuring before being issued as the instant TESS procurement.

Since the COTR was not involved in any aspect of the TESS procurement, and since the COTR was not employed by AJT, and did not otherwise assist AJT in the drafting of its proposal for this procurement, the organizational conflict of interest restrictions set forth at FAR 9.5 are inapplicable. See *Abt Assocs., Inc.*, B-253220.2, Oct. 6, 1993, 93-2 CPD p 269.

Although the protester contends that AJT's proposed employment of a current Air Force employee must have influenced the SSET to favor the AJT proposal, the record simply does not support this contention. CMT has not furnished any evidence to support this allegation, and we will not attribute bias in the evaluation of proposals on the basis of inference or supposition. See *TLC Sys.*, B-243220, July 9, 1991, 91-2 CPD p 37. The protester's speculation notwithstanding, the record contains no evidence of bias in the evaluation of either CMT's or AJT's proposal; instead, the record contains a well-documented, detailed evaluation and source selection analysis, showing that the Air Force conducted its evaluation reasonably and in accordance with the evaluation criteria. Under these circumstances, CMT's allegations of possible impropriety, unaccompanied by supporting evidence, amount to nothing

more than speculation, and as such, do not
provide a basis for protest. *ITT Fed. Servs.
Corp.*, B-253740.2, May 27, 1994, 94-2
CPD p 30.

The protest is denied.

These readings can be found in NCMA's online Research Articles Database. To access the database you must be an NCMA member. If you are not an NCMA member, you may be able to obtain equivalent readings by inserting relevant keywords into your web browser's search engine.

From NCMA's *Contract Management* magazine:

Baker, Keith, *Intellectual Property Clauses to Watch for in Government Contracts*, May 2011.
Three clauses that are potential "red flags" for contractors who desire IP rights similar to those in the *DFARS*.

Barnett-Rhodes, Amanda, *Ethics and Compliance in the Corporate Jungle: Attacking Social Influence, Conformity, and Groupthink as Root Causes*, September 2010.
How to best prepare employees to break free of the herd to comply and adhere to acceptable norms for ethical behavior while deviating from unethical norms and taking individual responsibility.

Beatty, Frank J. and Gregory A. Garrett, *Pre-Award Contract Audits*, February 2011.
A review of the procedures used by the U.S. Government to determine whether a prospective contractor is "responsible" enough to be awarded a contract.

Clinton, Kathy J. and M. Brent Armstrong, *The Federal Government's NAICS Code Process: Overdue for Change*, June 2011.
The NAICS code process should not be used to decrease competition, but this is what is occurring frequently across the U.S. government, which is neither in the best interests of the government nor the affected companies.

Curr, William Sims, *Transforming Ethics in Government Contracting*, April 2010.
A proposal of several changes designed to improve ethical behavior in the conduct of government contracting.

Currier, Michelle and Mark Lumer, *So You Think You Know the FAR?*, July 2010.
Put your knowledge to the test!

Darst, Brian, A. and Mark K. Roberts, *Government Contract Types: The U.S. Government's Use of Different Contract Vehicles to Acquire Goods, Services, and Construction*, December 2010.
Practical implications of selecting different contract vehicles and an examination of the impact these choices have on contract execution.

Dobriansky, John, *The Small Business Jobs Act of 2010*, March 2011.
What progress has been made so far? Where do we need to go from here to achieve its objectives?

Edwards, Vernon J., *Defining "Definitions,"* February 2011.
Recognition of definitions of words and terms in regulations, solicitations, and contracts is crucial to effective contract management and dispute avoidance.

Falcone, Ronald, *Empowering the Chief Acquisition Officer*, August 2010.
Chief Acquisition Officers (CAOs) need more than just a "seat at the table," they need an equal voice with regards to menu selections and choices.

Felber, Bryan, *When Is Competition not Competition?*, May 2011.
It is extremely important for buyers, subcontract administrators, and contracting officers to understand what a competition is. You may be surprised to find that some competitions aren't competitions at all.

Ford, John N. and David J Lundsten., *Reporting Executive Compensation and First-Tier Subcontracts*, April 2011.
An analysis of the newly revised FAR 4.14 and 52.201-10, which require contractor to report certain information on executive compensation and first-tier subcontractor awards.

Garrett, Gregory A. and Thomas Reynolds, *Government Contract Cost Accounting, Part I: The U.S. Federal Marketplace and the Need for Contract Cost Accounting*, July 2010.
An examination of the importance of utilizing government contract cost accounting to manage the growing number, value, and complexity of government contracts.

Garrett, Gregory A. and Frank J. Beatty, *Government Contract Cost Accounting, Part II: Cost Accounting Principles*, August 2010.
A description of the basic precepts of cost allowability, allocability, and reasonableness in the context of cost-reimbursable contracting, as well as the tenets of indirect cost rates for bidding and billing purposes.

Hillmer, Linda, *The Value of Making Small Business a Big Part of Your Procurement Strategy*, August 2011.
When guided by a strategic communications plan, websites and related tools are effective and efficient vehicles for improving communications between government and industry, as evidenced by recent efforts by the Air Force Office of Small Business Programs.

Krachman, Albert B., *Game Changer: The Presumed Loss Rule and Mis-Certification of Small Business Status*, May 2011.
All businesses, regardless of size status, must ensure that when contracting with the U.S. government, a small business's size status isn't compromised, or the Presumed Loss Rule can result in dramatic penalties.

Lane, Scott F., *Is Your Share of the Federal Budget Worth the Compliance Costs of Becoming a Government Contractor?*, June 2010.
A contract manager's guide to entering the massive government market with limited exposure to costly regulations.

Lawson, Lora, *FAR 15.4 Contract Pricing—Requiring Data Other Than Certified Cost or Pricing Data: Unveiling the Ingredient Costs of the Recipe*, February 2011.
Using cost analysis as the standard, vs. price analysis, yields substantial government contract cost savings, even in an environment of adequate price competition.

Lohier, Jean Marceau, *It's Time for Integrity in Government Contracting*, January 2011.
Enforcing FAR Part 3 and FAR 52.219-14 against the business community.

Lohier, Jean Marceau, *NAICS Code Interpretation: A World of Confusion*, November 2010.
It is imperative that the U.S. federal contracting office selects the NAICS and related size standards that best describe the goods or services being procured since failure to do so creates ambiguity and a world of confusion among the small, mid-size, and large business communities.

Marcinko, Thomas A., *Everything You Need To Know about Transparency—and have been too Afraid to Ask*, March 2011.
An explanation of the new subcontract award, executive compensation, and responsibility reporting requirements, as well as an exploration of the possible ramifications of making this information publically available.

Mendiburu, Steven R., *The New Preference for Fixed-Price Contracting*, May 2011.
Fixed-price contracting is now the preferred vehicle of choice by the U.S. gov-

ernment. Industry must now learn how to change their contracting approach in order to play in the fixed-price arena.

Miller, John "Johnny" E., *14 Important, Practical, and Useful Inventorship Issues*, October 2010.
A useful list of issues regarding U.S. inventions as a refresher for future discussions with your management about patents on inventions

Miller, Thomas H., *Are Contracting Professionals the Key to Achieving Carter Efficiencies Initiatives?*, August 2011.
How contracting professionals will be key players in determining the successful implementation of the Carter efficiencies initiatives, what challenges they will face, and what is being done to address those challenges.

Robey, Christopher, *A Strategic Planning Analysis of Recovery Act Procurement*, March 2011.
Contractor reporting mandated by the Recovery Act has expanded the accountability and transparency culture of federal procurement, with mixed results. A corporate-style strategic planning review is provided to clarify the extension of such requirement to a larger set of contractors through the Transparency Act.

Robey, Christopher, *Trouble at the Exit Ramp: Private Equity and Venture Capital in Government Contracting*, October 2010.
A review of the increasing importance and complexity of private equity in U.S. government contract financing.

Schenk, Claire M. and Scott F. Lane, *False Claims Act Whistleblowers in the Year 2011: Perils, Pitfalls, and Profits*, March 2011.
In order to identify risks early, contracting professionals must understand what false claims are, what the qui tam provisions mean, how liability has been recently expanded, and signals to initiate an internal investigation.

Sochon, Gloria, *Federal Awardee Performance and Integrity Information System (FAPIIS): Spotlight on Contractor Responsibility*, January 2011.
A review of the FAPIIS, the information that FAPIIS contains, how the government will use that information, and issues related to the protection and availability of the information.

Sochon, Gloria, *Federal Procurement Systems: Understanding their Purpose and Relationships*, April 2011.
Understanding the purpose of each federal government procurement system can facilitate the search for contracting opportunities, promote compliance with reporting requirements, reinforce the need for data accuracy and consistency, help locate information on trends, and just plain relieve frustration with the federal contracting process.

Sweatt, Glenn and Stephanie Tran, *Up in the Air*, March 2011.
An examination of the newly invigorated Fly America Act and its exemptions and waiver criteria.

Tillipman, Jessica and Damien Specht, *Venture Capital Investment & Small Business Affiliation Rules*, February 2011.
Why a limited exception is crucial to economic recovery efforts.

Virtue, Katie, *Implementation and Compliance Best Practices*, August 2010.
Contract rollouts within the procurement discipline have evolved to include pre-implementation, implementation, and compliance. This article reviews best practices in each of these three areas,

which will enable a company to plan for a smooth implementation and push compliance.

Vitasek, Kate and Mike Ledyard, *Vested Outsourcing: A Better Practice for Better Results*, November 2010.
Vested Outsourcing encourages both parties to act for mutual benefit--and in the process lay the foundation for sustained success.

Waeber, Kim, *"Medium-Sized" Businesses: Don't get Stuck in the Middle*, July 2010.
There are small businesses and large businesses, but what about "medium-sized" businesses? The government should level the playing field so more small businesses can make the transition to large business status.

Wells, Robert S., *The Contract Manager's Role in Ensuring Ethical Conduct on the World Stage*, June 2010.
As a contractor, receiving the required law of war training before serving with the U.S. Armed Forces during peace and stability operations isn't just a requirement, it's the right thing to do.

Williams, John G. and Gregory A. Garrett, *Government Contract Cost Accounting, Part 3: Software for Government Contract Cost Accounting*, September 2010.
Each contractor should ensure that their accounting processes and systems meet the unique set of requirements posed by their industry, business model, and the terms and conditions in their contracts.

Wolf, Christopher, Cost Limitations in Government Contracts, May 2010.
In order to avoid unnecessary financial losses, contractors must strictly comply with applicable limitations of cost/funds clauses.

From NCMA's *Journal of Contract Management*

Soll, Gabriel D., *The Diminished "Sanctity" of Government Contracts: A Comparative View of Changing Formation Regimes that Shows Strengthening of Overarching Goals*, September 2010, Volume 8, Issue 1.
This article traces the evolution of the latest wave of procurement reforms in the European Union relating to competition in and formation of government contracts, contrasting aspects of this reform to similar aspects of law and regulation in the United States.

Competency

2.0:

Acquisition Planning and Strategy

Process through which all activities and events are planned to award a contract.

2.1 Market Research

The process used for collecting and analyzing information about the entire market available to satisfy a buyer's need for the information required to establish the most suitable approach to acquiring, distributing, and supporting supplies and services.

In the expanded role of a business advisor, the contracting professional should consider an expanded concept of market research. Not only should the contracting professional determine the degree to which external sources could meet requirements, he or she should also look within the organization for information that might be of value in anticipating future requirements. It is within this context that market research can be viewed as having external and internal components.

LEXICON FOR MARKET RESEARCH:

External market research: Normally pertains to research activities undertaken once a requirement has been either defined or at least conceptualized. However, generalized external market research (undertaken in the absence of a requirement) can also be valuable to the contracting professional, particularly when one has also engaged in some level of internal market research. Whether it is used in response to a specific need or not, the external market research effort seeks to gain useful information about capabilities and limitations inherent in the commercial marketplace. The basic intent of external market research is to gain knowledge that will be used in determining the best method to obtain required goods and services consistent with pertinent law, regulation, and/or corporate policy. Just as the contracting professional can use internal market research to better understand and anticipate the actual and potential needs of the customer, external

39

market research should be used to better understand the actual and potential capabilities of external sources of supply. Standard external market research techniques include:

- Reviewing historical information on similar prior acquisitions for related market research information;

- Reviewing pertinent professional news, trade, association, or industry publications;

- Contacting knowledgeable third-party sources of unbiased information regarding potential sources;

- Attending trade or professional association shows and exhibits;

- Contacting customers of potential sources for past performance information;

- Reviewing catalogs and other printed or electronic information published by potential sources;

- Contacting potential sources for specific capabilities information or briefings; and

- Joining pertinent professional organizations and attending their meetings.

Though the amount of external market research conducted will vary according to the complexity of the anticipated effort and other issues, the results should be formally documented for current and future use.

Internal market research: For a contracting professional to be of maximum value to the management team and to the overall organization, he or she must be knowledgeable of the organization's mission. The contracting professional needs to know what products or services are generated by each segment of the organization; how these products or services are generated; who the organization's

customers are; what the organization's goals are; and what structures, processes, and procedures are in place to accomplish the goals. Fundamentally, the contracting professional needs to become immersed in the organization's activities and plans to the maximum extent possible. This level of involvement can usually be accomplished by activities such as:

- Reviewing historical information on prior acquisitions for internal customers;

- Attending regular management meetings of all internal customers;

- Receiving detailed briefings on the functions and processes of internal customers;

- Participating in short-term assignments of customer work units;

- Reading pertinent customer-oriented professional publications;

- Serving on cross-functional process improvement teams, or similar ad hoc teams, addressing issues that may have little or nothing to do with contracting; and

- Sharing information on contracting issues and trends with other managers.

The basic goal of internal market research is to learn as much as possible about the organization, how it does business, and how it has used goods and services acquired in the past. A secondary goal of internal market research is to develop good working relationships with the customer base.

Market survey: An attempt to ascertain whether other qualified sources capable of satisfying the buyer's requirements exist.

Monopsony: A market structure where a single buyer purchases a good or service, such as the federal government.

Request for information (RFI): May be used when the government does not presently intend to award a contract, but wants to obtain price, delivery, or other market information, or capabilities for planning purposes. Responses to these notices are not offers and cannot be accepted by the government to form a binding contract. There is no required format for RFIs.

2.2 Acquisition Methodology

A means of requesting or inviting offerors to submit offers, generally by issuing a solicitation. Solicitations basically consist of (1) a draft contract, (2) provisions for preparing and submitting offers, and (3) evaluation factors.

LEXICON FOR ACQUISITION METHODOLOGY:

Acquisition plan: A plan for an acquisition that serves as the basis for initiating the individual contracting actions necessary to acquire a system or support a program.

The acquisition plan should reflect a collaborative effort involving significant stakeholders. The level of detail provided in the acquisition plan will vary depending on the anticipated dollar value, level of complexity, degree of significance, and other appropriate factors. A written plan may not be required for simple, straightforward, low-dollar value purchases. In the absence of a written plan, the contracting professional should ensure that there is a common understanding and consensus among the stakeholders regarding the course of action to be taken. When required, written acquisition plans should clearly explain all pertinent issues relating to the acquisition, including:

- A description of the need to be satisfied. The description should be concise, yet complete enough to explain what the need is, how it came to be needed at the

current time, any pertinent history of related prior acquisitions, and how they were acquired.

- An explanation of conditions or constraints that relate to the proposed acquisition. These conditions or constraints might include the need for compatibility with existing or future equipment or systems; implementation constraints caused by space, personnel, or other limitations; budget constraints, particularly as they relate to lease vs. purchase decisions; and other known constraints that could influence cost, schedule, capability, or performance issues.

- The established cost targets for the acquisition, with sufficient explanation to support the targets. This section should include discussions of the following issues as appropriate: the make-or-buy decision, estimated life-cycle costs, design-to-cost, should-cost analysis, and other cost issues determined to be of significance.

- The required capabilities or performance to be acquired. This section should address such issues as speed, accuracy, reliability, ease of use, and other pertinent performance characteristics when acquiring goods. When acquiring services, the required performance standards or knowledge requirements that are required to provide the services should be discussed. This section should also explain how the goods or services being acquired relate to and will satisfy the need.

- Delivery or performance period requirements. This section should provide the required delivery date(s) or the required period of performance, as well as an explanation for why the dates or periods were selected. If an emergency or urgent condition exists that has influence on the delivery or performance requirements, explain that relationship, as well as the incremental impact that the emergency may have on cost considerations.

- Trade-offs related to the previously defined plans for cost, technical performance, capability, and schedule requirements. Explain what trade-off issues are likely to occur, the degree to which a trade-off decision may impact other plan components, and how trade-offs may impact the overall acquisition plan.

- A discussion of the level of risk associated with the technical, cost, schedule, and other pertinent aspects of the plan. This discussion should clearly define the anticipated risks; the strategies or actions planned or taken to eliminate, reduce, or mitigate risk to an acceptable level; and the likely consequences that might result from failure to achieve goals.

- The contracting plan of action. Taking into consideration all of the pertinent plan components mentioned above, the contracting plan of action should address such issues as:

  o Proposed sources that can provide the required goods or services;

  o The degree to which the acquisition will be subject to competition;

  o The contract type(s) proposed for use;

  o The source selection process, including an explanation of how the evaluation factors relate to the achievement of the goals of the acquisition;

  o How the contract will be administered after issuance;

  o Milestones or target dates for completion; and

  o Any other pertinent issues of concern.

The need for acquisition plans differs in the public and private sectors. In the public sector, such plans are normally required for significant or complex acquisitions. In the private sector, such plans may be created as the result of corporate policy or as a matter of professionalism or convenience. Regardless of whether they are required or desired, acquisition plans provide valuable information regarding the initial intent of a proposed acquisition and a basic roadmap to check against during the acquisition cycle.

Acquisition planning: The process by which efforts of all personnel responsible for an acquisition are coordinated and integrated through a comprehensive plan for fulfilling the buyer's need in a timely manner at a reasonable cost. It includes developing the overall strategy for management of the acquisition. Acquisition planning includes all activities and events required for both buyers and sellers to prepare for, negotiate, and form a binding contractual arrangement.

Planning is an essential preliminary component to the successful completion of virtually any effort. In the environments of government and business, planning is required to focus the application of usually scarce resources to the goal-directed activity necessary to accomplish the mission or functions of the organization. As it relates to the contracting profession, planning in general and acquisition planning in particular was a function that was often thought to begin at the point where a customer expressed a need for goods or services, or delivered a requirement to the contracting office.

Recent literature in the contracting profession has defined and described the need for the contracting professional to expand beyond the historical boundaries of the contracting office, and become a business advisor and part of the multi-disciplinary management team. As a result of this new environment, changes are required in the way contracting professionals perform acquisition planning. Acquisition planning should be viewed as a team effort, requiring the talents and input of many individuals other than the contracting professional, including: the customer; budget or finance experts; technical experts (IT, logistics); legal counsel; and other direct or indirect stakeholders. The planning process should begin before the traditional first customer contact, and should have an inward as well as outward focus, particularly as it relates to an important acquisition planning tool—market research.

Acquisition strategy: The conceptual framework for conducting systems acquisition. It encompasses the broad concepts and objectives that direct and control the overall development, production, and deployment of a system.

Contract bundling: The practice of combining requirements into one "umbrella" solicitation with the result that the offeror must be able to perform increasingly larger contracts covering multiple and diverse elements of performance.

Documenting requirements: Process for documenting requirements that meet the purchaser's or user's needs and representing those needs through measurable criteria.

Evaluation procedures: The solicitation package should clearly indicate the general procedures to be used to evaluate proposals and the decisions to be used as the basis for an award. The method of acquisition normally determines the basis for the award. The use of an invitation for bids (IFB) requires that the selection be based on price. The use of a request for proposal (RFP) indicates a negotiated procurement where various factors, with potentially different degrees of relative significance, will serve as the basis for award. The evaluation procedures can influence, either positively or negatively, the quality of proposals received from offerors.

Great care must be taken in determining evaluation factors. Too few factors may result in the receipt of inadequate proposals that are impossible to evaluate. Too many factors may result in the receipt of exceedingly complex proposals—or none at all. Though price will normally always be included as an evaluation factor, other factors such as cost realism, technical excellence, management capability, past performance, and other relevant factors can and should be included as appropriate. Cost or price is a required evaluation factor in federal government. Each evaluation factor should be independent of the other factors, again to reduce the potential for confusion. It is also important to advise potential offerors of the relative significance of the evaluation factors to each other. Though it is usually neither required nor desirable to provide all the details of the evaluation plan in the solicitation, it is important for potential offerors to understand how proposals will be evaluated, the factors that will make up the evaluation, and the relative importance of each evaluation factor to each other and to the overall acquisition.

Integrated project/product team (IPT): Team composed of representatives from appropriate functional disciplines working together to build successful programs, identify and resolve issues, and make sound and timely recommendations to facilitate decision making. There are three types of IPTs: Overreaching IPTs (OIPTs), which focus on strategic guidance, program assessment, and issue resolution; working-level IPTs (WIPTs), which identify and resolve program issues, determine program status, and seek opportunities for acquisition reform; and program-level IPTs (PIPTs), which focus on program execution and many include representative from both government and, after contract award, industry.

Negotiation: Permits bargaining and often affords sellers an opportunity to revise offers before final evaluation and contract award.

Objective: An objective is a brief statement of the goal to be achieved, the end product desired, or the basic purpose of the requirement.

Pre-award process (buyer): Process by which buyers develop a comprehensive plan for fulfilling requirements for products or services in a timely manner at a reasonable price; includes developing an overall strategy for the purchase, which is accomplished through researching the marketplace, developing strategy, initiating the procurement, and selecting a supplier.

Pre-award process (seller): Process by which sellers develop and execute a strategy for obtaining the award of a contract, including market strategies, pricing strategies, and responding to the procurement.

Pre-award surveys: An evaluation of a prospective contractor's ability to perform a specific contract, performed by the contract administration office or the purchasing office, with assistance from a audit organization, at the request of either office. The evaluation addresses the physical, technical, managerial, and financial capability of the prospective contractor. The adequacy of the contractor's accounting and management systems and procedures, and past performance record, is also addressed.

Publicizing: Issuing solicitation packages and the degree to which competitive proposals are sought often depends on the organization performing the buying function. Government contracting professionals are subject to a law- and regulation-based preference for fully competitive procurements. Though there are a number of authorized exceptions permitting less than full and open competition and sole-source acquisition, the general rule in government contracting is to seek the maximum level of meaningful competition whenever possible. Commercial contracting professionals sometimes work in organizations that also have a preference for competitive acquisition. However, sometimes other commercial considerations such as supply chain agreements, approved source lists, and other business decisions can have an influence on the degree to which competition is pursued. When competition is a goal, the buying organization normally uses publicizing as a technique to ensure adequate competition.

- **Government agencies**: Government contracting organizations are normally required to post solicitation packages exceeding certain dollar thresholds for full and open competition on an official Internet website. Though certain limitations can apply to these postings (including small business set-asides, restricting competition to firms that hold GSA Federal Supply Service (FSS) contracts, and other discriminators) the fundamental intent of these postings at a single location is to provide a uniform source of information to the business community in pursuit of a required or desired level of competition.

Solicitation packages that do not exceed certain dollar thresholds are normally competed by selecting an appropriate number of potential offerors and issuing the solicitation to them. Though the number of firms solicited usually varies depending on the dollar value and complexity of the acquisition, the intent is to seek a level of competition that will reasonably result in the receipt of multiple proposals, that will produce a competitive award, and will not cause undue administrative burden to the agency.

- **Commercial organizations**: Commercial contracting organizations may advertise their requirements in newspapers, trade journals, professional publications, and similar media. They may also provide the solicitation to capable firms in their supply chain, or as the result of other business agreements.

Commercial firms may also advertise business opportunities on their official Internet website, in much the same manner as government agencies sometimes do. Though the methods for publicizing active solicitation packages may vary, the basic purpose does not. When competition is required or desired, the solicitation should be advertised uniformly to ensure the target market of potential offerors is aware of the opportunity. Additionally, some other concepts are to be used to make the publicity effort more meaningful.

Solicitations should remain open or active for a period of time sufficient to permit potential offerors enough time to carefully and completely review and analyze all aspects of the requirement, make an informed bid/no-bid decision, and prepare and submit their best proposal. Though the contracting professional often faces internal pressures to reduce the acquisition cycle time, the length of time a solicitation remains open can have a direct impact on the number and quality of proposals received and the success or failure of the overall acquisition.

Contracting professionals should normally provide a period of time, within the solicitation period, for potential offerors to submit written questions and/or to attend pre-proposal conferences. These activities are often very valuable in clarifying the buyer's intent, as well as technical or other complex aspects related to the acquisition. These conferences can sometimes include a "walk-through" when the contract will be performed at the buyer's location, or other pertinent information that could be of value to potential offerors.

The need for changes or amendments to a solicitation may become evident after responding to written questions or after a pre-proposal conference. When appropriate, the solicitation should be modified to reflect the necessary changes and the due date for proposals should be extended to provide offerors the opportunity to respond to the changes.

The degree to which solicitation packages are publicized usually has a direct impact on both the quality and quantity of competitive proposals received. The solicitation phase is often a target when trying to reduce acquisition cycle time, primarily because a reduction in the length of time a solicitation remains open has little or no immediate adverse impact on the buying organization. Contracting professionals need to remain aware, however, that an inadequate solicitation period often affects the overall quality of the acquisition.

Request for proposals (RFP): A solicitation document used in other-than-sealed-bid procurements. RFPs are used in negotiated procurements to communicate buyer requirements to prospective sellers and to solicit proposals from them.

Request for quotations (RFQ): In federal contracting, this is a solicitation document used in other-than-sealed-bids procurements. Because an RFQ is merely a request for information, quotes submitted in response to it are not offers and consequently may not be accepted by the government to form a binding contract. In commercial contracting, this is a solicitation document used to request information; quotes submitted in response are typically counteroffers on seller's terms.

Request for technical proposal (RFTP): A solicitation document used in two-step sealed bidding. Normally in letter form, RFTPs ask only for technical information.

Price and cost breakdowns are forbidden in federal contracting, but for commercial contracting they are either budgetary or omitted at the RFTP stage. Also, in commercial contracting they may be used to prequalify contractors.

Requirements preparation: The preparation of the requirements, also referred to as solicitation preparation, is arguably the single most important function in the acquisition cycle. Although the acquisition planning activities have a significant impact on the success or failure of the proposed acquisition, requirements preparation usually provides the last major opportunity for the contracting professional to influence the solicitation package before it leaves the organization. It is therefore important that the contracting professional, in collaboration with the customer and required internal sources of specific expertise, craft a solicitation package that accurately reflects the customer's needs and communicates those needs and other related information clearly and concisely to potential offerors. The end goal should always be to satisfy the customer's need, at a fair price, with the minimum acceptable level of risk.

Once the solicitation package has been completed, there are a number of techniques that the buyer can use to validate the solicitation package's completeness and accuracy before it is formally issued. Some of these techniques include an independent technical review obtaining marketplace comments, and presolicitation notices and conferences.

- **Independent technical review:** The solicitation package can be reviewed by technical experts, legal counsel, and other resources within the organization to ensure it is complete and accurate. Normally, this independent technical review team is composed of people who had no prior involvement with the solicitation package.

- **Obtaining marketplace comments:** A draft of the solicitation package can be issued to potential offerors requesting review and comments or suggestions. This pre-release review sometimes yields useful suggestions for revision that might otherwise have been overlooked. However, the contracting professional needs to be aware of the possibility that potential offerors may use this opportunity for preliminary marketing purposes and may try to influence content changes in the solicitation that enhance their ability to successfully compete for the contract.

- **Presolicitation notices and conferences:** Presolicitation notices and conferences can be used to help identify potential interested sources and can provide a forum to explain technical or complicated aspects of the solicitation. These efforts can sometimes separate the interested potential sources from the merely curious ones.

Responsibilities: Contracting managers are responsible for ensuring performance of all necessary actions for effective contracting, ensuring compliance with the terms of the contract and safeguarding the interests of the government or company.

Scope: The scope is a general statement defining the parameters or boundaries of expected actions, required performance, or products required. Scope statements can be viewed as the "fenced-in area" in which the contractor performs.

Severable: A contract divisible into several parts; a default of one section does not invalidate the whole contract.

Source selection plan: The document that describes the selection criteria, process, and organization to be used in evaluating proposals for competitively awarded contracts.

Specifications: A description of the technical requirements for a material, product, or service that includes the criteria for determining whether the requirements a have been met. As used in the law relating to patents, manufacturing, and contracting contracts, a particular order or detailed statement, account description, or listing of various events.

Statement of work (SOW): The SOW is likely the single most important document in the solicitation package. The SOW is the document that describes the goods or services required in sufficient detail so as to provide potential offerors with a complete understanding of the requirement. Generally, there are three basic types of SOWs—design, performance, and functional. The differences among them relate to the degree to which the requirement is defined and explained, from specific to general. Each type of SOW has its own advantages and disadvantages, and SOWs often reflect elements of all three basic types in order to completely describe the requirement.

- **Design SOW**: A design SOW is most often used when the buyer requires a specific manufactured good. Design SOWs are extremely detailed, and usually define all required materials, production processes, and specifications such as size, shape, color, tolerances, etc. Design SOWs also frequently provide specific requirements related to quality, inspection, packaging, and related needs. The basic intent of a design SOW is to document the requirement with such specificity as to permit any competent seller to be able to provide the product, and that the end product will be exactly what the buyer required. The degree of precision inherent in design SOWs also presents challenges for the contracting professional. Design SOWs may restrict the competitive process by imposing too many specifications that result in no-bid

decisions from sellers that might otherwise be willing to provide the product. Design SOWs may also result in higher costs, since the seller may have to use materials and processes that are different from those used in the normal course of business. Additionally, the buyer assumes virtually total performance risk when contracting with design SOWs, since the seller is performing based on the buyer's design and specification requirements. As a result of these drawbacks, the use of design SOWs is commonly discouraged whenever a less restrictive type of SOW can be reasonably expected to provide the results required.

- **Performance SOW**: Performance SOWs are less restrictive than design SOWs. Performance SOWs define requirements in terms that relate to minimum acceptable standards or ranges of acceptable performance. A performance SOW may require a particular approach or a particular type of product, but it leaves most of the "how" decisions to the contractor. Performance SOWs are normally considered to enhance competition because they enable a contractor to utilize their inherent strengths and creativity to satisfy the requirement.

- **Functional SOW**: The functional SOW is the least restrictive of the three basic SOW types. Functional SOWs describe requirements in terms of the end purpose, expected result, or final objective rather than in terms of how the work effort is to be performed. Though the functional SOW may include needed quality standards or minimum essential characteristics, it focuses primarily on the "what" aspects of the requirement, not "how to." Functional SOWs provide the contractor with the maximum degree of flexibility and innovation in determining how best to satisfy the buying organization's needs. It is for this reason that functional SOWs are currently the most preferred type of SOW in most government and commercial contracting organizations.

In practice, SOWs rarely fall neatly into one of the three types discussed. Most SOWs reflect characteristics of at least two, if not all three, SOW types in order to adequately describe the requirement.

Statement of Work elements: Regardless of which type or types are used, SOWs normally contain at least some of the following elements:

- **Objective**: A brief statement of the goal to be achieved, the end product desired, or the basic purpose of the requirement.

- **Scope**: A general statement defining the parameters or boundaries of expected actions, required performance, or products required. Scope statements can be viewed as the "fenced-in area" in which the contractor performs.

- **Description of work required**: A sufficiently detailed explanation of what is required. The description often contains an explanation of interfaces that will impact the work effort, a history of how the required effort came to be needed, required place of performance, issues and problems that require resolution, and other pertinent information. To the maximum extent possible, the description should be outcome-focused, providing the contractor as much flexibility as possible for determining how to accomplish the work required to achieve the objective within the defined scope. When necessary specific performance elements can be prescribed, but they should be kept to a minimum.

- **Performance standards and reporting requirements**: An explanation of how the contractor's work effort will be evaluated, in terms of quantity, quality, frequency, or other appropriate measures. The performance standards should clearly define the expected, required ,or acceptable level of performance that will be expected from the contractor. The standards need to be achievable and measurable. Reporting requirements should explain how often and in what format any required progress or performance reports will be provided. Both performance standards and reporting requirements should be limited to the minimum necessary to achieve effective and efficient contract administration.

- **Staffing requirements**: If personnel with certain specific qualifications are required to perform the work (e.g., electrical engineer, certified public accountant, etc.), these qualifications should be included. However, in most cases, the contractor should have the option to propose staffing levels and composition to accomplish the required work.

- **Resources to be provided**: Specify any space, equipment, materials, services, information, or other resources that will be provided to the contractor.

- **Appropriate reference documents**: Provide a list of any pertinent reference documents that may have been discussed in the SOW, or that may be required by the contractor to ensure adequate performance or clarify contract requirements.

As previously mentioned, statements of work may be of varying lengths and levels of complexity, depending on the needs of the buying organization. While not all SOWs will necessarily contain all the elements noted, each SOW should be constructed so as to provide a complete, clear, and concise description of the requirement. Well-constructed SOWs reduce risk, enhance competition, and help achieve organizational goals.

Terms and conditions: In addition to the statement of work and contract type and method, terms and conditions are another component of the requirements package that help define the business relationship between the buyer and seller and the rights and obligations of both parties to the contract. The primary function of terms and conditions is to eliminate or reduce the risk of contract ambiguity, often the source of disputes and misunderstandings. Most contracting organizations include standard terms and conditions related to certain contract types in all solicitations and resulting contracts. In many cases, the selection of clauses that comprise the terms and conditions is an automated function that occurs within the buyer's contract writing software programs. In other cases, terms and conditions can be selected from a "shopping list" provided for the appropriate contract type. In still other cases, specific clauses must be crafted to meet an individual need, usually with the assistance of legal counsel and other professionals. Though frequently referred to as "boilerplate" and sometimes included in solicitations as little more than an afterthought, terms and conditions are another risk mitigating tool that can be used by the contracting professional to enhance the likelihood of success. A careful review of terms and conditions to be included in the solicitation can reveal gaps that could cause confusion, unnecessary terms and conditions that could adversely affect price or performance, or terms and conditions that conflict with each other. Terms and conditions should be reviewed to ensure each one serves a legitimate purpose, is required or provides a direct benefit to the acquisition in question, promotes an acceptable level of risk sharing between buyer and seller, and does not impose unreasonable burdens on prospective offerors.

2.3 Bid and Proposal Preparation

Activities and events required to submit an offer or quotation, usually in response to a customer request. Proposal preparation includes defining the proposal team, writing the proposal, and submitting the proposal. Typically, specific areas to focus on are the statement of work, invoicing and payment, and the contract type.

LEXICON FOR BID AND PROPOSAL PREPARATION:

Alternate bid/proposal: When one of two or more offers on the same item, submitted on different bases by the same seller, as provided by the invitation for bid.

Amendment: A change (correction, deletion, or addition) to any information contained in an invitation for bid (IFB) or request for proposal (RFP) (or previous amendment thereto). The amendment becomes part of the solicitation and any resulting contract.

Bid or no-bid decision: Determination made by seller's management whether or not to submit an offer, usually in response to a customer request.

Business development: A broad term applied to the process of strengthening ties with existing clients as well as cultivating customers in other market sectors. In order to accomplish this goal, business development normally crosses the traditional functions of sales, marketing, customer care, operations, and management to promote this process of expansion on more than one level. One of the foundational aspects of business development is to assess the current assets of the organization as they relate to the maintenance and expansion of the business. To this end, team members will work closely with sales and marketing professionals to identify the degree of penetration already enjoyed by the organization in various sectors of the consumer base.

- **Capture**: Positioning individuals in the buyers' organizations to help assure the proposal and the organization are preferred over that of the competition.

- **Capture management**: The process of winning more business.

- **Capture manager**: Person responsible to manage an opportunity from bid decision to contract award.

- **Capture plan**: Documented analysis, strategies, and actions initiated following the bid decision that details customer issues, considerations relating to competitor and internal positioning, approaches, and management tasks to be implemented to capture a particular opportunity.

- **Capture planning**: Process of assessing the customer and competitive environment and implementing strategies oriented toward capturing a specific business opportunity.

- **Capture strategy**: Plan to win a specific, defined opportunity.

- **Capture team**: Small group of individuals within a seller's organization who manage a capture strategy to contract award, typically including a capture manager, a technical lead, and the prospective program manager as a minimum, depending on the specific requirements of the pursuit.

Clarification: Used in negotiations for the sole purpose of eliminating minor irregularities, informalities, or apparent clerical mistakes in the proposal.

Color team reviews: Many organizations conduct color team reviews as part of their business development and proposal processes. These reviews are designed to help select the right opportunities on which to bid, confirm win strategies, address proposal and performance risk, and support development of high-quality proposals. While different organizations define color-team review labels differently, the most common teams and their definitions are:

- **Gold team**: Approves final proposal and price. This review by senior managers directly responsible for the offer and its execution confirms that the proposal contains acceptable profit and risk.

- **Purple team**: Assesses the opportunity for and alignment with organizational goals.

- **Pink team**: Ensures the proposal is complete and accurate. The pink team should include technical personnel who are familiar with the technology referenced in the proposal. If possible, pink team reviewers should be people who have had no involvement with the proposal up to this point, yet are technically competent in the areas it deals with. They should have no preconceived biases, but should understand the client and have a full understanding of the theme and issues. The pink team reviewers should read the proposal from beginning to end and compare it to the SOW, proposal preparation instructions, and evaluation criteria. In addition to checking the technical accuracy and validity of the proposal, the reviewers should also ensure the proposal responds to everything in the RFP and that the seller's message is clear.

- **Red team**: Ensures the proposal makes sense and solves the customer's business problem. Reviews to evaluate the proposal for customer focus, completeness, and clear communication of the winning strategy and solution by people who are independent of the proposal team and offer different perspectives. The red team is typically comprised of experts on the buyer, the buyer's industry, competitors, the organization, technology, approach, and on preparing and presenting winning proposals.

- **Others:**

  ○ **Black hat**: Predicts competitors' solutions.

  ○ **Green team**: Reviews cost/price proposal.

  ○ **White team**: Compiles "lessons learned" from capture planning through proposal development to contract award.

Compliance matrix: A common technique used to identify gaps in the seller's ability to meet the customer's needs as defined in the RFP. It lists all the solicitation references and functional requirements, along with indicators of the level of compliance (i.e., full, partial, or none).

Cost proposal: The document used to communicate estimated cost to perform the contract in suitable detail for the buyer's review and analysis. Sometimes it includes cost or pricing data.

Mailbox rule: Accepting an offer is effective when deposited in the mail if the envelope is properly addressed.

Market strategy: The action plan of how a company will sell its services or products. The strategy must consider the company's business environment, its abilities and competencies, the desires of top management, and overall mission objectives. Market strategy consists of four basic concepts: market segmentation, market positioning, market entry, and marketing mix.

Offer: Describes what the seller is willing to agree to and its terms; becomes part of the contract when accepted by the buyer.

Proposal: A written offer by a seller describing its offering terms. Proposals may be issued in response to a specific request or may be made unilaterally when a seller feels there may be an interest in its offer (see "unsolicited proposal"). When submitted in response to a government request for proposal (RFP), submissions are often required to be organized in three categories: technical, management, and cost.

Proposal evaluation: Once the offerors have submitted their proposals and the contracting officer has determined if the proposals are acceptable for evaluation, the evaluators read and assess the proposals in accordance with the RFP's evaluation criteria and the agency's procedures, which are sometimes documented in a source selection plan or a source selection evaluation guide.

Proposal manager: Person responsible for proposal development, including maintaining schedules, coordinating input, reviews, and strategy implementation; resolving internal problems; and providing leadership.

Proposal team: The first step in proposal preparation is to define who will be on the team. Possible candidates include the chief financial officer, proposal/capture manager, program manager, contracting, accounting, technical writers, and teaming partners.

Risk analysis: Managing factors that create the potential loss or injury in the performance of a contract. It includes all activities necessary to identify, analyze, plan, track, or control risk management activities. It also includes communication of risks and risk management internally and externally.

Risk management: The process for identifying, analyzing, and administering techniques to minimize potential financial loss from such exposure.

Should cost: Assessment of the costs of individual elements to comprise the price to win.

Storyboarding: Conceptual planning tool used to help proposal writers plan each proposal section before drafting text. It contains assignments, requirements, strategies, preliminary visuals, and content.

Teaming: Agreement among two or more prospective offerors to participate jointly in a business venture.

Unsolicited proposal: A proposal that is made by a prospective seller without prior formal or informal solicitation from the buyer.

2.4 Negotiation

Negotiation is the process by which two or more competent parties reach an agreement to buy or sell products or services. Contract negotiations may be conducted formally or informally, and may involve many people or just two—a representative for the buyer and a representative for the seller. Contract negotiation may take a few minutes or may involve lengthy discussions.

LEXICON FOR NEGOTIATION:

Acquisition team: Large and/or complex acquisitions usually require different people to participate in the negotiations, with each person contributing a special skill. Selection of team members depends on the nature of the acquisition and the experience that each member brings to the team. Team members on each side may include, but are not limited to, the contract professional, financial analyst, cost analyst, legal counsel, design engineer, production specialist, quality control specialist, and note taker. The negotiation teams for the buyer and seller each designate a lead negotiator for their team, which most often is the contract professional depending on the entity's practice and industry. In the case of federal contracting, the lead negotiator is always the contracting officer.

Adequacy of offer/conformance to requirements: Purchasing techniques that enable buyers to solicit input from multiple suppliers and create a solicitation document, taking the best from each. Accordingly, sellers are able to develop a compliance matrix that lists all solicitation and functional requirements, along with an assessment of the firm's competitive strengths and weaknesses.

Caucus: Used to break away from formal negotiations for the team to consider a point. When a counteroffer is made, a caucus can be used to confer with your negotiation team to consider all aspects of the counteroffer. A caucus is useful to discuss anything about the on-going negotiation you don't want the other team to hear. A caucus can be used when a team member wants to bring to the negotiator's attention an important fact, or if a fact needs to be checked with a team member, or if management approval is necessary in order to make a concession or counter-offer.

Concession strategy: The concession strategy is a plan of the goals and positions, and sometimes the underlying interests, you will be trading with the other party. Before entering into negotiations, at the very least you should have clarity on your and the other party's goals, and a sequence of which goals you want to trade or exchange. Concession strategies vary in detail.

Counteroffer: An offer made in response to an original offer that changes the terms of the original.

Documentation: As an agreement is reached, both parties must document it. The documentation must explain the facts upon which they based the agreement. The purpose of documentation is to establish that both parties accepted the final agreement. A lot of paperwork is accumulated by the end of negotiations and the negotiation documentation summarizes the agreements and concessions. It presents each step from solicitation to proposal to negotiation objectives to concessions to final agreement.

Although the narrative may have different formats or styles, the following identifies some basic information that documentation should include:

- A description of the supplies or services to be purchased, quantities, and delivery schedule;

- The solicitation/proposal number;

- The parties involved, including complete names, addresses, and phone numbers;

- The acquisition history, including information gathered;

- The negotiation objectives and their justifications; and

- A negotiation summary including:

  o Concessions made and their impact on negotiation objectives,

  o Major items discussed and the parties' positions and outcomes,

  o Use of and reliance upon data (including, but not limited to price/cost) submitted, and

  o A signed copy of the agreed-to final position.

Both parties keep this documentation in the contract file to explain the final agreement and why it is reasonable. It will allow other personnel who were not involved in the negotiations to track how the negotiators reached the final agreement.

Fact finding: The process of identifying and obtaining information necessary to complete proposal evaluation.

Negotiation objectives: Determining the issues to be negotiated and the minimum and maximum positions for each issue. They address strategies that provide the overall framework that will guide the conduct of the negotiation; includes both win-lose and win-win strategies and all tactics and countertactics necessary to achieve the desired result.

The facts are different for each negotiation even if the acquisition is for the same item as previously purchased. The market may be different, the delivery schedule may be different, or the economy may be different. All of these factors influence pricing decisions and negotiation objectives.

Establishing the negotiation objectives entails more than cost analysis and comparison. Most aspects of a solicitation are negotiable, such as the statement of work, contract type, delivery schedule, warranties, payment terms, terms and conditions, and reporting requirements. These aspects may be negotiable depending on the circumstances surrounding the acquisition.

Both buyers and sellers need to establish specific and realistic negotiation objectives. An objective of "the best price we can get" is neither specific nor realistic, as there would be no way of knowing if the result was the best price. Establishing negotiation objectives is an ongoing process because the negotiation objectives will change as the situation changes.

Based on the review of proposed costs, a negotiation objective is prepared based on the best information available. Since the circumstances change, the objective needs to be flexible. A way to ensure flexibility is to develop three positions in preparing an objective: the minimum objective, most likely objective, and maximum objective. By doing so, a range is established that permits movement one way or another depending on the situation. When the seller's objective overlaps the buyer's objective, both parties are satisfied with the final agreement.

Preparation: This is the most important step in the negotiation process. Buyers and sellers have unique advantages going into negotiations. Buyers know how much money is available, and the amount and nature of competition. Sellers know the basis for cost estimates and where there is flexibility in their proposal. Nonetheless, both parties must plan for negotiations. Thorough preparations can lead to smooth negotiations, a good contract, fewer changes, and successful performance.

The first step in the preparation process is to understand the acquisition. The buyer must know what is being bought, why it is needed, and whether it has been bought before. Although it is not always possible for every buyer to do an in-depth analysis of each acquisition, it is important to get to know as much as possible before entering negotiations. Sellers must also understand the acquisition. They should know the purpose of the acquisition; the buyer's objectives; whether the buyer is the end-user; if not the buyer, who is the end-user; and the end-user's needs.

Sole-source negotiation: The process for entering into or modifying a contract after soliciting and negotiating with only one source.

Standards: Used in competitive negotiations to evaluate a proposal. It includes both the maximum acceptable value and the minimum acceptable value for all selected evaluation criteria.

Strategy and tactics: Specific methods used during negotiations to reach agreement. The use and effectiveness of any strategy depends on a number of factors, including the nature of the acquisition and each party's long- and short-term objectives. In addition to the long- and short-term objectives, the parties must evaluate the nature of their relationship. On the one hand, if a long-term continuing relationship is important, then strategies and tactics used are usually cooperative. On the other hand, if the relationship is only a one-time, short-term relationship, then a more competitive strategy may be effective.

Four basic tactics are the cooperative mode, competitive mode, time restrictions, and deadlock.

1. The **cooperative mode** presumes that reasonable people are needed to achieve reasonable outcomes. The planning before the negotiation includes developing justifications and explanations for a party's position. This allows compromise and cooperation during negotiations because it allows the other party to understand and recognize the reasonableness and validity of the positions. Each party recognizes that the other party might have a position that meets the objectives of both parties, resulting in a mutually agreeable result. This tactic requires patience as the mutually agreeable result may not be presented immediately.

2. The **competitive mode** is used when each party views the other as an adversary and concessions are gained at the expense of the other party. Lack of planning can lead to this approach, such as not having justifiable reasons for a position. The ability to convincingly apply pressure is helpful in this mode. However, one should be careful not to issue threats; the other party may accept the threat rather than concede a point.

3. **Time restrictions** are usually present at any negotiation—the contract must be awarded so deliveries can be met or before funds expire. Learning to work under this pressure is important because concessions made due to time limits may not meet negotiation objectives. Extreme deadlines make adequate preparation difficult and may lead unprepared negotiators to make decisions based solely on time constraints. Time restrictions can be worked around by negotiating delivery schedule, inspection requirement, compensated overtime, or a letter contract. Time tactics can range from "my flight's scheduled to leave in an hour" to "the funding will not be available unless the contract is awarded today."

4. **Deadlock** is the inability to continue negotiations because the parties cannot or will not be flexible in their positions. If the negotiations break down and there is a deadlock, the party with time on its side usually benefits. Patience is also important when a deadlock occurs because new objectives must be established requiring additional management reviews. While objectives are re-established, both parties should consider how to allow the other party a "face-saving" way to concede: give the other party an opening, allowing a concession. After a deadlock happens, one party usually welcomes the other party back into negotiations. If the buyer has begun negotiating with a second seller, the position of the seller is greatly reduced when they enter back into negotiations. A deadlock can sometimes be resolved by introducing new people into the negotiation process to allow another perspective.

Technical leveling: Occurs when a buyer helps a seller bring its proposal up to the level of other proposals through successive rounds of discussion.

Technical transfusion: Occurs when technical information pertaining to a proposal is disclosed and results in improvement of a competing proposal.

2.5 Source Selection

Selection of the "winning" proposal is often referred to as the source selection, although the term is also sometimes used to represent all activities inherent in the evaluation process. The source selection is sometimes made by the contracting professional or the senior contracting professional in the organization, sometimes by a senior manager in the customer's organization, and sometimes by a neutral senior manager who has had no prior involvement in the acquisition process. Regardless of who makes the selection, the selection decision is normally intended to reflect the independent judgment of the selection official.

LEXICON FOR SOURCE SELECTION:

Award: The procurement decision to buy a supply or service from one or more companies on specified terms typically identified in the solicitation (IFB or RFP) including the dollar amount.

Best value: The expected outcome of an acquisition that provides the greatest overall benefit in response to the requirement. Price may not be the determining factor of contract award. The best value may mean awarding a contract to a company with higher technical capability at a higher cost.

Competitive range: The competitive range comprised of all of the most highly rated proposals.

Cost and price analysis: A review to determine and evaluate the cost elements in an offeror's or contractor's proposal to determine how well the proposed costs represent what the cost of the contract should be, assuming reasonable economy and efficiency. Factors to be considered in determining pricing and financial impact of a procurement include commodity markets, price lists, price quotations, negotiated pricing, inputs costs, transactions costs, relational costs, and landed costs.

Debriefing: An explanation given by the buyer or to an offeror detailing the reasons the offeror's proposal was unsuccessful.

Responsibility determination: The process by which a seller is found to be a capable party that has the financial resources, personnel, facilities, integrity, and overall capability to fulfill specific contractual requirements satisfactorily.

Discussions: Any oral or written exchanges between the buyer and the seller, other than those conducted to resolve minor clerical errors, that provide the offeror an opportunity to revise or modify its proposal. In federal government contracting, discussions are held only with companies that are in the competitive range.

Effective competition: This exists when two or more responsible sellers acting independently contend for a contract that results in the buyer receiving either (1) the lowest cost or (2) the optimal combination of technical design coupled with a cost-effective price.

Evaluation factors: Factors that are tailored to each acquisition and the consideration of each proposal and that establish a baseline for proposal evaluation for recommendations regarding the source selection decision. Price, or cost to the buyer, and quality are addressed. Although evaluation factors are tailored to each acquisition, buyers tend to focus on the same broad categories: technical, management (including key personnel and security), cost or price, and past performance. The following is a presentation of some typical evaluation considerations:

- **Management considerations**: An offeror's management proposal identifies its plan for efficiently managing the work proposed in its technical proposal. A management proposal may cover the vendor's proposed organizational structure and essential management functions and how it will integrate these management functions.

- **Past performance**: Relevant information concerning how well an offeror has performed similar work in the past is often used as a significant evaluation factor. Offerors are normally required to submit past performance data that references other contracts they have performed that are similar in nature to the current requirement. When required by the solicitation, the evaluation plan must address how past performance issues will be evaluated, including the effect (usually neutral) of an offeror having little or no pertinent past performance. Evaluation factors for past performance normally require the evaluators or the contracting professional to attempt to verify the accuracy of past performance information submitted by an offeror. This is usually accomplished by contacting the sources provided by the offeror and obtaining answers to an established set of past performance questions.

- **Price**: Price (or cost) should always be an evaluation factor. In some cases, such as sealed bidding, price is the only factor. In negotiated procurements, price is always included, but may be of secondary or even lesser significance compared to other evaluation criteria.

- **Technical considerations**: An offeror's technical proposal describes how well it understands the statement of work and the RFP requirements. The evaluation team reads and analyzes the technical proposal to evaluate the offeror's comprehension of the requirements set forth in the RFP. Although costs are analyzed separately from the technical proposal, they may signify the offeror's understanding of the resources, personnel, and material required to perform the contract.

The evaluation plan should also address the relative significance of all evaluation factors to be used as a basis for selection, as well as the relative significance of price factors to non-price factors. This factor-ranking process is particularly important in negotiated procurements, because the award is often made to some offeror other than the lowest price. As with all other evaluation factors, the relative significance of the factors should have also been addressed in the solicitation.

Evaluation process: The process used to evaluate offers against established selection criteria in accordance with the source selection plan.

Implied acceptance: In the case of a bilateral contract, acceptance of an offer need not be expressed, but it may be shown by any words or acts indicating the offeror's assent of the proposed bargain.

Lease or buy decision: The decision concerning whether to contract for the possession and use of an asset owned by another party for a period of time in return for lease payments, as opposed to purchasing the asset.

Life-cycle cost: The total cost of a system, building, or other product computed over its useful life. It includes all relevant costs involved in acquiring, owning, operating, maintaining, and disposing of the system or product over a specified period of time, including environmental and energy costs.

Lowest priced technically acceptable (LPTA): A negotiated acquisition method that is appropriate when best value is expected to result from selecting the techni-

cally acceptable proposal with the lowest evaluated price.

Oral presentations: May substitute for, or augment, written information. Use of oral presentations as a substitute for portions of a proposal can be effective in streamlining the source selection process. Oral presentations may occur at any time in the acquisition process, and are subject to the same restrictions as written information, regarding timing and content. Oral presentations provide an opportunity for dialogue among the parties.

Proposal evaluation: Assessing proposals and the offeror's ability to perform the prospective contract successfully. The buyer evaluates competitive proposals and then assesses their relative qualities solely on the factors and subfactors specified in the solicitation. Evaluations may be conducted using any rating method or combination of methods, including color or adjectival ratings, numerical weights, and ordinal rankings. The relative strengths, deficiencies, significant weaknesses, and risks supporting proposal evaluation is documented and added to the contract file.

Responsive: When a seller materially complies with a solicitation and is capable of being made compliant through discussions.

Source selection authority (SSA): Can refer either to an individual or a team. While any organization wanting to outsource or subcontract a project or portions of a project may use the term *SSA*, most often it is used in a government context. A key factor of selection authority responsibility involves identifying requirements and communicating those requirements such that offerors clearly understand the project. As offers come in, the SSA has the responsibility of making value judgments with the objective of selecting the proposal providing the best value to the buying organization.

Source selection board: Any board, team, council, or other group that evaluates bids or proposals for the purpose of selecting a contract/contractor.

Source selection decision: The source selection authority's (SSA) decision is based on a comparative assessment of proposals against all source selection criteria in the solicitation. While the SSA may use reports and analyses prepared by others, the source selection decision represents the SSA's independent judgment. The source selection decision is documented, and the documentation includes the rationale for any business judgments and tradeoffs made or relied on by the SSA, including benefits associated with additional costs. Although the rationale for the selection decision must be documented, that documentation need not quantify the tradeoffs that led to the decision.

Source selection objective: The objective of source selection is to select the proposal that represents the best value.

Source selection plan: Incorporates the required elements of an acquisition plan, thus satisfying the requirement. A written source selection plan is particularly important for a complex negotiated acquisition that will take a long time to complete. Organizations normally do not require source selection plans for less costly acquisitions; the dollar thresholds vary by organization. Documenting key elements of the source selection is an important part of the planning process. This documentation can be done either in a separate source selection plan (SSP), if required by the agency, or as a supplement to the acquisition plan. The source selection plan should discuss the acquisition strategy, including the requirements, expected competition, and the method of procurement. It serves several purposes, including:

- Defining a specific approach for soliciting and evaluating proposals;

- Describing the evaluation factors and subfactors, their relative importance, and the methodology used to evaluate proposals; and

- Providing essential guidance to the RFP authors.

Suggested topics to be covered in a source selection plan include, but are not limited to:

- A description of what the agency is buying;

- The acquisition's goals;

- Evaluation procedures, including whether award will be made based on the identified lowest priced technically acceptable offer or on a trade-off evaluation; and

- Proposed evaluation factors and subfactors, their relative importance, and associated standards. The relative importance of the following factors should be identified, as applicable:

  o Price or cost;

  o Technical proficiency;

  o Management;

  o Past performance; and

  o The proposed acquisition strategy, including anticipated contract type.

Source selection team: Multidisciplinary team responsible for evaluating offers and identifying the most advantageous offer through proposal evaluation, to include an assessment of both the proposal and the offeror's ability to successfully accomplish the prospective contract.

Trade-off: The selection among alternatives with the intent of obtaining optimal, achievable system configuration. Often, a decision is made to opt for less of one parameter in order to achieve a more favorable overall system result.

2.6 Protest

A protest is a written objection by an interested party to (1) a solicitation or other request by an agency for offers for a contract for the procurement of property or services; (2) the cancellation of the solicitation or other request; (3) an award or proposed award of the contract; or (4) a termination or cancellation of an award of the contract, if the written objection contains a allegation that the termination or cancellation is based in whole or in part on improprieties concerning to award of the contract.

The period immediately following contract award is the time frame when contracting professionals are most likely to be presented with potentially time consuming and damaging issues, sometimes generated by both the successful offeror as well as unsuccessful offerors. These issues are usually presented by offerors as either mistakes or protests. Though they can also surface in the pre-award phase, charges of mistakes or protests usually are reserved for the immediate post-award period. An awareness of the more common types of mistakes and protest-related issues can be used by the buyer when crafting solicitation packages to hopefully avoid ambiguities and prevent or reduce the frequency of such issues arising in the post-award environment.

In federal government contracting, if a seller alleges a mistake, it is incumbent on the seller to present clear and convincing evidence to support the allegation that a mistake was made. Protests are formal challenges to some aspect or aspects of the acquisition process. Like mistakes, protests can be lodged in either the pre-award or post-award phase. Though the specific grounds for a protest can vary widely and will depend on the particular circumstances of an acquisition and the seller's perceptions, protests generally relate to some of the following issues:

Typical Pre-Award Protest Issues:

- **Restrictive requirements:** The protestor may claim that the requirements or specifications are unnecessarily restrictive and thereby prohibit or limit meaningful competition.

- **Inappropriate sole-source requirement:** A protestor may claim that a requirement advertised as a sole-source procurement is not, in fact, a valid use of sole source authority and that the possibility for competition exists.

- **Ambiguous or erroneous evaluation criteria:** A protestor may claim the criteria to be used to evaluate proposals is flawed, inaccurate, or ambiguous in some material way so as to negatively impact the protestor's ability to fairly compete.

- **Ambiguous or incomplete requirements:** The protestor may claim that the statement of work is so incomplete or ambiguous so as to preclude a clear understanding of the full nature and scope of the requirement to be performed.

- **Exclusion from the competitive range:** A protestor may claim their exclusion from the competitive range, when such a range was pre-established, was inappropriate or that the establishment of a competitive range was not revealed or sufficiently clear in the solicitation.

Typical Post-Award Protest Issues:

- **Unfair evaluation criteria:** The protestor may assert that one or more of the criteria used to evaluate proposals were unreasonable, unfair, or otherwise inappropriate.

- **Failure to evaluate as advertised:** The protestor may claim that the method used to actually evaluate proposals was significantly different than the evaluation criteria specified in the solicitation.

- **Unreasonable best value analysis:** A protestor may indicate that, in a best value procurement, the cost/tradeoff analysis used to justify an award to other than the highest rated or lowest price proposal was flawed, inaccurate, or otherwise unreasonable in some material way.

- **Unequal treatment:** A protestor may claim that other offerors received some form of special treatment or that all offerors were not treated equally, thereby adversely impacting the protestor's ability to compete effectively.

- **Failure to conduct meaningful discussions:** A protestor may claim that they were not the recipient of meaningful discussions during pre-award negotiations, which unfairly prevented them from having the opportunity to submit a more competitive, revised proposal.

Regardless of the specific nature of a pre-award or post-award protest, the underlying issue usually relates to some real or perceived flaw, error, or shortcoming in some facet of the pre-award process. A thorough and comprehensive acquisition planning effort and the logical implementation of the acquisition plan in the solicitation phase can result in a better procurement and fewer post-award issues to resolve. Once a protest is received, the buyer should take all reasonable and appropriate steps necessary to resolve the issue at the lowest possible level.

Alternative dispute resolution (ADR): Administrative procedures established within an agency as an alternative to outside protest forums.

Arbitration: The use of an impartial third party to whom the parties to an agreement refer their disputes for resolution. Some contracts contain provisions that provide for binding arbitration of unsettled grievances.

Competition in Contracting Act of 1984 (CICA): Revised the *FAR* to encourage competition for the award of all types of government contracts. The purpose was to increase the number of competitors and to increase savings through lower, more competitive pricing. The following are found in the CICA provisions:

- Contracting officers shall provide for full and open competition through the use of the competitive procedure or combination of competitive procedures that is best suited to the circumstances of the contract action. The competitive procedures are sealed bidding and competitive proposals.

- To ensure enhancement of competition, the statute requires the government to obtain full and open competition and has only a limited number of exceptions to this rule. The agencies are not permitted to use sole-source procurements unless the written authorization of the agency head is obtained *and* specific statutory or regulatory authority exists for sole source or limited competition. Every deviation from the requirement for full and open competition must be documented in writing and authorized by the appropriate government official. Therefore, agencies rarely seek to limit competition.

- In addition, CICA requires each agency and procuring activity to establish a competition advocate within its organization to review and challenge any procurement that limits competition.

- CICA also amended the protest procedures that are contained in Part 33 of the FAR. Specifically, it established that a protest before contract award to the Government Accountability Office (GAO) will cause the award to be suspended until GAO rules on the protest.

Contra proferentem: A legal phrase used in connection with the construction of written documents to the effect that an ambiguous provision is construed most strongly against the person who wrote the language.

Contract Disputes Act of 1978 (CDA): The CDA establishes procedures and requirements for asserting and resolving claims subject to the CDA. The CDA allows contractors with a dispute to seek redress outside the judiciary system, thereby saving the government and the contractor time and money. The main provisions of the CDA include:

- Strengthening the authority and capabilities of the Board of Contract Appeals (BCA);

- Giving contractors the option of direct appeal to the U.S. Claims Court, bypassing the BCA;

- Providing the government with the right to seek judicial review of adverse BCA decisions;

- Providing contracting activities with more flexibility in negotiating and settling contract disputes;

- Establishing new BCA procedures for handling small claims;

- The payment of interest on contractor claims;

- Establishing a requirement for certification of contract claims; and

- A civil penalty for contractor claims that are fraudulent or based on a misrepresentation of fact.

The disputes clause applies to all government contracts, either expressed or implied. This clause requires the contractor to pursue resolution of its claims through the administrative procedures delineated in the CDA. Contractors are required to continue contract performance pending resolution of a dispute, unless the dispute arises outside the contract or in breach of the contract.

Contract interpretation: Determining the meaning of a contract or a term in the contract based on the original intent of the parties. Contract interpretation may begin by attempting to give all parts of the contract some meaning (as opposed to some sections being rendered meaningless through certain interpretations), and by the assertion of the specific over the general.

Forums: The administrative and judicial bodies that adjudicate disputes and protests.

Forums for contract disputes:

- **Boards of Contract Appeals (BCA)**: The Contract Disputes Act of 1978 (CDA) waives sovereign immunity for contract claims (not protests) to the BCA and suits before the Court of Federal Claims. The CDA formalized the patchwork system for handling disputes over contract performance and related matters. Two BCAs exist—the Civilian Board of Contract Appeals and the Armed Services Board of Contract Appeals.

- **Court of Federal Claims (basic process):** Complaint must be filed within the statutory one-year period. Hearing is before one judge who may or may not disagree with the other judges on the court. No defined amount of time dictates how long the court may take in resolving the appeal.

It is a United States federal court that hears monetary claims against the U.S. government. The court is established pursuant to Congress's authority under Article I of the *U.S. Constitution*. Unlike judges of courts established under Article Three, judges on the Court of Federal Claims do not have life tenure. Instead they serve for 15-year terms and are eligible for reappointment. The sixteen judges of the court are nominated by the president and confirmed by the Senate.

- **The Court of Appeals for the Federal Circuit:** The Federal Circuit can hear appeals from both the boards and the COFC. The contractor has 120 days from the date of the board's denial of the contractor's appeal to appeal to the Federal Circuit. The contractor has 60 days from the date of entry of the COFC's judgment to appeal to the Federal Circuit.

The United States Court of Appeals for the Federal Circuit was established under Article III of the Constitution on October 1, 1982. The court was formed by the merger of the United States Court of Customs and Patent Appeals and the appellate division of the United States Court of Claims. The court is located in the Howard T. Markey National Courts Building on historic Lafayette Square in Washington, DC.

The Federal Circuit is unique among the thirteen Circuit Courts of Appeals. It has nationwide jurisdiction in a variety of subject areas, including international trade, government contracts, patents, trademarks, certain money claims against the United States government, federal personnel, veterans' benefits, and public safety officers' benefits claims. Appeals to the court come from all federal district courts, the United States Court of Federal Claims, the United States Court of International Trade, and the United States Court of Appeals for Veterans Claims.

Forums for government contract protests:

- **Agency protests:** Typically, the contracting officer or other cognizant government official within the agency handles all protests. Whomever handles the protest must seek and consider legal advice regarding all protests filed with the agency. Protesters do not need to exhaust administrative remedies, they can go directly to the GAO or court.

- **Government Accountability Office (GAO):** The Competition in Contracting Act of 1984 (CICA) authorizes the GAO to hear bid protests. The GAO is an independent, nonpartisan agency that works for Congress. Often called the "congressional watchdog," GAO investigates how the federal government spends taxpayer dollars. The head of GAO, the comptroller general of the United States, is appointed to a 15-year term by the president from a slate of candidates Congress proposes.

Interested party: An actual or prospective offeror whose direct economic interest would be affected by an award of the contract or by failure to award the contract.

Interveners: Awardees of the protested procurement or all other offerors who had a "reasonable prospect" of receiving an award.

Order of precedence: A solicitation provision that establishes priorities so that contradictions within the solicitation can be resolved.

Prime-sub disputes: Traditional disputes between prime and sub are settled at the local state court level. However, if the sub has a protestable event against the government, the prime must protest on behalf of the sub because the sub is not in privity with the government.

Procedures: The processes used by the administrative and judicial forums to resolve protests.

1. A form of written approval signed by an authorized government official that is required by statute or regulation as a prerequisite to taking certain contracting actions is called

   a. determination and findings.
   b. justification and approval.
   c. accord and satisfaction.
   d. determination of the facts.

2. Full and open competition means that

   a. all small businesses are permitted to compete.
   b. three or more sources are solicited.
   c. all responsible sources are permitted to compete.
   d. the procurement does not have a restrictive specification.

3. The overall plan for meeting the requirement in the most effective, economical, and timely manner is the

   a. source selection plan.
   b. acquisition strategy.
   c. capture management.
   d. market research.

4. In government contracting, what is the method of acquisition used when contract award will be made on the basis of price and other price-related factors?

   a. simplified acquisition
   b. commercial item acquisition
   c. sealed bid
   d. negotiation

5. A life cycle process used by both small and large businesses that ensures consistency and discipline to aggressively pursue and win contract opportunities is called

   a. contingency planning.
   b. operational planning.
   c. tactical planning.
   d. capture planning.

6. This government acquisition method includes the following purchasing methods: government-wide purchase card, imprest fund, blanket purchase agreements and purchase orders.

   a. simplified acquisition
   b. commercial item acquisition
   c. sealed bid
   d. negotiation

The following scenario and associated follow-on questions is a new, additional style of CPCM question you can expect to see beginning with the 2012 exam. The questions appear after the scenario.

Use the information provided in the following scenario to answer questions 7–10. The questions ask you to apply your knowledge of contract management to the given scenario. These questions require candidates to understand the concepts and terminology and apply that knowledge to answer the question correctly.

Scenario

A federal agency issued a request for proposal (RFP) for the supply and delivery of natural gas to 91 facilities nationwide. The RFP stated that following competitive negotiations, award would be made to the offeror whose proposal conformed to the solicitation requirements and was most advantageous to the government, price and other factors considered.

The RFP's evaluation factors listed in descending order of importance were: (1) past performance, (2) evidence of ability to purchase natural gas and transportation below the Federal Energy

Regulatory Commission index price, (3) quality, and (4) price. The agency received seven proposals and two of those proposals are the subject of this scenario—SDS and Tiger.

The evaluators initially found that SDS's proposal was technically deficient because it did not have past-performance delivery information and did not show an ability to procure natural gas below the index price. SDS's proposal received 35 of the 90 available technical points. In contrast, Tiger's proposal received all 90 available technical points. Despite the technical deficiencies in its proposal, SDS's proposal was included in the competitive range for discussions.

After discussions SDS submitted additional information in a revised technical proposal, but it did not establish the ability to obtain gas and gas transportation prices below the index price. For example, the revisions indicated that discounted prices are generally available, but did not detail the terms or state if SDS would be eligible for such discounts. Evaluators reviewed the revised proposal and SDS's score for the past-performance factor increased from 12 to 32 (out of 40 possible points).

The SDS proposal's technical score was still considered extremely low and it was the highest priced, so the contracting officer determined that SDS had no reasonable chance for award. The contracting officer advised SDS that its proposal was no longer in the competitive range. The contracting officer determined that Tiger was the only offeror whose proposal was within the competitive range and provided only that firm the opportunity to submit a final proposal revision. After evaluating the revised proposal, the contracting officer awarded the contract to Tiger.

SDS argues that no matter how low its proposal's evaluation rating was compared to Tiger's, the agency was required to retain its proposal in the competitive range since it was the second-highest rated.

Scenario Questions

7. Why would the agency make past performance the most important evaluation criteria?

   a. Since past performance is a mandatory evaluation factor in government best value contracts, the agency made it the most important because of a bad experience with the incumbent contractor.
   b. Past-performance information is one indicator of an offeror's ability to perform the contract successfully.
   c. Past performance need not be evaluated if the contracting officer documents the reason past performance is not an appropriate evaluation factor for the acquisition.
   d. The source selection team will be able to electronically access the various agency contractor information systems and download the required information.

8. Was the agency correct to exclude SDS from the second competitive range determination?

   a. No. The competitive range consists of all offerors with a reasonable chance of winning the contract award.
   b. No. The competitive range must have more than one offeror to be valid.
   c. Yes. The competitive range consists only of all of the most highly rated proposals, and it is appropriate to have only one offer in this range.
   d. Yes. The competitive range consists of all responsive and responsible offerors, but the range should be limited to 10 offers for purposes of efficiency.

9. Why would the agency use an indefinite delivery/indefinite quantity contract type for this scenario?

    a. A definite quantity of supplies or services will be required during the contract period and the supplies or services are regularly available or will be available after a short lead time.
    b. It is not possible at the time of placing the contract to estimate accurately the extent or duration of the work or to anticipate costs with any reasonable degree of confidence.
    c. The agency cannot predetermine, above a specified minimum, the precise quantities of supplies or services that the agency will require during the contract period.
    d. The required supplies or services can be acquired at lower costs and, in certain instances, with improved delivery or technical performance by relating the amount of profit or fee payable under the contract to the contractor's performance.

10. Why would SDS submit additional information in a revised technical proposal after discussions?

    a. SDS was responding to a request for best and final offers.
    b. The contracting officer requested a revision in order to document negotiations.
    c. There were clerical errors in the original proposal submission.
    d. The contracting officer asked SDS to clarify the relevance of their past performance.

1. A form of written approval signed by an authorized government official that is required by statute or regulation as a prerequisite to taking certain contracting actions are

   a. **(Correct) determination and findings.**
   b. Justification and approval. *A document to justify procurement using other than full and open competition. This document is required prior to commencing negotiation for a contract resulting from an unsolicited proposal or any other contract award that does not provide for full and open competition.*
   c. Accord and satisfaction. *A method of discharging a claim whereby the parties agree to give and accept something in settlement of the claim and perform the agreement. The accord is the agreement and the satisfaction is the execution or performance.*
   d. Determination of the Facts *is not a recognized term.*

(Source: *NCMA Desktop Guide to Basic Contracting Terms*)

2. Full and open competition means that

   a. all small businesses are permitted to compete. *It is the policy of the government to provide maximum practicable opportunities in its acquisitions to small business. Contracting officers may set aside solicitations to allow only such business concerns to compete.*
   b. three or more sources are solicited. *There is no numerical requirement for competition.*
   c. **(Correct) all responsible sources are permitted to compete.**
   d. the procurement does not have a restrictive specification. *Specifications should not be written to restrict competition.*

(Source: *NCMA Desktop Guide to Basic Contracting Terms*)

3. The overall plan for meeting the requirement in the most effective, economical, and timely manner is the

   a. source selection plan. *The source selection plan documents key elements of a source selection.*
   b. **(Correct) Acquisition strategy**
   c. Capture management *encompasses activities a seller does to raise its win probability.*
   d. Market research *is the process used to collect and analyze information to help determine the most suitable approach to acquiring, distributing, and supporting supplies and services.*

(Source: Rumbaugh, Margaret G. *Understanding Government Contract Source Selection.* (Vienna, VA: Management Concepts, Inc.) 2010.)

4. In government contracting, what is the method of acquisition used when contract award will be made on the basis of price and other price-related factors?

   a. simplified acquisition
   b. commercial item acquisition
   c. **(correct) sealed bid**
   d. negotiation

(Source: FAR 6.401)

5. A life cycle process used by both small and large businesses that ensures consistency and discipline to aggressively pursue and win contract opportunities is called

   a. contingency planning *involves developing alternative plans for various business conditions.*
   b. operational planning *establishes the methods used for the near future to achieve the tactical plan.*

c. tactical planning *focuses on a short-term period that are consistent with the firm's strategic plan.*

d. **(Correct) capture planning**

(Source: Rumbaugh, Margaret G. *Understanding Government Contract Source Selection.* (Vienna, VA: Management Concepts, Inc.) 2010.

6. This government acquisition method includes the following purchasing methods: government-wide purchase card, imprest fund, blanket purchase agreements and purchase orders.

   a. **(Correct) Simplified Acquisition**
   b. commercial item acquisition. *Agencies shall acquire commercial items or non-developmental items when they are available to meet the agency's needs.*
   c. sealed bid. *Sealed bidding is an acquisition method that uses competitive bids, public opening, and award.*
   d. negotiation. *Negotiation is an acquisition method that is used when the conditions required for sealed bidding do not exist.*

(Source: FAR 13.3)

7. Why would the agency make past performance the most important evaluation criteria?

   a. Since past performance is a mandatory evaluation factor in government best value contracts, the agency made it the most important because of a bad experience with the incumbent contractor.
   b. **(Correct) Past performance information is one indicator of an offeror's ability to perform the contract successfully.**
   c. Past performance need not be evaluated if the contracting officer documents the reason past performance is not an appropriate evaluation factor for the acquisition.

d. The source selection team will be able to electronically access the various agency contractor information systems and download the required information.

8. Was the agency correct to exclude SDS from the second competitive range determination?

   a. No. The competitive range consists of all offerors with a reasonable chance of winning the contract award.
   b. No. The competitive range must have more than one offeror to be valid.
   c. **(Correct) Yes. The competitive range consists only of all of the most highly rated proposals, and it is appropriate to have only one offer in this range.**
   d. Yes. The competitive range consists of all responsive and responsible offerors, but the range should be limited to 10 offers for purposes of efficiency.

9. Why would the agency use an indefinite delivery/indefinite quantity contract type for this scenario?

   a. A definite quantity of supplies or services will be required during the contract period and the supplies or services are regularly available or will be available after a short lead time.
   b. It is not possible at the time of placing the contract to estimate accurately the extent or duration of the work or to anticipate costs with any reasonable degree of confidence.
   c. **(Correct) The agency cannot predetermine, above a specified minimum, the precise quantities of supplies or services that the agency will require during the contract period.**
   d. The required supplies or services can be acquired at lower costs and, in certain instances, with improved delivery or technical performance, by relating the amount of profit or fee payable under the contract to the contractor's performance.

10. Why would SDS submit additional information in a revised technical proposal after discussions?

   a. SDS was responding to a request for best and final offers.
   b. **(Correct) The contracting officer requested a revision in order to document negotiations.**
   c. There were clerical errors in the original proposal submission.
   d. The contracting officer asked SDS to clarify the relevance of their past performance.

Additional information for a better understanding of the decision:

Matter of: SDS Petroleum Products, Inc. File: B-280430 Date: September 1, 1998 * Redacted Decision.

Digest

Exclusion of protester's proposal from competitive range was not improper where agency reasonably concluded that the proposal failed to demonstrate the ability to purchase and transport natural gas at certain rates and terms, as required by the solicitation.

Decision

SDS Petroleum Products, Inc. protests the exclusion of its proposal from the competitive range, and the subsequent award of a contract to Tiger Natural Gas, Inc., under request for proposals (RFP) No. 693-16-98, issued as a competitive section 8(a) set-aside by the Department of Veterans Affairs for the supply and delivery of natural gas to 91 facilities nationwide.

We deny the protest.

On February 3, 1998, the contracting officer prepared and furnished to the Small Business Administration (SBA) an offering letter in which he determined that adequate competition existed among 8(a) contractors to set aside this national procurement for the 8(a) program. Previously, the agency had procured its gas supplies through four regional contracts by means of unrestricted procurements. By letter dated February 4, the SBA accepted the offer for a competitive 8(a) procurement.

The RFP was issued on February 24 and, as amended, contemplated award of an indefinite-delivery, indefinite-quantity (ID/IQ) contract for a base period of 1 year, with four 1-year options. The RFP stated that, following competitive negotiations, award would be made to the offeror whose proposal conformed to the solicitation requirements and was most advantageous to the government, price and other factors considered. Section M of the RFP contained the following evaluation factors, listed in descending order of importance: (1) past performance from January 1, 1995 to present; (2) evidence of ability to purchase (a) natural gas and transportation below the Inside FERC (Federal Energy Regulatory Commission) index price 1 and (b) natural gas transportation below tariff rate; (3) quality; and (4) price.[2]

Seven proposals were received by the May 11 closing time. The evaluators initially found that SDS's proposal was technically deficient because it contained no past performance delivery information and failed to show an ability to procure natural gas below the index price or natural gas transportation below the tariff rate. SDS's proposal received 35 of the 90 available technical points (price was worth 10 points), and under the index factor, only 3 of 30 possible points. In contrast, Tiger's proposal was found to contain detailed and extensive documentary evidence of its ability to procure gas below the index price and transportation below the tariff rate. Tiger's proposal received all 90 available technical points. (The other proposals scored very low technically and are not relevant here.)

Despite the serious technical deficiencies in its proposal, SDS's proposal was retained in the competitive range for purposes of discussions. By letter dated May 18, the contracting officer advised SDS that its proposal was deficient under the past performance and index factors. Revised proposals were due on May 26. In the meantime, on May 21, amendment No. 7 was issued, making certain changes to RFP sections C, G, and H, and clarifying the minimum and maximum order quantities.

On May 23, SDS submitted additional information in a revised technical proposal, specifically, two signed natural gas contracts containing prices below-index price and letters purportedly demonstrating its ability to obtain below-tariff rate transportation under similar contracts. On May 28, the evaluators reviewed the revised proposal. SDS's score for the past performance factor increased from 12 to 32 (out of 40 possible points). However, its score for the index factor was unchanged, the evaluators concluding that, although SDS had submitted additional information in this area, it was not sufficient to establish the ability to obtain gas and gas transportation prices below the index price and tariff rate. The results of the evaluation of Tiger's and SDS's revised proposals were as follows:

Offeror Technical Score Price for Base Load Gas

Tiger 90 $6.6 million

SDS 55 [DELETED] million

Based on these results--SDS's proposal's technical score still was considered extremely low and it was the highest-priced--the contracting officer determined that SDS had no reasonable chance for award. Consequently, by letter dated June 1, the contracting officer advised SDS that its proposal no longer was in the competitive range. The contract-

ing officer determined that Tiger was the only offeror whose proposal was within the competitive range, provided only that firm the opportunity to submit a best and final offer (BAFO), evaluated the BAFO, and made award to Tiger. This protest followed a debriefing provided to SDS by the agency.

Noting that the RFP did not specify that a certain amount of evidence was required to meet the index factor requirements, SDS asserts that its revised proposal included adequate evidence of its ability to purchase natural gas below the index price and transportation below the tariff rate. SDS concludes that, had its proposal been evaluated properly, the proposal would have been retained in the competitive range, and it would have had the opportunity to submit a BAFO.[3]

In reviewing competitive range determinations, our Office will not independently reevaluate proposals; rather, we will examine the record to ensure that the evaluation was reasonable and in accordance with the solicitation's evaluation criteria. Cobra Techs., Inc., B-272041, B-272041.2, Aug. 20, 1996, 96-2 CPD Para. 73 at 3.

Here, the evaluation and the agency's decision to exclude SDS's proposal from the competitive range were reasonable. The index factor was intended to indicate whether an offeror would be able to obtain and transport natural gas at favorable prices, which would result in savings to the government. As discussed, SDS initially provided no evidence supporting its ability to obtain such favorable prices. In its revised proposal, SDS submitted as evidence two gas purchase contracts, one dated 1995 and one dated 1998. Agency Report (AR), Tab 19. The agency determined that two contracts, one from 3 years ago, were not sufficient to clearly establish an ability to obtain favorable pricing on a large-scale basis (the contract here would cover 91 installations). Further, while these contracts established prices of [DELETED] and [DELETED] below the index price, the agency noted that they did not specify an actual price, and SDS did not provide other evidence of the actual prices paid under the contracts. In contrast, Tiger submitted evidence of hundreds of actual prices below the index prices, for delivery of natural gas at numerous points nationwide. The rationale underlying the agency's position is a reasonable one--if a firm's ability to obtain discounted natural gas prices on a large-scale, continuing basis is to be demonstrated through prior contracts, then the firm must present substantial numbers of contracts with clear evidence of the prices paid. We find the agency reasonably determined that two contracts, with no evidence of the prices actually paid, were insufficient to evidence an ongoing ability to obtain discounted natural gas on a large-scale basis.

As evidence of its ability to purchase gas transportation below the tariff rate, SDS submitted an "example" purportedly showing an "approximate" discount from the tariff rate, along with a commercially available sample gas transportation report. AR, Tab 19. SDS also submitted letters from six vendors that would sell gas and/or transportation for the contract, but these letters did not specify a price or state which pipelines would be used. Three of the letters indicated generally that discounted prices are available--but did not detail the terms or state whether SDS would be eligible for such discounts--and three of the letters merely referenced the tariff, with no indication that discounts would be available. In its comments on the agency report, the protester ignores these weaknesses in its submitted information, and does not attempt to explain how its submissions adequately met the solicitation requirements; rather, the comments are general and merely express disagreement with the agency's determination. Again, we think the agency reasonably concluded that the evidence provided--an example showing only

an approximate discount, and letters from suppliers with no evidence that discounted transportation would be obtained--while perhaps relevant to SDS's ability to obtain below-tariff rate transportation, simply was inadequate to establish an ability to obtain discounted prices in performing the contract.

SDS seems to argue that, no matter how low its proposal's evaluation rating relative to Tiger's, the agency was required to retain its proposal in the competitive range since it was the second-highest rated. We find no merit in this argument, which is apparently based on the recent rewrite of Part 15 of the Federal Acquisition Regulation (FAR) that changed the language governing competitive range determinations. The earlier language, FAR Sec. 15.609(a) (June 1997), stated that the competitive range "shall include all proposals that have a reasonable chance of being selected for award" and that "[w]hen there is doubt as to whether a proposal is in the competitive range, the proposal should be included." The current language, which governs this procurement, states, "Based on the ratings of each proposal against all evaluation criteria, the contracting officer shall establish a competitive range comprised of all of the most highly rated proposals, unless the range is further reduced for purposes of efficiency pursuant to paragraph (c)(2) of this section."[4] FAR Sec. 15.306(c)(1) (FAC 97-02). We do not read the revised language to require agencies to retain in the competitive range a proposal that the agency reasonably concludes has no realistic prospect of award, even if that proposal is, as here, the second-highest rated proposal.

The explanatory preamble published at the time the final version of the FAR Part 15 rewrite was issued makes clear that the intent of the revised language was to permit a competitive range more limited than under the prior "reasonable chance of being selected for award" standard. That preamble states that

71

the drafters had elected to require contracting officers to retain in the competitive range "only" the most highly rated offers rather than include in that range the potentially broader range of proposals that could be viewed as having a reasonable chance of award. 62 Fed. Reg. 51,224, 51,226 (1997). Specifically, the preamble stated that the new language would "ensure that offerors with little probability of success . . . are advised early on that their competitive position does not merit additional expense in a largely futile attempt to secure the contract." Id.

Accordingly, we conclude that the Part 15 rewrite does not require that agencies retain in the competitive range a proposal that is determined to have no reasonable prospect of award simply to avoid a competitive range of one. We have long held that there is nothing inherently improper in a competitive range of one, Cobra Techs., Inc., supra, at 3, and we do not view the Part 15 rewrite as effecting a change in that regard; conducting discussions and requesting BAFOs from an offeror with no reasonable chance of award would benefit neither the offeror nor the government. See 62 Fed. Reg. 51,226 (retaining marginal offers in competitive range imposes additional and largely futile effort and cost on government and industry).

SDS also argues that amendment No. 7, issued May 21, 5 days before revised proposals were due, on May 26, made such substantial changes to the solicitation that cancellation of the RFP and resolicitation were required. In procurements where proposals are requested, alleged improprieties which do not exist in the initial solicitation but which are subsequently incorporated into the solicitation must be protested not later than the next closing time for receipt of proposals following the incorporation. 4 C.F.R. Sec. 1.2(a)(1). If SDS believed that the changes made by amendment No. 7 were improper or required resolicitation, it was required to protest on this ground prior to the next clos-

ing date, May 26. As SDS did not do so, its protest on this basis is untimely and will not be considered.[5]

Finally, SDS argues that the agency failed to provide critical information in its letter offering this requirement for the 8(a) program, which prevented SBA from determining that the placement of the procurement in the 8(a) program would have an adverse impact on other small business programs or on other individual small businesses, such as the incumbent. Since SDS is an 8(a) firm and the procurement was set aside under the competitive 8(a) program, SDS could not have been competitively prejudiced by any improper action related to the decision to accept this procurement in the 8(a) program, and is not an interested party to raise this issue on behalf of non-8(a) small business firms. Stated differently, a protester is not an interested party to raise issues affecting other firms in which the protester has no direct economic interest. 4 C.F.R. Sec. 21.0(a); see XMCO, Inc., B-228357, Jan. 26, 1988, 88-1 CPD Para. 75 at 5.

The protest is denied.

Comptroller General of the United States

Endnotes:

1. Inside FERC is a publication that contains the market prices for natural gas for delivery to specific geographical areas. In this decision, all references to the index refer to the Inside FERC index.

2. Price, the least important factor, consisted of a base load gas (based on fixed unit prices proposed by offerors) of 2.0 million MMBTU (equivalent to 1,000,000 BTU) and an ID/IQ portion of 9.4 million MMBTU based on index-priced gas. Thus, according to the agency, approximately 82 percent of the natural gas prices would be affected by a firm's abil-

ity to purchase gas at below-index rates. Contracting Officer's Statement at 2. The calculation of savings to the government from a below-index purchase was based on a formula contained in RFP Sec. C.

3. In its comments on the agency report, SDS asserts for the first time that (1) in assigning Tiger's proposal the maximum score under the index factor, the agency improperly considered basic ordering agreements--which are not contracts--as evidence of Tiger's ability to purchase natural gas below the index price; and (2) the index factor should have been evaluated as a price factor rather than a technical factor. SDS was aware of these bases of protest, at the latest, upon its receipt of the agency report, yet it did not assert these bases of protest within 10 calendar days after its receipt of the report. In this regard, SDS's comments were not received within the normal 10-calendar-day period, see 4 C.F.R. Sec. 21.3(i) (1998), due to our granting an extension request by SDS. Since a time extension for purposes of filing comments does not waive the timeliness rules with regard to new grounds of protest, Anchorage Enters., Inc., B-261922, Nov. 7, 1995, 95-2 CPD Para. 211 at 3 n.2, we dismiss these bases of protest as untimely.

4. Because the ratings are to reflect assessment against "all evaluation criteria" and cost (or price) must always be one of those criteria, 41 U.S.C. Sec. 253a(c) (1)(B) (West Supp. 1998), FAR Sec. 15.304(c)(1) (FAC 97-02), the assessment of which are the "most highly rated proposals" must reflect cost (or price) as well as other evaluation criteria.

5. The protester also argues that, even if the evidence it furnished was deemed inadequate, it still should have received award of the fixed-price, base load gas portion of the contract. However, the RFP required a single award and, in any event, the protester's price was not low for the base load gas quantity.

*DOCUMENT FOR PUBLIC RELEASE

The decision issued on the date below was subject to a GAO Protective Order. This redacted version has been approved for public release.

Comptroller General of the United States
Matter of: SDS Petroleum Products, Inc.
September 1, 1998
Comptroller General (C.G.)
B-280430, 1998 WL 637020 (C.G.)

These readings can be found in NCMA's online Research Articles Database. To access the database you must be an NCMA member. If you are not an NCMA member, you may be able to obtain equivalent readings by inserting relevant keywords into your web browser's search engine.

From NCMA's *Contract Management* magazine:

Bjorklund, Ray, *Analyzing the 2011 Federal Budget: Learning to Compete in a Zero-Sum Game*, August 2010.
With cuts in many areas of the federal budget and shifting priorities in others, contractors may have to rethink--and readjust--their business strategies accordingly.

Broderick, Deborah, Reinventing the G-Man: *Bringing Change to FBI Procurement*, June 2011.
How the FBI is strengthening its procurement processes by strengthening its employees.

Caisse, Lauren J., *Teaming Agreements: To Team or Not to Team?*, April 2010
A practical guide to forming contractor team arrangements.

Esperne, Eric, *Opportunities for Making Risk Management Happen Now Through Kaizen*, May 2010.
How current contract risk management approaches by the U.S. government and multinational corporations can be immediately improved using kaizen.

Esperne, Eric, *The Contracts Risk Management Framework, Part 1 of 2: Translating Risk Management into Contract Management*, August 2010.
A building process for implementing a contracts risk management framework in government and industry.

Esperne, Eric, **The Contracts Risk Management Framework, Part 2 of 2: Translating Risk Management into Contract Management using the Example of the United Kingdom**, September 2010.
The U.S. and UK government contract management frameworks are very different and have different histories. Notwithstanding these differences, the U.S. acquisition community can and should study the benefits of the UK's contracts risk management resources and thought leadership, as well as those of the EU.

Garrett, Gregory A., *What Small and Emerging Government Contractors Must Know to Win Business with the U.S. Government, Part 1*, October 2010.
A brief overview of the process of winning U.S. government contracts.

Garrett, Gregory A., *What Small and Emerging Government Contractors Must Know to Win Business with the U.S. Government, Part 2: Becoming a Qualified U.S. Government Contractor*, November 2010.
Understanding the rules of the game: the top 25 questions involved with becoming a qualified government contractor answered.

Garrett, Gregory A., *What Small and Emerging Government Contractors Must Know to Win Business with the U.S. Government, Part 3: Building Contractor Teaming Agreements*, December 2010.
A review of the key elements of contractor teaming arrangements used to perform government contracts, as well as a discussion of the lessons learned and best practices of forming business partnerships in the federal government marketplace.

Garrett, Gregory A., *Working with Government Auditors*, January 2011.
A review of various practices contractors can follow to ease the tension often associated with the DCAA audit process.

Ipsaro, Michael, *How an IGCE Can Help You Assess Cost/Price Reasonableness During Source Selection*, July 2011.
To improve the odds of a successful source selection, an accurate assessment of cost/price reasonableness and realism is essential. This article will explain the usefulness of the IGCE as a tool to aid the assessment.

Ipsaro, Michael, *How an Independent Government Cost Estimate Can Help You Determine How Much Your Contract Should Cost*, June 2011.
A credible IGCE will result in the avoidance of, or mitigation against, major risks and adverse consequences, improving the probability of acquisition and program management success.

Knott, Claudia "Scottie" and John Qua, *Strategic Sourcing with the AbilityOne Program*, June 2010.
The Department of Defense and Ability-One Program are currently involved in a strategic effort focused on customer solution delivery while providing employment opportunities for people who are blind or severely disabled.

Reid, Tom, *Industry Motivation in Negotiations*, July 2010.
When we realize that the party on the other side of the table is motivated by a variety of things, we can more easily determine how best to meet those interests and structure a deal that is more beneficial to both parties.

Rhodes, Amanda Barnett, and Carl R. Eckert, *Social Psychology and Contract Negotiation: Symphony of Group Dynamics and Interpersonal Relations*, April 2010.
Theories of social psychology offer insight into how to effectively initiate, prepare for, and conduct negotiations.

Segel, Kenneth R., *Negotiating Fixed-Price Incentive (Firm Target) Contracts: The Next Wave in Government Contracting*, July 2011.
The U.S. government now encourages the use of FPIF contracts, and contract managers must be fully aware of the intricacies associated with the FPIF type contract, as well as the administrative oversight required to effectively manage them.

Shreni, Suresh, *Transforming from Transactional Procurements to Strategic Acquisitions*, March 2011.
How the IRS Procurement Office has been able to take great strides in improving business outcomes and customer and contractor relationships by focusing on strategic initiatives.

Solloway, Jr, Charles D., *Charade Discussions: Are You a Player in this No-Win Game?*, June 2011.
A particular area of protest vulnerability in the awarding of U.S. government contracts is the failure to hold meaningful discussions, which results in" charade discussions."

Terzano, Mark, *"Greening "a Protest Response: Team Collaboration Tools Encourage Environmental Sustainability*, April 2011.
Use of collaborative tools can improve acquisitions and enhance project efficiency, effectiveness, and team cohesion, all while protecting the environment.

Ukelson, Jacob, *The Value of Adaptive Case Management for Contract Management*, July 2010.
Adaptive case management is a valuable tool for not only managing the contract document, but also the contract creation process.

From NCMA's *Journal of Contract Management*:

Liounis, Nancy L., *Privatization at the Federal Level: Contracting-out by the U.S. Department of Defense*, September 2010, Volume 8, Issue 1.
DOD uses privatization of government functions to save money and because regulations require outsourcing of commercial activities. However, more scrutiny shows that DOD's willingness to privatize is also caused by politics, agency attitudes, budget pressures, and other factors.

Westergren, Brad, *Leading Outsourced Outsourcers*, September 2010, Volume 8, Issue 1.
This article addresses alternatives for leading the right-sourced federal contracting community.

Wydler, Ginny, *Acquisition Strategy: Best Practices for Successful Source Selection*, September 2010, Volume 8, Issue 1.
A review of some current best practices for executing major systems acquisitions which need to be considered for a successful source selection. Through a case study and after-action review, the article also offers lessons learned from first-hand experience.

Competency

3.0:

Post-Award

The post-award phase of contract administration includes all the tasks that both buyer and seller perform to complete the contract. It encompasses all dealings between the parties from contract award until contract completion and acceptance. It includes invoicing and making payments, resolving disputes, and terminating the contract. As such, the post-award phase constitutes a large part of the activity in the contracting process.

3.1 Contract Administration

Once contract award is complete, the contractor begins performance. If an unsuccessful offeror files a protest, they may try to stop contract performance (called a "stay" in federal government contracts), but there is a strict time limit to make this happen. Unless there has been a stay of contract performance, the awardee may continue with contract performance while the protest is decided. The broad goals of contract administration are to ensure the buyer obtains the needed work on time and at the level of quality called for by the contract, and that the seller receives proper compensation in a timely manner. However, as circumstances change, it is often necessary to change the contract. (Changing contract requirements requires a new competition.) A large part of contract administration is in adapting to changing circumstances. This may require changing contract delivery requirements when they do not reflect the current needs of the user, or terminating the contract when the goods or services are no longer required.

The range and extent of contract administration activities required will vary greatly, depending primarily on the complexity, dollar value, and priority of the contract. It is also important to note that effective contract administration is a shared responsibility of both the buyer and seller. The contract specifies the duties, obligations that both parties are responsible for, and benefits to which both parties are entitled. Contract administrators oversee performance to ensure that both parties comply with the contract. Contract administration can be straightforward, particularly when the contracting parties are individuals or small organizations; larger companies, agencies, and organizations tend to have more complex processes. Contracting professionals in large, complex organizations frequently find themselves simultaneously responsible for administration activities on multiple contracts, and usually require some technical assistance and ongoing input from their internal customers, internal professional resources, management, and other stakeholders. Managing multiple contracts and depending on external resources makes contract administration challenging for both buyers and sellers.

LEXICON FOR CONTRACT ADMINISTRATION:

Cooperation and good faith: Cooperation during contract administration is not only mandated by common sense, but it is a legal requirement. The buyer's rights to insist upon strict compliance with contract requirements and to enforce all seller obligations do not relieve the buyer from its duty to cooperate with the seller to perform the work. Similarly, the seller is obligated to work to meet the buyer's expectations. Lack of cooperation frequently causes disputes.

- **Bad faith performance:** This violates community standards of decency, fairness, or reasonableness. It may be overt or may occur from inaction. Examples of bad faith include evading the spirit of the bargain, slacking off performance, rendering of imperfect performance willfully, abusing power to specify terms, and interfering with the other party's performance.

- **Good faith performance:** Emphasizes faithfulness to an agreed common purpose and consistency with the justified expectations of the other party.

- **Good faith in enforcement:** The obligation of good faith and fair dealing extends to asserting contract claims and defenses. The obligation is violated by dishonest conduct such as conjuring up a fictitious dispute, asserting an interpretation contrary to one's own understanding, or falsifying facts.

Timely identification and resolution of problems: Even the best of working relationships will not yield good contract administration unless the parties properly document contractual events, identify problems in a timely manner, and work out mutually agreeable solutions.

- **Problem identification:** When either party identifies a problem during contract performance, they should immediately notify the other party. Early communication regarding problems is especially important when a seller believes the buyer caused the problem. If this is true, the seller may be entitled to additional compensation under one of the standard clauses, and the buyer may be able to minimize the compensation amount by implementing a cost-effective solution to the problem.

- **Problem resolution:** Promptly identifying problems is of little use if they are not resolved in a timely manner. Avoid simply filing memoranda or reaching verbal or side agreements that are not incorporated into the contract. Effective problem solving involves both parties agreeing to a resolution that is formally documented in the contract.

3.2 Contract Performance and Quality Assurance

Effective contract performance requires the contractor to perform contractual requirements in accordance with the contract's terms. Effective quality assurance provides confidence that materials, data supplies, and services conform to established technical requirements in a planned and systematic manner.

Contract administrators oversee contract performance to ensure that contract requirements are met. An essential element of successful contract administration is establishing and maintaining effective communications. Maintaining a productive, two-way professional dialogue between buyer and seller during the period of contract performance is perhaps the most difficult—but potentially the most beneficial—aspect of contract administration. All too often, other business priorities and demands seem to force the contracting professional to relegate many administration activities to a lower priority. When this occurs, contract performance may suffer.

The communications, reporting, and observation aspects of contract administration form the basis for many of the other administration functions to be discussed later in this chapter.

LEXICON FOR CONTRACT PERFORMANCE AND QUALITY ASSURANCE:

Acceptance: That act of an authorized buyer representative by which the buyer assents to ownership of existing and identified supplies, or approves specific services rendered as partial or complete performance of a contract.

Acceptance sampling: A statistical quality control technique used to evaluate the overall condition of a given lot by inspecting only a portion or sample of the lot.

Compliance system: Information technology system that translates contract requirements (such as pricing, warranty, service requirements, and product changes) into executable instructions to internal systems. It includes connectivity to enterprise resource planning (ERP) tools and other customer-resource management tools that the organization uses to communicate internally and externally.

Critical dependencies: The interrelationships existing within or among processes that are primary drivers of defects or errors in a product or service.

Critical success factors: Indicators developed by a customer that specify the defect-free character of a product or service.

Customer service: Interaction with the designated end users of the contracted products and services; includes actions to resolve customer complaints and facilities' use of products or access to services.

Data management: Use of commercially available software tools to manage contract information, including repositories for contract documents, reporting systems, contracting process management, and portfolio management.

Documentation: A continuous stream of pertinent documentation should be generated and maintained throughout the life of the contract. The documentation can take many forms; formal correspondence, memoranda for the record, telephone logs, e-mails, personal notes, journal entries, etc. The documentation serves as a written record of all meetings, discussions, issues, problems, solutions, and agreements. The record can be used as a ready reference source to reflect the intent of the parties over time as a means to guide future actions based on agreements reached in the past or as evidence in the event of litigation. Creating such documentation is effective only if the requesting organization actually reads the reports provided. Simply filing reports without reading them is not effective contract administration.

Indemnification: Protections provided by the parties to each other; also to restore a loss, either in whole or in part, by payment, repair, or replacement. It can be a contract provision whereby one party engages to secure another against an anticipated loss resulting from an act of forbearance on the part of one of the parties or some third party.

Inspection: The examination (including testing) of supplies and services (including, when appropriate, raw materials, components, and intermediate assemblies) to determine whether the supplies and services conform to the contract requirements.

International Organization for Standardization (ISO) Standards: The ISO Standards are families of standards consisting of standards and guidelines that relate to management systems and related supporting standards on terminology and specific tools, such as auditing (the process of checking that the management system conforms to the standard).

Observation: In addition to the information provided by a contractor in various meetings and reports, observation is a tool often used by the buyer's contract professionals and management staff to validate information received from other sources.

- **Direct observation**: The actual physical presence of the contracting professional or other appropriate manager, on site, to visually check on progress or compare actual work completed to planned work completed.

- **Indirect observation**: Usually obtained through the receipt of various types of reports from the contractor, from reviews or audits performed by either the buyer's management staff or by internal or external auditors, from various forms of pre- and post-production testing and sampling, and a variety of other methods. Indirect observation can provide valuable information regarding issues such as cost, schedule, and quality that might not

otherwise be available. If the work effort is primarily physical in nature, indirect observation is often augmented by direct observation.

Performance bond: A type of bond that secures the fulfillment of all the undertakings, covenants, terms, conditions, and agreements contained in the contract.

Periodic status review meetings: Updated information on status, issues, and concerns should be shared between the buyer and seller during periodic face-to-face meetings. The frequency, content, and required attendees for these meetings should be mutually agreed upon and each should have a written agenda. These meetings should augment any written reports required and help serve as a means to continue an open and honest dialogue for issues related to contract performance.

Pre-performance meeting: This meeting can help avoid problems during contract performance. A pre-performance meeting can set the foundation for good communication between the buyer and seller. When conducted, this meeting should be chaired by contracting professionals from the buyer and seller and include appropriate managers and staff personnel from the buyer's organization (i.e., the customer who will interface with and receive the benefits from the contractor's work) and appropriate managers and staff personnel from the seller's organization (i.e., the contractor's resources that will interface with and perform work for the customer).

A pre-performance meeting includes a detailed review of the contract including all work to be performed and related terms and conditions. The intent of this review is to achieve a clear, mutual understanding of what needs to be done and who will do the work. It could include establishing a procedure for documenting written and oral communication. The meeting may also include a discussion about progress reporting requirements to include the frequency, format, and content of required reports, procedures for reporting unusual or urgent issues, and similar subjects. Attendees should also agree on methods and processes to resolve minor disagreements or questions about contract interpretation, with provisions for escalation when appropriate. The subjects discussed and agreements reached during these meetings should be thoroughly documented, approved by both the buyer and seller, and distributed throughout both organizations.

Reporting: Contracts sometimes require contractors to provide reports to the buyer about performance and financial status to ensure contract completion on time and within budget. When required by the contract, the contractor should provide written status reports to keep the buyer's contracting professionals and customers aware of progress and issues. These reports can be narrative, statistical, or a combination of the two, consistent with the need for the information.

Warranty: A promise or affirmation given by a seller to a buyer regarding the nature, usefulness, or condition of the supplies or performance of services furnished under the contract. Generally, a warranty's purpose is to delineate the rights and obligations for defective items and services and to foster quality performance.

3.3 Subcontract Management

Subcontract management describes the role a contractor has in ensuring subcontractor performance in accordance with their contract with the prime. In a subcontract, the prime contractor delegates some of the required work to another company, the subcontractor. Subcontracting usually occurs where the contracted work such as the construction of a building requires a variety of skills. Responsibility for fulfilling the original contract remains with the original contracting party, the prime contractor.

Although the contractual relationship between the buyer and the seller (i.e., the prime contractor) is normally the most important aspect of contract administration, the buyer also needs to pay attention to the relationship between the seller and its subcontractors. In many cases, the ability of a prime contractor to successfully meet contractual obligations is at least partially, and sometimes significantly, dependent on the ability of subcontractors to meet contractual obligations to the seller. In some cases, the subcontractor is simply a supplier of goods or raw materials to the seller for use in production or fabrication. In other cases, the subcontractor may perform specialized intellectual or highly technical work for a seller in direct support of the seller's contract with the buyer. Though in both cases, the seller's ability to successfully perform is dependent on the action of their subcontractors. The buyer should normally be more attuned to and concerned with subcontractor performance when that performance plays a direct and significant role in the overall contract performance.

In some cases, particularly in certain types of government contracting, the government organization may require that it consent to subcontracts anticipated by the prime contractor. In other cases, the government may require that the seller's purchasing system be periodically reviewed by government personnel. In both of these cases, the primary intent of the oversight is to ensure that government funds provided to the prime are used appropriately.

In other cases, it may be a matter of prudent management, whether in the public or private sector, for a buyer to be cognizant of the relationships between sellers and their subcontractors. When a subcontractor's performance is anticipated to have a significant impact on the prime contractor's ability to perform, the buying organization may consider including subcontractors in some or all of the communications-related activities, particularly the face-to-face meetings. Including the subcontractor in meetings can enhance the level of open communications, provide both the buyer and seller with a more complete understanding of all actions required for performance, alert both the buyer and seller to issues and potential subcontractor problems that may be referred to their level, encourage the seller to maintain an effective relationship with their subcontractors, provide the subcontractor with valuable insight regarding the nature of the relationship between the prime contractor and the buyer, and can assist the subcontractor in understanding how their performance affects the seller and successful contract completion.

When a prime contractor uses a subcontractor, the buying organization needs to exercise a degree of caution because the buyer has no privity of contract with the subcontractors. Buyers should therefore be careful when communicating and meeting with subcontractors. The prime contractor should always be the conduit through which information from the both the buyer and the subcontractor is relayed to the other party. The buyer should not allow a subcontractor to bring issues or problems with the seller to the buyer for resolution. The buyer should normally not meet with the subcontractor without representatives of the seller present. The buyer should, by word and deed, clearly communicate to the subcontractor that the buyer's contractual relationship with the seller forms the framework for the relationship. The buyer should also be careful not to give the appearance of undercutting the authority of the seller over its subcontractors.

LEXICON FOR SUBCONTRACT MANAGEMENT:

Bill of materials (BOM): A descriptive and quantitative listing of materials, supplies, parts, and components required to produce a designated complete end-item.

Commodity warehousing, Just in Time (JIT): Physically holding raw materials and commodities until ready for use. Although the storage of materials for use in the production process is basically the same as storing finished products, raw-materials storage and finished-goods storage differ in terms of the type of facility each requires, the value of the stored items, and product perishability. The basic JIT concept is an operations management philosophy whose dual objectives are to reduce waste and to increase productivity. Operationally, JIT minimizes inventory at all levels; materials are purchased, transported, and processed just in time for their use in a subsequent stage of the manufacturing process.

Concerted refusal to deal: An agreement or understanding by which two or more companies jointly refuse to do business with a specific third party.

Consent to subcontract: Some government contracts require the government to consent to a prime contractor's subcontract. Consent is required when subcontract work is complex, the dollar value is substantial, or the government's interest is not adequately protected by competition and the type of prime or subcontract.

Contractor's Purchasing Systems Review: An evaluation of the efficiency and effectiveness with which the prime contractor spends government funds and complies with government policy when subcontracting.

Critical subcontract: A subcontract, the failure of which seriously jeopardizes the successful completion of a program within cost, schedule, quality, and/or technical performance specifications.

Flow down: The transfer and translation of prime contract requirements to subcontracts.

Local buying: Patronizing local suppliers can have the following benefits: improved community relations, smaller quantities of materials can be provided at lower prices, local inventories can be adapted for continuing local users, minimal transportation costs, and shorter lead times.

Make-or-Buy Program: The part of a contractor's written plan for the development or production of an end item outlining the subsystems, major components, assemblies, subassemblies, and parts intended to be manufactured, test-treated, or assembled by the seller (make) and those the seller intends to procure from another source (buy).

Material Management and Accounting System (MMAS): The contractor's system for planning, controlling, and accounting for the acquisition, use, and disposition of material. Such a system may be manual or automated and may be integrated with planning, engineering, estimating, purchasing, inventory, and/o r accounting systems, etc.—or may be essentially a stand-alone system.

Outsourcing: The contractual process of using another party to provide goods, services, or both that were previously done internally in an organization.

Price fixing: Any agreement, understanding, or arrangement among competitors to raise, lower, fix, or stabilize prices, as well as any agreement between a supplier and customer as to the price at which the customer may resell goods purchased.

Prime contractor: The entity an agent for the buyer enters into a prime contract with to obtain supplies, materials, equipment, or services of any kind.

Privity of contract: The direct legal (contractual) relationship that exists between parties that allows either party to (a) enforce contractual rights against the other party and (b) seek remedy directly from the other party with whom this relationship exists.

Section 8(a) subcontract: A subcontract between the Small Business Administration and a socially and economically disadvantaged business concern named after the section of the Small Business Act that authorized it.

Specialized, long lead items: Lead time management of critical materials and deliverables. Procurement lead time starts when a material requirement is identified and spans the time until a significant portion of the material is delivered. Procurement lead time has two components: administrative lead time and production lead time. Administrative lead time begins with the identification of a material requirement and continues until a contract is awarded for the creation of the material. Production lead time is the time from contract award until material delivery.

Subcontract: A contract between and buyer and seller in which a significant part of the supplies or services being obtained is for eventual use in a prime contract.

Subcontracting preference: A government policy that encourages prime contractors to assist minority companies by requiring that prime contractors develop subcontracting plans. On all contracts over the simplified acquisition threshold, contractors must agree to allow small and small disadvantaged businesses (SDBs) opportunities to participate in contract performance.

Supplier goods, services: Management of any contract, agreement, or purchase order (and any preliminary contractual instrument other than a prime contract) calling for the performance of any work or the making or furnishing of any material required for the performance of a prime contract; includes managing the purchase of supplies that are consumed in becoming incorporated in other property, thus losing identity.

Supply chain function: Management of the flow and storage of materials (raw materials, semi-finished goods, and finished products) from vendor sources through to the ultimate customer. It includes both inbound logistics (materials management and procurement) and outbound logistics (customer service and channels of distribution).

Any written alteration in the specification, delivery point, rate of delivery, contract period, price, quantity, or other provision of an existing contract that is accomplished in accordance with a contract clause. Contract changes may be unilateral or bilateral.

In a perfect world, the buyer and seller negotiate and agree on all aspects of a contract: the contract is issued, the contractor performs flawlessly, all required work is completed on or ahead of schedule and at or below expected cost, all goods and services are received, the contractor is paid accurately and promptly, and both sides happily move on to the next matter of business. Though the perfect contract is a goal both buyers and sellers should pursue, the reality is that we live in an imperfect world and the parties need to deal with inevitable changes that may occur during contract performance. Generally, there are three types of changes: directed changes, constructive changes, and cardinal changes.

Both parties to a contract should adhere to an agreed-upon change management process that fairly and equitably deals with the impacts of change on contracts.

LEXICON FOR CONTRACT CHANGES AND MODIFICATIONS:

Adjusted ceiling: A negotiated adjustment to the ceiling price due to changes; reflects a change in the negotiated maximum liability of the buyer. This term applies to incentive contract types.

Adjusted target: Accumulated price resulting from changes to the basic contract for in-program changes, changes in scope, and/or terminations reflecting the current negotiated target price for work authorized. This term applies to incentive contract types.

Administrative changes: Unilateral contract changes, in writing, that do not affect the substantive rights of the parties, such as a change in the paying office or the appropriation data.

Alternate item: An item selected by the responsible engineering activity in lieu of the forecast item.

Amendment: A change (correction, deletion, or addition) to a solicitation before it is due. The amendment becomes part of the resulting contract.

Authorized work: Definitized work that is on contract. Work for which written authorization exists but the contract costs have not been definitized.

Bilateral change: Formed by the exchange of promises to perform reciprocal obligations for the other party.

Cardinal changes: Changes beyond the scope of the contract that materially alter the nature of the contract that the parties entered into. A cardinal change could be considered a breach of contract.

Change orders: Written orders signed by an authorized buyer pursuant to a contract clause that modifies contractual requirements within the scope of the contract.

Changes clause: A standard clause in government contracts. There are several versions corresponding to the specific type of contract, but all have certain common characteristics. The clause, which is mandatory for most government contracts, provides a contractual grant of authority to the government by its supplier. It gives the government the right to unilaterally alter specific matters affecting the performance of the contract.

Claim: A written demand or written assertion by one of the contracting parties seeking, as a matter of right, the payment of money in a sum certain, the adjustment or interpretation of the contract terms, or other relief arising under or relating to the contract. A claim arising under a contract, unlike a claim relating to that contract, is a claim that can be resolved under a contract clause that provides for the relief sought by the claimant. A voucher, invoice, or other routine request for payment that is not in dispute when submitted is not a claim.

Compensable delays: A delay for which the buyer is contractually responsible and that excuses the seller's failure to perform and is compensable.

Consequential damages: Costs resulting from a particular cause. For example, a product's failure may mean the purchaser not only has incurred the added cost necessary to replace the product, but also has lost income that would have resulted had the product not failed. The lost income would be a consequential damage. The extent to which consequential damages may be recovered depends on the language contained in the contract and the law in a particular jurisdiction.

Constructive changes: Oral or written acts or omissions by employees or agents of the buyer that are of such a nature that they have

the same effect as written change orders. A constructive change is a change resulting from buyer actions or directives that impact the cost or schedule for performance. A constructive change generally occurs when the buyer impliedly or expressly orders the seller to perform work that is not in the contract. In government contracting, equitable adjustment is granted for constructive changes only if the change caused injury or liability to the seller.

Deductive change: A change resulting in a reduction in contract price because of a net reduction in a contractor's work.

Delays:

- **Federal**: Contractual provision designed to protect the contractor from sanctions for late performance. To the extent that it has been excusably delayed, the contractor is protected from default termination, liquidated damages, or excess costs of procurement or completion. Excusable delays (e.g., acts of God or the public enemy, acts of the government in either its sovereign or contractual capacity, fire, flood, quarantines, strikes, epidemics, unusually severe weather, or freight embargoes) may also lead to recovery of additional compensation if the government constructively accelerates performance.

- **Commercial**: Late delivery of products and services and implications to contract management; includes time requirements of obligations, impracticability, and other standards of delivery performance.

Differing site conditions: A provision in construction contracts that provides for adjustment of the contract price should the contractor discover physical conditions of an unusual nature that differ from those normally encountered.

Directed change: Most contracts contain a changes clause that gives the buyer the right to direct changes during contract performance. The clause describes what type of changes the buyer can direct, the procedure for ordering the change, and a provision for "equitable adjustment" to the contract amount or period of performance if there is a resultant change in cost or schedule. A directed change usually must be within the original scope of the contract.

Economic price adjustment: An alteration permitted and specified by contract provisions for the upward or downward revision of a stated contract price upon the occurrence of certain specifically defined contingencies.

Engineering change proposal: A document proposing any design change requiring revision to contract specifications or engineering drawings. An engineering change proposal may be originated by either party to a contract. The proposal requires detailed documentation and evaluation of technical, cost, and schedule effects.

Equitable adjustment: The compensation or price adjustment to which a seller is entitled upon the occurrence of a constructive change or special event.

Force majeure clause: A French term that refers to an unexpected or uncontrollable event that upsets the plan or releases one from obligation.

Liquidated damages: A contract provision providing for the assessment of damages on the seller for its failure to comply with certain performance or delivery requirements of the contract. It is used when the time of delivery or performance is of such importance that the buyer may reasonably expect to suffer damages if delivery or performance is delinquent.

Modified total cost basis: A means of pricing equitable adjustments. Under this approach, information on specific costs incurred is included in addition to a total cost portion of the claim.

Offsets: A cost balancing action whereby a claim may be cancelled or lessened by a counterclaim.

Option: A unilateral right in a contract by which for a specified time the buyer may elect to purchase additional quantities of the services or supplies called for in the contract, or may elect to extend the period of performance in the contract.

Show cause letter: A written delinquency notice informing a contractor of failure to perform within the specific terms of the contract, and advising that the government is considering termination for default. It affords the seller the opportunity to show cause why it should not be terminated.

Stop-Work Order:

- **Federal:** Under a negotiated fixed-price supply, cost-reimbursement supply, research and development, or service contract, a contract clause that permits the contracting officer to order the contractor to stop work if a work stoppage is required for reasons such as state-of-the-art advancements, production or engineering breakthroughs, or realignment of programs.

- **Commercial:** Instruction served on the seller by the buyer requiring that the seller cease to perform the contract and take alternative steps to limit the risk and liabilities of the parties. This is usually governed by predetermined protocols set forth in the contract. In the event of such termination, the contractor must immediately stop all work and immediately have all of its suppliers and subcontractors stop all work.

Supplemental agreements: Contract modifications that are accomplished by the mutual consent of the parties.

Unilateral change: Formed by the exchange of a promise of one party for an action by the other party.

3.5 Property Administration

Property Administration includes the processes used by prime contractors to account for and manage all property, both real and personal. This includes facilities, material, special tooling, special test equipment, and agency-peculiar property.

Generally speaking, most contracts require total performance from the contractor. That is, under the requirements and terms and conditions contained in the contract, the contractor is usually required to provide all of the resources required for successful performance. In some cases, however, the buyer may provide various forms of property to a contractor or subcontractor. The fundamental reason for the buyer to provide property to the seller is cost savings. It may be less expensive for a buyer to provide property to a contractor for use during performance than it would be for the contractor to purchase the property, particularly when the property can be re-used for future contracts. The post-award administration of property is a highly specialized aspect of contract administration, normally handled by a trained sub-specialist within the buyer's contracting organization. However, there are some general concepts related to property that are important, including ownership, accountability, competitive advantage, and property administration.

When buyer-furnished property is provided to a contractor, several property administration issues are normally part of the acquisition. The availability of buyer-furnished property is usually included in the solicitation, and potential offerors are normally provided an opportunity to review and inspect the property to verify its existence and condition.

The buyer is most often responsible for the delivery of buyer-furnished property to the contractor. The buyer should ensure that delivery delays do not occur and that the property delivered is suitable for use as intended. Late delivery and defective property may adversely affect contractor performance and have cost and schedule impacts.

The contractor is usually required to have a system in place to ensure that all property provided by the buyer is accounted for, maintained as appropriate, and used as specified in the contract. Both the buyer and seller should periodically review or audit these control systems to ensure they are operating properly.

Upon completion or termination of a contract, the contractor is usually held responsible for requesting property disposition instructions from the buyer for disposing of the property as directed.

LEXICON FOR PROPERTY ADMINISTRATION:

(See 4.10, Government Property, for additional information.)

Abstract of title: A condensed history of the title to property from past records.

Accountability: The buying organization usually retains internal organizational accountability for all property the buyer provides to a seller. But the seller is required to document the property receipt and record relevant facts about the property, such as its condition, if overages, shortages, or damages occurred. In addition, the seller should maintain the property in its possession. The contractor's maintenance program shall enable the identification, disclosure, and performance of normal and routine preventative maintenance and repair.

Acquisition cost: The cost to acquire a tangible capital asset, including the purchase price of the asset and costs necessary to prepare the asset for use. Costs necessary to prepare the asset for use include the cost of placing the asset in location and bringing the asset to a condition necessary for normal or expected use.

Bill of sale: A written document formally transferring ownership of personal property specified in the document from the seller to the buyer.

Competitive advantage: Particularly as it relates to government contracting, the possession of buyer-furnished property can provide an incumbent contractor with a competitive advantage when competing with other sellers for future contracts. Contracting professionals often "level the playing field" in such cases by taking the value of the property into account when evaluating competing offers.

Demilitarization: Rendering a product unusable for military use, and not restorable to, the purpose for which it was designed or is customarily used.

Discrepancies incident to shipment: Any differences (e.g., count or condition) between the items documented to have been shipped and items actually received.

Ownership: Usually the buyer retains ownership (title) of all rights to buyer-provided property. The question of ownership of property acquired by the seller to perform the contract is sometimes more complex, and may be dependent upon the type of contract the seller is performing under.

Property administration: When a buyer furnishes property to a contractor, several property administration issues are normally part of the acquisition. The availability of buyer-furnished property is usually included in the solicitation, and potential offerors are normally provided an opportunity to review and inspect the property to verify its existence and condition.

The buyer is most often responsible for delivering buyer-furnished property to the contractor. The buyer should be careful to ensure that delivery delays do not occur, since that may adversely affect contractor performance.

The contractor is usually required to have a system in place to ensure that all property provided by the buyer is accounted for, maintained as appropriate, and used as specified in the contract. Both the buyer and seller should periodically review or audit these control systems to ensure they are operating properly.

Property control system: Procedures that meet the requirements of government property clauses to control, protect, and maintain all government property.

Property records: The records created and maintained by the contractor in support of its stewardship responsibilities for the management of government property.

Provide: To furnish, as in government-furnished property, or to acquire, as in contractor-acquired property.

Title: The legal right to control and dispose of property.

3.6 Transportation

When contracting for goods, the costs associated with transportation are sometimes little more than a minor afterthought for many contracting professionals. However, transportation issues can sometimes represent a significant expense, particularly when a large quantity of goods is purchased, or when the goods are extremely heavy, cumbersome, fragile, subject to spoilage, or otherwise difficult to transport. Transportation is another technical subspecialty and many organizations have some expertise in their transportation, logistics, or shipping and receiving functions that the contracting professional can consult to evaluate the cost considerations of various transportation options. Some of the more common transportation considerations include required receipt dates, mode of transportation, transportation-related services, and responsibility for transportation charges.

LEXICON FOR TRANSPORTATION:

Assignment: Transference of a property right or title to another party. In shipping, it is commonly used with a bill of lading, which involves transfer of rights, title, and interest for the purposes of endorsement. Such endorsement gives, to the party named, the title to the property covered by the bill of lading.

Bailment: A temporary transfer of possession of personal property without a change of ownership for the specific purpose and with the intent that possession will revert to the owner at a later date.

Bill of lading: A transportation document, used as a receipt of goods, as documentary evidence of title for clearing customs and generally used as a contract of carriage.

- **Commercial bill of lading (CBL)**: Unlike the government bill of lading, is not an accountable transportation document.

- **Government bill of lading (GBL)**: An accountable transportation document, authorized and prepared by a government official.

Carrier (or commercial carrier): A common carrier or a contract carrier.

Common carrier: A person holding himself or herself out to the general public to provide transportation for compensation.

Consignee: A person, group of persons, or organization that receives supplies and services and that is named on the bill of lading.

Contract carrier: A person providing transportation for compensation under continuing agreements with one person or a limited number of persons.

Demurrage: A fee charged by a carrier against a consignee, consignor, or other responsible party to compensate for the detention of the carrier's equipment in excess of allowable free time for loading, unloading, reconsigning, or stopping in transit.

Government rate tender: An offer by a common carrier to the United States at a rate below the regulated rate offered to the general public.

Household goods: Personal property other than real estate, belonging to an individual or their immediate family, including (but not limited to) appliances, books, clothing, furnishings, and furniture; and paid for by

- The householder, except such term does not include property moving from a factory or store, other than property that the householder has purchased with the intent to use in his or her dwelling and is transported at the request of the householder, and the transportation charges are paid to the carrier by the householder; or

- Another party.

Free on Board (FOB): A term used in conjunction with a physical point to determine the responsibility and basis for payment of freight charges and, unless otherwise agreed, the point at which title for goods passes to the buyer or consignee.

- **FOB Destination:** The seller is responsible for paying transportation costs associated with delivering the goods from their facility to the place or places specified by the buyer in the contract. Such costs are normally included in the seller's price. An advantage to the buyer is that the title to the goods does not pass from the seller to the buyer until the goods have been received, thereby insulating the buyer from in-transit loss or damage issues.

- **FOB Origin:** The buyer is responsible for paying transportation costs associated with delivering the goods from the seller's facility to the place or places specified by the buyer in the contract. This option may be advantageous to the buyer when the buyer can obtain the transportation at lower costs than the seller could, or when the buyer has its own transportation capability. Title to the goods transfers from the seller to the buyer when the goods leave the seller's facility.

Mode of transportation: Means of moving freight traffic using transportation methods such as bills of lading, parcel post, bus service, air cargo, rail freight, carload and less than carload, motor freight, freight forwarder, and pipeline. The mode of transportation (i.e., rail, motor freight, air, etc.) is sometimes dictated by the nature of the goods being purchased, and is always a factor in determining appropriate transportation methods. Consistent with other contract requirements and industry standards, the mode of transportation selected should reflect a thoughtful balance between speed, reliability, need, and cost.

Noncontiguous domestic trade: Transportation (except with regard to bulk cargo, forest products, recycled metal scrap, waste paper, and paper waste) subject to regulation by the Surface Transportation Board involving traffic originating in or destined to Alaska, Hawaii, or a territory or possession of the United States.

Released or declared value: The assigned value of the cargo for reimbursement purposes, not necessarily the actual value of the cargo. Released value may be more or less than the actual value of the cargo. The released value is the maximum amount that could be recovered by the agency in the event of loss or damage for the shipments of freight and household goods.

Required receipt date: The date that goods are due to be received at the place designated by the buyer is sometimes a determinant of transportation costs. The buyer and seller should be aware of the potential for increased transportation costs that may be a result of a specific receipt date, particularly when the delivery schedule is aggressive, or when the delivery schedule is accelerated by modification due to a change in plans or to overcome some issue or problem in production.

Transportation: Applying transportation and traffic management considerations in the acquisition of supplies and acquiring transportation-related services.

Transportation-related services: Procedures for the acquisition of related services such as stevedoring, storage, packing, marking, and ocean freight forwarding.

3.7 Disputes

Disputes are legal disagreements between the parties regarding their rights under a contract that begin when a recipient denies claim submitted against it by the another contracting party.

Notwithstanding the advantages that can result from the buyer and seller adopting a collaborative and cooperative approach toward all aspects of contract management, sometimes issues arise during contract performance that are difficult to resolve. As a general rule, buyers and sellers should always seek to resolve differences in the least formal and most collaborative manner possible. Though formal legal action is always a possibility, both buyers and sellers should be hesitant to pursue resolution through legal proceedings for many reasons, including time, expense, uncertainty of outcome, and the effect on the business relationship.

Formal legal proceedings often require many months or years to resolve. Preparing for and participating in legal proceedings can require expending substantial funds, which can sometimes have a negative impact on other aspects of the organization's business.

Few, if any, organizations will pursue legal action if they do not believe they will prevail. However, in most actions, there are winners and losers, and parties to litigation often find themselves the recipient of unpleasant surprises. Since legal proceedings are by nature adversarial, they can have a permanently negative effect on the relationship between the litigants. This negative effect can prevent the parties from engaging in mutually beneficial business relationships in the future.

In recent years, both government and commercial contracting organizations have made progress toward pursuing a variety of informal, less formal, and formal dispute resolution methods in lieu for formal legal proceedings, including informal collaboration, negotiation, and alternate dispute resolution.

Alternative dispute resolution, for example, is a procedure that is used in lieu of litigation to resolve issues in controversy, including but not limited to settlement negotiations, conciliation, facilitation, mediation, fact finding, mini-trials, and arbitration.

LEXICON FOR DISPUTES:

Accord and satisfaction: A situation where two people agree that one of them has a right of action against the other, but they accept a substitute or different act or value as performance.

Accrual of a claim: The date when all events that fix the alleged liability of either the government or the contractor and permit assertion of the claim were known or should have been known. For liability to be fixed, some injury must have occurred. However, monetary damages need not have been incurred.

Alternative dispute resolution: Any procedure that is used in lieu of litigation to resolve issues in controversy, including but not limited to settlement negotiations, conciliation, facilitation, mediation, fact finding, mini-trials, and arbitration.

When the less formal methods of collaboration and negotiation between the parties does not produce a satisfactory result, Alternative dispute resolution procedures can often be used to arrive at a mutually agreeable solution. ADR encompasses practices for managing and quickly resolving disputes at modest cost and with minimal adverse impact on the relationship between the contracting parties.

These processes significantly broaden dispute resolution options beyond litigation or traditional unassisted negotiation. Some ADR procedures, such as binding arbitration and private judging, are similar to expedited litigation in that they involve a third-party decision maker with authority to impose a resolution if the parties so desire. Other procedures, such as mediation and the minitrial, are collaborative, with a neutral third party helping a group of individuals or entities with divergent views to reach a goal or complete a task to their mutual satisfaction.

Some examples of ADR techniques include interest-based negotiation, mediation, minitrial, nonbinding arbitration, and binding arbitration.

Appeal: When a contractual party resorts to a superior court to review the decision of a lower court or administrative agency.

Arbitration: Process involving the use of an impartial third party to whom the parties to an agreement refer their disputes for resolution.

- **Binding arbitration**: Parties that submit to binding arbitration submit their disputes to a neutral third person or panel for a decision that both parties must accept. Binding arbitration is commonly used in private-sector contracting, but is rarely used in government contracting due to the absolute nature of the binding decision.

- **Nonbinding arbitration**: Involves an evidentiary hearing before a third party, composed of one or more arbitrators, that draws conclusions regarding the issues in dispute. These hearings typically include broad fact-finding activities, which assist in educating the third party about the matters in dispute. Upon completion of presentations by each party, the third party renders its decision. The parties are not bound by the arbitrator's decision and either or both sides may reject it. The intent of nonbinding arbitration is to predict the likely adjudicated outcome of the case as an aid to settlement.

Contract Disputes Act of 1978: Establishes procedures and requirements for asserting and resolving claims in government contracts that are subject to the act. The act provides for

- Paying interest on contractor claims,

- Certifying contractor claims, and

- Imposing a civil penalty for contractor claims that are fraudulent or based on a misrepresentation of fact.

Damages: Compensation of a specific value, as determined by a court, to be paid for loss or injury suffered by one party to a contract as a result of the other party's breach of the contract.

- **Consequential damages**: Those damages not directly associated with the seller's breach, but traceable to it nonetheless because the seller had reason to know of the buyer's general or particular needs at the time of contracting. Consequential damages also include injury to person or property proximately resulting from any breach of warranty.

- **Incidental damages**: Includes damages resulting from a seller's breach; for example, expenses reasonably incurred in inspection, receipt, transportation (including care and custody of goods rightfully rejected), any commercially reasonable charges, expenses or commissions in connection with effecting cover, and any other reasonable expense incident to the delay or other breach.

Liquidated damages: A contract provision assessing damages on the contractor for its failure to comply with certain performance or delivery requirements of the contract; used when the time of delivery or performance is of such importance that the buyer may reasonably expect to suffer damages if the delivery or performance is delinquent.

- **Money damages**: Includes compensatory damages for the purpose of putting the non-breaching party in the position that he or she would have been in if the contract had not been breached.

- **Punitive damages**: In the case of fraud or malice, punitive damages may be awarded to the non-breaching party to punish the party that breached; meant to discourage him or her from committing the same offense again.

Defective certification: A certificate which alters or otherwise deviates from the language in the *FAR* or which is not executed by a person duly authorized to bind the contractor with respect to the claim. Failure to certify shall not be deemed to be a defective certification.

Differing site conditions: A provision in construction contracts that adjusts the contract price should the contractor discover physical conditions of an unusual nature that differ from those ordinarily encountered.

Discovery: A pretrial or prehearing procedure designed to promote full disclosure of all relevant facts related to a contract dispute.

Dispute: A disagreement between the parties regarding their rights under a contract that originates when a claim is denied by the other party against which the claim is made.

Equitable remedies: Includes an order of specific performance, restitution and recession. In the case of goods or real property, an order of specific performance can require the breaching party to perform in accordance with the contract.

- **Rescission**: Allows the cancellation of the contract, usually when mutually agreed to between the parties. In some cases, the contract or statutes allow unilateral rescission for a specified period of time, such as in the case of mortgages and real estate purchases.

- **Restitution**: Seeks to restore the non-breaching party to the position he or she was in before the formation of the contract.

Extraordinary contractual relief: Form of relief for contractors under federal law giving the president the power to authorize federal agencies to enter into contracts, or amendments or modifications of contracts, without

regard to other revisions of law relating to the making, performance, amendment, or modification of contracts, when the president believes the action will facilitate national defense.

Forums: The administrative and judicial bodies that adjudicate disputes.

Issue in controversy: A material disagreement between the buyer and the contractor that may result in a claim, or is all or part of an existing claim.

Latent defect: A type of defect that existed at the time of acceptance but would not have been discovered by a reasonable inspection.

Mediation: A private, informal process in which the parties are assisted by one or more neutral third parties in efforts to achieve settlement. Mediators do not judge or arbitrate; rather they advise and consult impartially with the parties in an attempt to bring about a mutually agreeable resolution.

Minitrial: A structured process where the attorney for each party presents an abbreviated version of that side's case. This information exchange allows each party to hear the strength and weaknesses of the other party's case as well as their own. Following the presentation, the attorneys meet to see if they can negotiate a settlement. A neutral party can oversee the process if desired, and provide an opinion on what the potential court outcome might be.

Misrepresentation of fact: A false statement of substantive fact, or any conduct that leads to the belief of a substantive fact material to proper understanding of the matter in hand, made with intent to deceive or mislead.

Negotiation: Another method preferred by both buyers and sellers to resolving disputes. Negotiation is often preferred because most parties are familiar with and experienced in the process, and because it is much more efficient and less expensive than other dispute resolution processes. Agreements resulting from negotiations can be easily implemented as contract modifications.

Traditional negotiation involves each side beginning with a proposed solution, followed by a series of counter-proposals, offers and counteroffers, argument, persuasion, and concessions until an acceptable compromise is reached. Interest-based negotiation is a more collaborative process that involves the parties becoming educated about the needs, concerns, and interests of the other, followed by joint problem solving to identify the most acceptable way to meet all or most of the interests of both parties.

Patent defect: A type of defect that can be discovered without undue effort.

Substantial performance: The doctrine that prohibits termination of a contract for default if a contractor's performance deviates only in minor respects from the contract's requirements.

3.8 Organizational Conflict of Interest

An organizational conflict of interest (OCI) exists when the nature of the work to be performed under a proposed contract may, without some restriction on future activities, result in an unfair competitive advantage to the contractor, or impair the contractor's objectivity in performing the contract work. OCI refers to conflict of interest relating to the government. The term is used similarly in the private sector. Parties must remain impartial and trustworthy. When one of the parties is not objective, that would constitute conflict of interest. Given the number of mergers, acquisitions, and consolidations that have taken place in recent years, contractors risk being told they are ineligible to compete for a contract because they or their predecessors have an unfair competitive advantage over other firms.

It is essential that a potential OCI be identified as early as possible during acquisition planning so steps can be taken to avoid, mitigate, or neutralize the OCI. Early identification of a potential OCI will reduce the possibility of delays and disruptions during the acquisition process.

LEXICON FOR ORGANIZATIONAL CONFLICT OF INTEREST:

OCI categories: Potential OCI problems are unequal access to information, impaired objectivity, and biased ground rules.

Mitigation plans: To help mitigate or eliminate an OCI, most plans include some or all of the following elements:

- **Confidentiality agreements**: Employees are required to execute special confidentiality agreements, with penalties for noncompliance ranging from disciplinary action to termination. Confidentiality agreements require the employee to notify a high-ranking corporate official should any person not working on the contract attempt to solicit information or influence the work being performed under the contract.

- **Disclosure of relevant information**: This requirement tends to dictate that companies have systems in place to be able to screen not only new work against contracts already in place containing OCI provisions, but also new solicitations with OCI provisions that might conflict with future plans of other parts of the business.

- **Divestiture of a company**: A new company can be created with a completely separate board of directors.

- **Firewalls**: The written agreement between the conflicted entities usually relies on a combination of procedures and physical security to establish organizational "firewalls" to avoid potential, real, or perceived OCIs from affecting the business activities of either party.

- **Removal of conflict**: Oftentimes, staff members have been supporting a particular program or agency for most of their careers, and their particular expertise and knowledge would have dire consequences for the program should their efforts be interrupted. In these cases, the affected individual(s) can be hired by another, nonconflicted entity to perform the same work. However, the buyer must be careful to keep the employees "whole" from a salary and benefits perspective.

- **Separation of personnel**: Eliminating communication between personnel from the conflicted entity and the organization can effectively eliminate the potential for bias.

- **Work-switch**: Depending on who has the conflict, work can be switched between the prime and the subcontractor.

Personal benefit: OCI exists when personal or professional interests of a person affect the person's ability to be objective.

OCI compliance requirements: The types of individuals or entities who are required to comply with OCI laws are government contractors, sub-contractors, and affiliates of contractors—any entities owned by the prime contractor and chief executives and directors.

3.9 Contract Closeout

Contract closeout is the process of declaring that the obligations under a contract have been satisfied and that a procurement file is both physically and administratively complete. A closeout can occur when (1) the contractor's supplies or services have been

accepted and paid for, and (2) all documentation on the procurement is finalized and properly assembled.

Contracting activities are responsible for initiating each contract closeout. This administrative process should begin as soon as possible after the contract is physically complete, which means the seller has delivered the required supplies and the buyer has inspected and accepted them; or the seller has performed and the buyer has accepted all services required by the contract and made final payment, and the base period and any option periods exercised have expired.

Contract closeout consists of completing a number of procedural and administrative tasks to change the status of a contract from active to complete. These required tasks normally include:

- Verifying that all required goods or services have been received and accepted;

- Verifying that all contractor invoices have been received and paid;

- Returning or disposing of any buyer-furnished property;

- Settling subcontracts by the seller;

- Agreeing that no claims, issues, or unresolved matters exist by both parties;

- Signing and issuing a formal contract completion notice; and

- Deobligating excess funds remaining on the contract (federal contracting) by the buyer.

Upon completion of all required closeout actions, completed contract files should be retained for the appropriate period of time required by law, regulation, or corporate policy.

Administrative closeout: Process of ensuring that all documentation—including releases, audits, reports, and final invoices—has been completed and that contract files have been properly stored or disposed of.

Contract cost: The aggregate dollar amount paid to the seller.

Contract fulfillment: The joint buyer and seller actions taken to successfully perform and administer a contractual agreement and meet or exceed all contract obligations.

Excess and remaining funds: Generally, fixed-price contracts have an unliquidated balance equal to $0.00 when the contract becomes physically complete. However, there are instances where the contract allows for variances in quantity shipped, the contractor has rounded on the invoice, or performance on a specific contract line item number (CLIN) was not necessary (e.g., fixed funds provided for maintenance or service on computer hardware).

- **Excess funds:** Funds relating to a specific line item or deliverable that was not performed on a contract. These funds are deobligated funds by contract modification.

- **Remaining funds:** Funds left on a contract due to quantity variances or price rounding and where all contract performance required by the contract has been completed and paid in full. These funds are annotated accordingly and are automatically removed.

Payment: Fulfillment of financial obligations of the contract; includes consideration, exchanges, compromise, and release of claims, part-payment, and forbearance.

Physical completion: When the contractor has completed required deliveries and/or performed all services, all options have expired, or the contract has been terminated.

Quick closeout: A faster method of completing the closeout process for a cost-reimbursement contract. Final indirect rates are negotiated on a contract basis, rather than by fiscal year as in regular closeout methods. Quick closeout can only be done in limited circumstances: if the contract is physically complete, the amount of unsettled indirect costs to be allocated to the contract is relatively insignificant, and an agreement can be reached on a reasonable estimate for allocable dollars.

Records retention:

- **Federal:** The record retention requirements addressed by the FAR apply to both prime contracts and subcontracts. Contractors must make books, records, documents, and other supporting evidence available to the comptroller general and contracting agencies for a certain period after final payment. The calculation of a retention period starts at the end of the contractor's fiscal year in which an entry is made that charges a cost to a government contract.

- **Commercial:** Controls over the creation, maintenance, and use of records relating to a contract; includes determining a period of active access and procedures for disposition of records at the end of that period, either by destruction or by retirement to archives.

Subcontractor costs: The prime contractor is responsible for auditing subcontractors and generally closing subcontracts using procedures similar to the government.

3.10 Contract Termination

In some cases, it becomes necessary to end performance on a contract before the contractual period of performance ends. In federal contracting, action is taken pursuant to a contract clause in which the contracting officer unilaterally ends all or part of the work. In commercial contracting, action is taken pursuant to a contract clause in which either party exercises a legal right to terminate the contract.

LEXICON FOR CONTRACT TERMINATION:

Anticipatory profit: Profit payable for work not performed. It is viewed as a reasonable sanction to be imposed upon defaulters in ordinary contractual relationships.

Avoidable costs: Those costs that will not continue if an ongoing operation is changed or deleted.

Bilateral notice: Termination of a contract by mutual consent. Typically initiated by one party by notice of the exercise of a contractual right to termination based on particular circumstances. Generally, both the circumstances permitting the termination and the process for termination are predetermined in the contract.

Cancellation: The withdrawal of the requirement to purchase goods and/or services by the buyer.

Force majeure: A clause that allows for nonperformance for excusable conditions.

No-cost cancellation: A type of quasi-termination that usually occurs shortly after contract execution, often because the seller realizes that they will be unable to perform. If both parties agree, no debts or obligations are due, and if the buyer can obtain performance from other sources, a no-cost cancellation can be a quick and efficient way to sever a contractual relationship.

Other work: Any current or scheduled work of the contractor, whether government or commercial, other than work related to the terminated contract.

Plant clearance period: The period beginning on the effective date of contract completion or termination and ending 90 days (or such longer period as may be agreed to) after receipt by the contracting officer of acceptable inventory schedules for each property classification. The final phase of the plant clearance period means that period after receipt of acceptable inventory schedules.

Settlement agreement: A written agreement in the form of a contract modification settling all or a severable portion of a settlement proposal.

Settlement proposal: A proposal for effecting settlement of a contract terminated in whole or in part, submitted by a contractor or subcontractor. A settlement proposal is included within the generic meaning of the word "claim" under false claims acts.

Stop work order: A request for interim work stoppage as a result of nonconformance, lack of funding, or technical considerations.

Subcontractor's rights: A subcontractor has no contractual rights against the government upon the termination of a prime contract. A subcontractor may have rights against the prime contractor or intermediate subcontractor with whom it has contracted. Upon termination of a prime contract, the prime contractor and each subcontractor are responsible for the prompt settlement of the settlement proposals of their immediate subcontractors.

Substantial performance: Doctrine that prohibits termination of a contract for default if a contractor's performance deviates only in minor respects from the contract's requirements.

Termination by mutual consent: Commonly used in the commercial contracting environment, termination by mutual consent is a bilateral agreement indicating that the parties no longer wish to be bound by the contract, and terminating both parties respective rights and obligations. Termination by mutual consent clauses are sometimes included in the basic contract, though they can also be negotiated and executed during the period of performance.

Termination claim: Any claim or demand by a prime contractor for compensation because of the termination before completion of any contract or subcontract for the convenience of the government.

Termination for convenience: In government contracting, the government buyer always has the unilateral right to terminate a contract for the convenience of the government, when the contract no longer serves the best interests of the government. Terminations for convenience often result from a change in government priorities, program termination or downsizing, or other significant events that were not anticipated at the time of contract formation. When the government pursues a termination for convenience, a termination settlement is negotiated with the seller.

Termination for default: Also referred to as *termination for cause*; is normally a right of law as well as a right vested as the result of the inclusion of appropriate terms and conditions in the contract. Termination for default can result from one party's failure to perform one or more actions required by the contract. Typical reasons to terminate for default include:

- **Failure to adhere to schedule:** If a seller fails to completely perform during the specified period of performance, that failure may be justification for a default termination. The buyer should exercise good business judgment in this situation to determine if the failure is significant enough to justify the termination.

- **Failure to comply with other terms and conditions:** The seller's failure to comply with the contract's significant terms and conditions can justify a default termination. This is another area in which the buyer should exercise sound business judgment and good faith in determining if the seller's failures are damaging enough to warrant termination.

- **Failure to perform:** The seller's failure to provide the required goods or services is a valid reason to terminate for default.

- **Repudiation:** A contract may be terminated for default if either the buyer or seller clearly indicates to the other party, by word or deed, that they cannot or will not perform.

Termination inventory: Any property purchased, supplied, manufactured, furnished, or otherwise acquired for the performance of contract that was subsequently terminated and properly allocable to the terminated portion of the contract. It includes government furnished property (GFP). It does not include facilities, material, special test equipment, or special tooling that is subject to a separate contract or to a special contract requirement governing its use or disposition.

Torncello rule: In *Torncello v. United States* (1982), the court ruled that the termination for convenience clause could not be used to avoid anticipated profits, unless there had been some change in circumstances between the time of award of the contract and the time of termination.

Unilateral nonperformance: Termination of a contract by one of the parties. Right to terminate, notice required, and procedures for termination are typically specified in the contract. Most commonly, this is available as a remedy for the seller's nonperformance or the buyer's failure to pay.

Unsettled contract change: Any contract change or contract term for which a definitive modification is required but has not been executed.

Work-in-process inventory: The cost of uncompleted goods still on the production line.

1. Organizational conflict of interest means

   a. a person is unable to render impartial assistance or advice to the government because of activities or relationships with other persons.
   b. the person/firm is involved in litigation with the contracting agency. An OCI can exist without being involved in litigation.
   c. the person's placement in their organizational structure would result in bad management of the contract. Impartiality is the key concept for OCI, not management decisions.
   d. a government technical advisor's role in source selection must be limited. Technical advisors with a conflict of interest should recuse themselves from participating in a source selection.

2. A direct contractual relationship between parties that allows the parties to enforce contractual rights and seek remedies is called

   a. partnership.
   b. memorandum of understanding.
   c. privity of contract.
   d. program directive.

3. The government exercises influence on subcontracts through

   a. flow-down clauses.
   b. privity of contract.
   c. the Christian doctrine.
   d. alpha contracting.

4. The process of settling all outstanding contractual issues to ensure that each party has met all of its obligations and documenting the contract file accordingly is

   a. contract termination.
   b. contract closeout.
   c. contract management.
   d. collective bargaining.

5. Which of the following is an excusable delay in government contracting?

   a. weather
   b. fire
   c. defective specifications
   d. key personnel termination

The following scenario and associated follow-on questions is a new, additional style of CPCM question you can expect to see beginning with the 2012 exam. The questions appear after the scenario.

Use the information provided in the following scenario to answer questions 6–10. The questions ask you to apply your knowledge of contract management to the given scenario. These questions require candidates to understand the concepts and terminology and apply that knowledge to answer the question correctly.

Scenario

Memorex Corporation protests a modification issued by a federal agency under a contract option to acquire USB flash drives. The modification substituted a newer type of drive and changed the terms of the contract. Memorex contends that the agency should have procured the newer model flash drives competitively rather than by modifying the option.

The agency awarded a contract to Storage Technology Corporation (STC) to purchase storage resource management solutions including data back-up and storage. Ten months later, the agency exercised an option in the contract to acquire more storage resources to provide additional storage. Then the agency deferred delivery of the option quantity to a later date.

After the agency exercised the option, but before delivery of the option quantity, the agency experienced problems with the already-installed initial quantity and decided it could not accept the option quantity.

The agency also determined that it could not establish STC responsibility or liability under the purchase contract for the problems with the storage resource management solutions. While the agency was debating whether to terminate the option and expect a claim from STC, or to negotiate a settlement, the agency declined to accept delivery under the option on the last extended delivery date. STC asserted that the agency's failure to take delivery was a breach of the contract. The agency and STC eventually agreed to modify STC's contract.

The modification substitutes USB flash drives for the storage resource equipment and converts the option from a negotiated acquisition to a commercial item contract.

Memorex contends that the modification so changed the nature of the contract that it should have been the subject of a competitive procurement.

Questions

6. What should the agency have done when they determined that the contract terms did not establish responsibility or liability for the problem with the original drives?

   a. Issue a "show cause" notice to begin termination for default proceedings for failure to deliver supplies in the time specified.
   b. Reject the disk drives and require the contractor to repair them at their own expense.
   c. Terminate the contract for convenience and resolicit the requirement.
   d. Terminate the contract for default and charge STC excess reprocurement costs.

7. Did the agency breach the contract by not taking delivery of the option quantity?

   a. Yes. The agency issued the contract modification exercising the option thereby making it a contractual requirement.
   b. Yes. the agency's new computer center was not available to receive the shipment, thereby creating an excusable delay.
   c. No. Both parties agreed to the delay and extension using a bilateral modification.
   d. No. Memorex protested the option exercise modification making it null and void.

8. Is Modification 10 within the scope of the contract?

   a. Yes. Both parties agreed to the terms.
   b. Yes. Exercising an option is a unilateral right of the government.
   c. No. It substantially changed the purpose or nature of the contract.
   d. No. It established stringent performance requirements.

9. Does Memorex have standing to file a protest against Modification 10?

   a. Yes. Memorex is an interested party as a potential offeror in a new procurement.
   b. Yes. Memorex could become a subcontractor to STC for the new work.
   c. No. It is past 10 days after contract award so the protest is not timely.
   d. No. GAO does not consider protests against contract modifications.

10. What method of acquisition is best suited for this scenario?

   a. Indefinite delivery/indefinite quantity
   b. commercial item acquisition
   c. sealed bidding
   d. negotiated acquisition

1. Organizational conflict of interest means

   a. **(Correct) a person is unable to render impartial assistance or advice to the government because of activities or relationships with other persons.**
   b. the person/firm is involved in litigation with the contracting agency. *An OCI can exist without being involved in litigation.*
   c. the person's placement in their organizational structure would result in bad management of the contract. *Impartiality is the key concept for OCI not management decisions.*
   d. a government technical advisor's role in source selection must be limited. *Technical advisors with a conflict of interest should recuse themselves from participating in a source selection.*

(Source: FAR 2.101 and 9.5)

2. A direct contractual relationship between the parties that allows the parties to enforce contractual rights and seek remedies is called

   a. partnership. *A partnership occurs when two or more entities combine capital and/or services to carry on a business for profit.*
   b. memorandum of understanding. *A memorandum of understanding is a document that outlines the terms of a transaction or contract.*
   c. **(Correct) privity of contract.**
   d. program directive. *A program directive gives specific contract operational instructions that may be issued to inform organizations of program requirements.*

(Source: Rumbaugh, Margaret G. *Understanding Government Contract Source Selection.* (Vienna, VA: Management Concepts, Inc.) 2010.)

3. The government exercises influence on subcontracts through

   a. **(Correct) flow-down clauses.**
   b. privity of contract *is a direct contractual relationship between the parties that allows the parties to enforce contractual rights and seek remedies.*
   c. the Christian doctrine *is a principle that maintains that if a significant clause is required to be included in a government contract, the contract will be read to include it, even though the clause is not physically incorporated in the document.*
   d. alpha contracting *is an acquisition streamlining technique.*

(Source: Rumbaugh, Margaret G. *Understanding Government Contract Source Selection.* (Vienna, VA: Management Concepts, Inc.) 2010.)

4. The process of settling all outstanding contractual issues to ensure that each party has met all of its obligations and documenting the contract file accordingly is

   a. contract termination. *Ending contract performance by either convenience of the government or default of the contractor.*
   b. **(Correct) contract closeout.**
   c. contract management. *The oversight of a contractor's (supplier's) performance pursuant to the fulfillment of the terms, conditions, and specifications of a contract.*
   d. collective bargaining. *Agreement that regulates terms and conditions of employment between an employer and a labor union.*

(Source: NCMA Desktop Guide to Basic Contracting Terms)

5. Which of the following is an excusable delay in government contracting?

a. weather. *Weather must be unusually severe to be an excusable delay.*
b. **(Correct) fire**
c. defective specifications. *A contractor is entitled to an equitable adjustment under the changes clause for the increased costs of performance due to defective specifications, but it is not an excusable delay.*
d. key personnel termination. *Prime contractors are expected to replace key personnel in a timely manner so performance is not delayed.*

(Source: FAR 52.249-14)

6. What should the agency have done when they determined that the contract terms did not establish responsibility or liability for the problem with the original drives?

    a. Issue a "show cause" notice to begin termination for default proceedings for failure to deliver supplies in the time specified.
    b. Reject the disk drives and require the contractor to repair them at their own expense.
    c. **(Correct). Terminate the contract for convenience and resolicit the requirement.**
    d. Terminate the contract for default and charge STC excess reprocurement costs.

7. Did the agency breach the contract by not taking delivery of the option quantity?

    a. **(Correct) Yes. The agency issued the contract modification exercising the option thereby making it a contractual requirement.**
    b. Yes. The agency's new computer center was not available to receive the shipment thereby creating an excusable delay.
    c. No. Both parties agreed to the delay and extension using a bilateral modification.

d. No. Memorex protested the option exercise modification making it null and void.

8. Is Modification 10 within the scope of the contract?

    a. Yes. Both parties agreed to the terms.
    b. Yes. Exercising an option is a unilateral right of the government.
    c. **(Correct) No. It substantially changed the purpose or nature of the contract.**
    d. No. It established stringent performance requirements.

9. Does Memorex have standing to file a protest against Modification 10?

    a. **(Correct) Yes. Memorex is an interested party as a potential offeror in a new procurement.**
    b. Yes. Memorex could become a subcontractor to STC for the new work.
    c. No. It is past 10 days after contract award so the protest is not timely.
    d. No. GAO does not consider protests against contract modifications.

10. What method of acquisition is best suited for this scenario?

    a. Indefinite delivery/indefinite quantity
    b. **(Correct) Commercial Item Acquisition**
    c. sealed bidding
    d. negotiated acquisition

Use the full text of the scenario case to better understand the correct answer choices.

(Though the terminology of the products involved in this case were changed for the purposes of updating the scenario questions, the contracting terminology and concepts remain intact.)

Memorex Corporation 61 Comp. Gen.
42, B-200722, 81-2 CPD P 334 October 23, 1981 Comptroller General's
Decision B-200722, October 23,
1981, 61 Comp. Gen. 42

Matter of: Memorex Corporation,
October 23, 1981

Memorex Corporation (Memorex) protests a modification issued by the social security administration (the agency), department of health and human services, under a contract option for the acquisition of disk drives, a type of information storage device used with computers. The modification substituted a newer type disk drive and changed the terms of the contract. Memorex contends that the agency should have procured the newer model disk drives competitively rather than by modifying the option. We agree with Memorex.

Background

On January 18, 1978, the agency awarded a contract to storage technology corporation (STC) for the purchase of STC 8800 disk drives to provide 30.4 billion characters of disk storage capacity. On October 28, 1978, the agency exercised an option in the contract to acquire additional STC 8800 disk drives to provide a further 30.4 billion characters of storage. The agency deferred delivery of the option quantity as the result of delays in the availability of the agency's new computer center. After the agency exercised the option, but prior to delivery of the option quantity, the agency experienced problems with the already installed initial quantity of STC 8800 drives and eventually decided it could not accept the option quantity. the agency also determined that it could not establish STC responsibility or liability under the purchase contract for the problems with the model 8800 drives. While the agency was debating whether to terminate the option and expect a claim from STC,

or to negotiate a settlement, the agency declined to accept delivery under the option on the last extended delivery date. STC asserted that the agency's failure to take delivery was a breach of the contract. On September 23, 1980, the agency and STC agreed to modification 10 to STC's contract.

Modification 10 provides for the substitution of STC 8650 disk drives for the older model 8800 equipment and converts the option from an outright purchase to a "lease-to-ownership" plan which contemplates government ownership of the disk drives at the end of a 5-year lease period. The cost of the 5-year lease of the 8650's is more than $200,000 greater in absolute terms than the purchase option cost of 8800's. (the agency asserts that the cost is lower when compared on a present value basis—purchase price of the 8800's versus the amount of cash, adjusted for interest, required to pay the lease costs for the newer 8650's over the 5-year period.) Approximately nine of modification 10's 46 pages establish stringent performance requirements for the 8650's over the 5-year lease and specify the agency's remedies for unsatisfactory performance.

Memorex contends (1) that the option was improper; (2) that the exercise of the option was improper; and (3) that modification 10 so changed the nature of the contract that it should have been the subject of a competitive procurement. the agency contends (1) that Memorex is not an interested party under our bid protest procedures, 4 C.F.R. part 21(1981); (2) that Memorex's various protests are untimely under our procedures; (3) that the modification was a matter of contract administration not for consideration by our office; and (4) that the modification was proper, in any event. Stc has offered additional reasons as to why Memorex's protest is untimely. We will confine our discussion to those issues which we consider dispositive of the protest.

Timeliness of Memorex's protest

Memorex filed an initial short protest with our office on October 7, 1980, contesting, in part, the agency's "failure to obtain competition" under modification 10. On October 17, 1980, Memorex filed a substantial expansion of its protest, charging in part that the substitution of equipment, the change from straight purchase to lease-to-ownership, and the increase in price, so substantially changed the nature of the option that competition was required. the agency contends that this aspect of Memorex's protest cannot be deduced from Memorex's October 7 protest and is therefore untimely because it was not raised until October 17, more than 10 working days after Memorex received a copy of modification 10 on September 26. STC adds that we should not consider Memorex's letter of October 17 because Memorex did not submit these "details" of its protest within the 5 working days contemplated under our procedures.

Our bid protest procedures, 4 C.F.R. part 21(1981), generally require that initial protests to our office contain a concise statement of the grounds for the protest, supported to the extent feasible, and also provide that any additional details required by our office must be furnished within 5 working days of the protester's receipt of our request for the statement. 4 C.F.R. 21.1(c), 21.2(d). With certain exceptions not relevant here, protests must be filed within 10 working days of the date on which the protester knew or should have known of the basis for its protest. C.F.R. 21.2(b)(2). Although each new basis for protest must independently satisfy our timeliness criteria, we will generally consider later-filed materials and/or arguments which merely provide further support for an already timely protest. Kappa systems, inc., 56 Comp. Gen.. 675(1977), 77-1 CPD 412.

We find this protest to be timely. Memorex's timely initial protest letter of October 7 specifically objects to the agency's failure to conduct a competition for the disks acquired under the modified option. Despite STC's suggestion to the contrary, we find Memorex's October 17 submission to be only an explanation of the rationale for Memorex's fundamental objection which, we note, the protester provided voluntarily and not at our request. Consequently, this material will be considered.

Interested party

the agency argues that Memorex is not an "interested party" as required under our procedures (4 C.F.R. 21.1(a)(1981)) in order to have its protest considered by our office because Memorex did not compete in the original procurement.

The protest is that changes to the contract were so substantial that the contract should be terminated and a new competition conducted for the modified requirements. As a potential offeror on a new procurement, Memorex has a direct and established interest in the opportunity to compete for the award. Consequently, Memorex is an interested party. Webcraft Packaging, Division of Beatrice Foods, Co., B-194087, August 14, 1979, 79-2 CPD 120.

Contract administration

We do not consider protests against contract modifications unless it is alleged that the modification went beyond the scope of the contract and should have been the subject of a new procurement. Webcraft Packaging, Division of Beatrice Foods Co., supra; Brandon applied systems, Inc., 57 Comp. Gen. 140(1977), 77-2 CPD 486. This contention is the substance of Memorex's protest. Therefore, the protest is appropriate for our consideration.

Change v. New procurement

We have consistently held that preservation of the integrity of the competitive procurement system requires that contracting parties not make changes to contracts which have the effect of circumventing the competitive procurement statutes. Lawson division of Diebold, incorporated, b-196029.2, June 30, 1980, 80-1 CPD 447; American air filter, 57 Comp. Gen. 285(1978), 78-1 CPD 136. This principle is violated when a modification so substantially changes the purpose or nature of a contract that the contract for which the competition was held and the contract which is to be performed are essentially different. Webcraft packaging, division of Beatrice foods co., supra. We find this to be the case here.

Modification 10's conversion of the option from a purchase to a 5 year lease-to-ownership plan with continuing performance requirements has shifted the burden and risk of nonperformance from the government to the contractor. STC's only continuing responsibility in connection with the original option was to provide maintenance services and the agency's only remedy for an inoperable disk was to obtain credits against the maintenance agreement. Under modification 10, however, STC has a continuing obligation to assure continuous satisfactory performance of the disks measured by objective standards; if a piece of equipment fails and cannot be repaired, STC must replace it. If a piece of equipment is unsatisfactory, even though it is repaired, the agency may deduct a portion of the rental charge. If deficiencies warrant, the agency may terminate the contract for default and hold STC liable for the excess costs of reprocurement. In effect, the agency now has acquired a right to continued satisfactory performance which it did not possess under the original option. STC has assumed correspondingly enlarged contractual obligations. We conclude that a change of this magnitude in the fundamental relationship of the contracting parties goes beyond the scope of the original contract and has resulted in a contract which is substantially different from that originally competed.

Memorex's protest is sustained.

The agency should initiate a competitive procurement for the disk drives. Because the agency has expressed a particular need for uninterrupted system availability, we will not object if in conducting the competitive procurement the agency elects to provide for the phased introduction of the replacement equipment. If STC is presently performing, STC's contract should be modified to reflect the lower price. If STC is unsuccessful, the lease would be terminated for the convenience of the government in accordance with the "no-cost" termination provisions in the contract option. We recognize that implementation of this decision may result in the revival of STC's breach claim. However, that matter is for consideration under the disputes clause of the contract.

Key Points

A potential competitor for equipment which has been the subject of a contract modification is an "interested party" to challenge the modification as a change beyond the scope of the contract requiring a new competition.

Although protests against contract modifications usually are matters of contract administration which we will not review, we will consider protests which contend that a modification went beyond the scope of the contract and should have been the subject of a new procurement.

New competition recommended a modification which converts a contract for the acquisition of disk drives from a purchase, with virtually no post-acquisition government right to assure equipment performance, to a 5-year lease-to-ownership plan, with expansive rights in the government to enforce newly added performance requirements over the full term of the lease, so substantially alters the rights of the parties as to be beyond the scope of the original contract and results in a contract substantially different from that for which the competition was held. Therefore, a new competition should be conducted.

These readings can be found in NCMA's online Research Articles Database. To access the database you must be an NCMA member. If you are not an NCMA member, you may be able to obtain equivalent readings by inserting relevant keywords into your web browser's search engine.

From NCMA's *Contract Management* magazine:

Davidson, Samuel G., *Requests for Equitable Adjustment: Are You a Winner or a Sinner?*, May 2010.
How to be a winner in the REA process.

Dobriansky, John, *Government Contract Management—Changes and Impact on Subcontractors*, January 2011.
While large prime contractors have the financial and human capital resources to assess, integrate, manage, and comply with new statutory and regulatory requirements, major prime subcontractors often don't, and have to founder with the statutory and regulatory changes.

Foley, Michael, *Contract Administration of Unpopulated LLCS—Managing the Contract, Performance Reporting, and Compliance*, December 2010.
The business of doing business with the U.S government in the absence of any employees.

Garrett, Gregory A., *Contract Administration, Part I: People, Processes, and Best Practices*, March 2010.
It is vitally important to have the right people and processes in place to manage the growing number, value, and complexity of U.S. government contracts.

Garrett, Gregory A., and Rene G. Rendon, *Contract Administration, Part 2: Managing Contract Changes*, April 2010.
Contract changes management is a critical part of contract administration, contract management, and ultimately, project management.

Garrett, Gregory A., *Contract Administration, Part 3: Contract Interpretation Guidelines and Best Practices*, April 2010.
Successful contract administration involves an understanding of the guidelines typically used in contract interpretation and some of the proven-effective best practices to mitigate potential contract misinterpretations.

Graham, J. Hatcher, *Contractor Performance Assessment Reports: Past Performance Evaluations and What to Do*, January 2011.
Past performance evaluations have become critical in today's "best value" awards. So what do you do when you receive a negative past performance review that you feel is unwarranted?

Harper, Veronica Cole, *Managing Change during Contract Performance*, June 2011.
There are four critical steps applicable to contract administration and oversight that contractors can take to manage formal and informal change during contract performance.

Kamradt, Mike, Sihyun Choi, and Jim McIntosh, *Modeling COR/COTR Resource Needs: Improved Contract Performance through Enhancing Time Availability*, May 2010.
An analysis of a category-level resource planning model that predicts the time COR/COTRs need to successfully manage contracts.

Meeks, Annie, *The Buck Stops...Where? Post-Award Accountability for Large Service Contracts*, June 2011.

Seven practical and proven suggestions for both public and private sector organizations to ensure accountability, transparency, and compliance.

Nagle, James F., *Resolving Disputes on Public Contracts*, September 2010.
Like the common cold, claims will probably always be with us. But the preventative and curative methods mentioned in this article may well help to avoid or quickly resolve them.

Reid, Tom, *It's a Termination! What Now?*, July 2011.
A termination is an extraordinary event and immediately declares a contract physically complete. Professional contract managers will be prepared for such eventualities and will have a plan to attack the issues and resolve the many lingering situations.

Reid, Tom and Gregory A. Garrett, *Terminating Subcontracts: Challenges and Best Practices*, August 2011.
Best practices for subcontract managers that will make the settlement with subcontractors more efficient and minimize the trauma and drama that often accompany a government termination for convenience.

Sacilotto, Kara M. and Daniel P. Graham, *FAR Councils Release Rewrite of OCI Rules*, July 2011.
A new proposed rule makes significant changes, both structurally and substantively, to the current FAR regime for addressing OCIs.

Salamone, Marie and Mitchell Plank, *Incurred Cost Audits*, March 2011.
An examination of incurred cost audits and best practices for compliance.

Wall, Olga and Krista Pages, *Understanding the Defense Base Act: Defusing a Liability Time Bomb*, June 2010.

Learn how to protect your company and avoid costly mistakes by ensuring that mandatory DBA coverage is obtained and claims are filed promptly.

Competency

4.0:

Specialized Knowledge Areas

Specialized knowledge areas include those that require additional specialized knowledge over and above the knowledge that a person of ordinary experience possesses. Additional professional skills are necessary for contract managers to (1) perform efficiently and effectively in a specific industry or work environment (i.e., construction) or (2) interact productively with other specialized professionals (i.e., finance).

Certain types of contracting actions require highly specialized experience and knowledge to perform effectively. This section presents a brief overview of various contracting specialty areas. Some of the areas relate exclusively to government contracting, others relate exclusively to commercial contracting, and some have a degree of application to both the government and commercial sectors.

4.1 Research and Development (R&D)

When an organization buys research and development services, it is difficult to define the requirement other than to describe the problem. This situation creates a departure from the general guidelines used when contracting for other types of products or services because the contract specialist cannot clearly define the requirement, define specific acceptance criteria, or negotiate a price based on the market. R&D contracting necessitates a different philosophy than is necessary for other types of procurement.

- **Federal**: The primary purpose of federal government R&D contracts and programs is to advance scientific and technical knowledge and apply that knowledge to achieve organizational and national goals. Unlike most other type of contracts, R&D contracts are intended to achieve objectives for which the work or methods cannot be precisely defined in advance. It is also frequently difficult to estimate the effort required for various

R&D technical approaches, particularly when some of the approaches may offer little or no early indications or assurances that they will be successful. Due to this level of uncertainty, contracting professionals should use R&D contracting in a manner that will encourage the best scientific and industrial sources to participate and the contracts should be structured so that they provide an environment in which the work can be pursued with reasonable flexibility and minimum administrative burden.

- **Commercial**: In the commercial world, the phrase *research and development* has a special commercial significance apart from its conventional meaning of research and technological development. In the commercial context, R&D normally refers to future-oriented, long-term activities in science and technology. Profits are not realized until after a successful discovery, development, and application of a new technology, which only occurs after diligent and systematic research.

A clear and complete statement of work (SOW) detailing the area of exploration for basic research, or the end objectives for development and applied research, is essential. The SOW should provide contractors with the freedom required to exercise innovation and creativity, while adhering to the overall objectives of the R&D effort.

The fundamental nature of R&D contracting usually precludes using the sealed bid acquisition method, and often makes fixed-price contracts inappropriate. Because of the typical absence of precise specifications and the associated difficulties in estimating costs, R&D contracts are often cost-reimbursement contracts, sometimes with appropriate incentives. Contracting professionals should consult extensively with internal technical experts regarding the appropriate contract type.

R&D solicitations should generally be distributed only to sources that have been identified; as a result of publicizing requirements, consultation with internal technical personnel, conducting market research, and other means as technically qualified to perform the required work. Such evaluations of technical competence usually include factors such as present and past performance of similar work, professional stature and reputation, relative position in a particular field of endeavor, ability to acquire and retain the technical capability required to perform the work, and other relevant factors. If it is not practicable to initially solicit all apparently qualified sources, a reasonable number should be solicited to obtain meaningful competition.

Generally speaking, R&D contracts are most often awarded to offerors that propose the best ideas or concepts and have the highest competence in the specific field involved. However, the buyer should use caution and not obtain technical capabilities that clearly exceed those required by the solicitation or those required for successful performance of the requirement. It is also customary to evaluate the offerors proposed cost or price as a means to verify that the offeror has a clear understanding of the scope of the project, perception of risks involved, and the ability to organize and perform the work.

LEXICON FOR RESEARCH AND DEVELOPMENT:

Applied research: The effort that (1) normally follows basic research, but may not be severable from the related basic research; (2) attempts to determine and exploit the potential of scientific discoveries or improvements in technology, materials, processes, methods, devices, or techniques; and (3) attempts to advance the state of the art. When being used by contractors that must comply with cost principles, this term does not include efforts whose principal aim is the design, development, or testing of specific items or services to be considered for sale; these efforts are within the definition of "development.".

Computer-aided design/computer-aided manufacturing (CAD/CAM): These systems provide a means of standardization in the manufacturing predesign stage to facilitate data transfer between various manufacturers.

Cooperative agreement: A legal instrument used principally for transferring money, property, or services between the parties to accomplish a specific purpose of support or stimulation where substantial involvement and cooperation are expected between the parties.

Development: The systematic use of scientific and technical knowledge in the design, development, testing, or evaluation of a potential new product or service (or of an improvement in an existing product or service) to meet specific performance requirements or objectives. It includes the functions of design engineering, prototyping, and engineering testing; it excludes subcontracted technical effort that is for the sole purpose of developing an additional source for an existing product.

Grant: A legal instrument for transferring money, property, or services to the recipient to accomplish a public purpose of support or stimulation where there is no substantial involvement between the federal agency and recipient during performance.

Independent Research and Development (IR&D):

- **Federal:** Contractor effort that is neither sponsored by a grant nor required in performing a contract and that falls within any of the following four areas: basic research, applied research, development, and systems and other concept formulation studies (see also CMBOK 1.4.1.4, Independent Research and Development).

- **Commercial:** Effort that is neither sponsored by a grant nor required in performing a contract and that falls within any of the following four areas: basic research, applied research, development, and systems and other concept formulation studies that are pursued independently by an organization to further a specific business purpose (see also CMBOK 1.4.1.4, Independent Research and Development).

Nondevelopmental item: A generic term describing either a commercial product or an item developed and used prior to a planned acquisition. Its use reduces R&D costs and speeds up the acquisition process.

R&D contract: A contract for basic research (directed toward improving or expanding new scientific discoveries, technologies, materials, processes, or techniques) or development (directed production of or improvement in useful products to meet specific performance requirements through the systematic application of scientific knowledge).

R&D programs (government): The primary purpose is to advance scientific and technical knowledge and apply that knowledge to the extent necessary to achieve agency and national goals. Unlike contracts for supplies and services, most R&D contracts are directed toward objectives for which the work or methods cannot be precisely described in advance. It is difficult to judge the probabilities of success or required effort for technical approaches, some of which offer little or no early assurance of full success. The contracting process shall be used to encourage the best sources from the scientific and industrial community to become involved in the program and must provide an environment in which the work can be pursued with reasonable flexibility and minimum administrative burden.

R&D solicitation:

- The **evaluation factors** used to determine the most technically competent usually include the offeror's:

  o Understanding of the scope of the work;

  o Accomplishing the scientific and technical objectives of the contract or the merit of the ideas and concepts proposed;

  o Proposing experienced and competent technical personnel who are available to work on the contract;

  o Proposing novel ideas in the specific branch of science and technology involved; and

  o Having access to necessary research, test, laboratory, or shop facilities from any source.

- **Evaluation:** Generally speaking, R&D contracts are most often awarded to offerors that propose the best ideas or concepts and have the highest competence in the specific field involved. However, the contracting professional should be careful and not obtain technical capabilities that clearly exceed those required by the solicitation or those required for successful performance of the requirement. It is also customary to evaluate the offerors' proposed cost or price as a means to verify that the offeror has a clear understanding of the scope of the project, perception of risks involved, and the ability to organize and perform the work.

Recoupment: The recovery by the government of government-funded nonrecurring costs from contractors that sell, lease, or license the resulting products or technology to buyers other than the federal government.

4.2 Architect and Engineer (A&E) Services and Construction

Architect and Engineer (A&E) Services: A&E services include professional services of an architectural or engineering nature required to be performed or approved by a person licensed, registered, or certified to provide such services or are associated with research, planning, development, design, construction, alteration, or repair of real property or other related professional services, such as studies and surveys. Construction means alteration or repair, including dredging, excavating, and painting of buildings, structures, or other real property.

Contracts for architect, engineering, and construction services are highly technical in nature and are often awarded by specialized contracting professionals with extensive experience in and knowledge of the skills and abilities required for successful performance.

Federal government A&E services are procured using qualification-based selection (QBS) pursuant to the Brooks Act. There are seven basic steps involved in pursuing federal design work under QBS:

1. Public solicitation for architectural and engineering services,

2. Submission of an annual statement of qualifications and supplemental statements of ability to design specific projects for which public announcements were made,

3. Evaluation of both the annual and project-specific statements,

4. Development of a short-list of at least three submitting firms in order to conduct interviews with them,

5. Interviews with the firms,

6. Ranking of at least three of the most qualified firms, and

7. Negotiation with the top-ranked firm.

Normal evaluation and selection criteria for architect and engineering services usually include having:

- The professional qualifications necessary for satisfactory performance of the required services;

- The specialized experience and technical competence in the type of work required;

- The capacity to accomplish the work in the required time;

- The past performance in both the government and commercial sectors in terms of cost control, quality of work, and compliance with performance schedules; and

- The proximity to the general geographical area of the project and knowledge of the local conditions.

The selection process usually results in the preparing a selection report that ranks competent contractors in order of preference. The contracting professional then begins specific negotiations with the contractor(s) to agree upon terms and conditions and award a contract.

In commercial construction contracting, there are both formal and informal policies and procedures used in acquiring construction services. Construction contracts are subject to many outside restraints that have an impact on the successful contract performance, such as inspections, permits, and licenses. Careful planning is necessary to ensure adequate coordination of the acquisi-

tion. In government contracting, sealed bid procedures are normally used for construction contracts.

LEXICON FOR ARCHITECT AND ENGINEER (A&E) SERVICES AND CONSTRUCTION:

Advisory and assistance services: Services provided under contract by nongovernmental sources to support or improve organizational policy development, decision making, management and administration, program and/or project management and administration, or R&D activities. It can also refer to the furnishing of professional advice or assistance rendered to improve the effectiveness of federal management processes or procedures (including those of an engineering and technical nature). In rendering the foregoing services, outputs may take the form of information, advice, opinions, alternatives, analyses, evaluations, recommendations, training, and the day-to-day aid of support personnel needed for the successful performance of ongoing federal operations. All advisory and assistance services are classified in one of the following subdivisions:

1. **Management and professional support services**: Contractual services that provide assistance, advice, or training for the efficient and effective management and operation of organizations, activities (including management and support services for R&D activities), or systems. These services are normally closely related to the basic responsibilities and mission of the agency originating the requirement for the acquisition of services by contract. Included are efforts that support or contribute to improved organization of program management, logistics management, project monitoring and reporting, data collection, budgeting, accounting, performance auditing, and administrative technical support for conferences and training programs.

2. **Studies, analyses, and evaluations:** Contracted services that provide organized, analytical assessments/evaluations in support of policy development, decision making, management, or administration. Included are studies in support of R&D activities. Also included are acquisitions of models, methodologies, and related software supporting studies, analyses, or evaluations.

3. **Engineering and technical services:** Contractual services used to support the program office during the acquisition cycle by providing such services as systems engineering and technical direction to ensure the effective operation and maintenance of a weapon system or major system as defined in OMB Circular No. A-109 or to provide direct support of a weapon system that is essential to research, development, production, operation, or maintenance of the system.

Architect and design services: Professional services of an architectural or engineering nature that are required to be performed or approved by a person licensed, registered, or certified to provide such services or are associated with research, planning, development, design, construction, alteration, or repair of real property, or other related professional services such as studies and surveys.

Bid bond: In government contract administration, an insurance document in which a third party agrees to pay a specific amount of money, if the bonded (insured) bidder fails to sign a contract as bid and accepted by the government.

Bid guarantee: A form of security accompanying a bid or proposal as assurance that the bidder will not withdraw its bid during the specified time period and will execute a written contract and will furnish such bonds as may be required.

Bond: A written instrument executed by a bidder or contractor/supplier (the principal) and a second party (the surety or sureties) to ensure fulfillment of the principal's obligations to a third party (the obligee or government) identified in the bond. If the principal's obligations are not met, the bond ensures payment, to the extent stipulated, of any loss sustained by the obligee.

Brooks Act: The Brooks Act establishes federal policy concerning the selection of firms and individuals to perform architectural, engineering, and related services for the federal government. It is the policy of the federal government to publicly announce all requirements for architectural and engineering services, and to negotiate contracts for architectural and engineering services on the basis of demonstrated competence and qualification for the type of professional services required and at fair and reasonable prices.

Construction and demolition materials and debris: Materials and debris generated during construction, renovation, demolition, or dismantling of all structures and buildings and associated infrastructure.

Construction contract award process: The following process is also normally used by the government as part of a construction contracting effort:

- **Presolicitation notice:** A presolicitation notice, containing sufficient detail to identify the nature, volume, location, and schedule for the requirement. These notices are usually issued well in advance of the invitation to bid in order to stimulate the interest of the greatest number of prospective bidders.

- **Invitation for bids:** The solicitation instrument used in sealed bidding method of procurement. It should allow sufficient time for bidders to perform the many tasks and issues associated with the bid process including site inspection, obtaining required subcontracting bids, examining plans and specifications, and preparing the required estimates.

- **Pre-bid conferences**: Pre-bid conferences are often held to ensure that all prospective bidders have a clear and complete understanding of all aspects of the requirement.

- **Notice of award**: Done in writing or electronically; contains the following information: Identify the invitation for bids; identify the contractor's bid; state the award price; advise the contractor that any required payment and performance bonds must be promptly executed and returned to the contracting officer; and specify the date of commencement of work, or advise that a notice to proceed will be issued.

- **Pre-construction orientation**: A pre-construction conference is often held with the successful offeror before the construction effort begins to again ensure that there is a complete understanding of all issues related to the effort.

Construction contracts: The traditional method of construction contracting that uses the phases of design, bid, and build for construction projects. Construction means alteration of the landscape, assembly and fitting out of structures, installation of furnishing and fixtures, decoration, or repair of real property.

Design: The process that defines a construction requirement, including the functional relationships and technical systems to be used, producing the technical specifications and drawings, and preparing the construction cost estimate.

Design-bid-build: The traditional construction delivery method where design and

construction are sequential and contracted separately with two contracts and two contractors.

Design-build: A method of construction contracting that combines the architectural, engineering, and construction services required for a project into a single agreement.

Miller Act: The Miller Act (40 U.S.C 270a-270f) requires performance and payment bonds for any construction contract exceeding a specified threshold ($150,000), except that this requirement may be waived (1) by the contracting officer for as much of the work as is to be performed in a foreign country upon finding that it is impracticable for the contractor to furnish such bond, or (b) as otherwise authorized by the Miller Act or other law.

Qualifications-based selection: Qualifications-based selection (QBS) establishes the procurement process by which architects and engineers (A/Es) are selected for design contracts with federal design and construction agencies. The Brooks Act establishes a qualifications-based selection process, in which contracts for A/Es are negotiated on the basis of demonstrated competence and qualification for the type of professional services required at a fair and reasonable price. Under QBS procurement procedures, price quotations are not a consideration in the selection process. This QBS process, as established by the Brooks Act, has long been enthusiastically supported by every professional A/E society.

Plans and specifications: Drawings, specifications, and other data for and preliminary to the construction.

Record drawings: Drawings submitted by a contractor or subcontractor at any tier to show the construction of a particular structure or work as actually completed under the contract.

Two-phase design-build: A selection procedure that selects a number of offerors, based on qualifications, in the first phase to submit detailed proposals for evaluation and award in the second phase.

4.3 Information Technology (IT)

The acquisition and collection of technologies that deal specifically with processing, storing, and communicating information; includes all types of computer and communication systems. It involves those special policies and procedures applicable to the acquisition and use of computers, telecommunications, and related resources.

IT requirements often present a unique set of challenges for the contracting professional. The rapid pace of technological advancements often makes it difficult to acquire state-of-the-art information technology items without exposing the buying organization to a significant amount of inherent risk.

Common risk elements include schedule risk, risk of technical obsolescence, cost risk, technical feasibility, dependencies among new projects and existing projects or systems, the number of simultaneous high-risk projects to be monitored, funding availability, and program management risk.

Typical techniques to manage and mitigate risks associated with information technology acquisitions include prudent project management, thorough acquisition planning related to budget planning, continuous collection and evaluation of risk-based assessment data, prototyping systems prior to implementation, post-implementation reviews to determine actual costs and benefits, using quantifiable measures to assess risks and returns, and the use of modular contracting.

LEXICON FOR INFORMATION TECHNOLOGY:

ANSI X12: A set of standards promulgated by the American National Standards Institute for use in formatting and handling purchasing related documents transmitted by electronic data interchange (EDI).

Chief Information Officer Council: The Chief Information Officers (CIO) Council was established by Executive Order 13011, Federal Information Technology, on July 16, 1996. A charter for the council was adopted on February 20, 1997, and later codified by the E-Government Act of 2002. The CIO Council serves as the principal interagency forum for improving practices in the design, modernization, use, sharing, and performance of federal government agency information resources. The council's role includes developing recommendations for IT management policies, procedures, and standards; identifying opportunities to share information resources; and assessing and addressing the needs of the federal government's IT workforce.

Data rights: The rights of ownership under any contract of recorded information, regardless of the form of media on which it may be recorded.

Electric commerce: Marketing goods and services over the Internet by exchanging information between buyers and sellers, while in the process minimizing paperwork and simplifying payment procedures; includes both business-to-consumer (B2C) and business-to-business (B2B) transactions.

Encryption: A method of data secrecy in which the message to be sent is coded using a key available only to the sender and receiver.

Information life cycle: The stages through which information passes, typically characterized as creation or collection, processing, dissemination, use, storage, and disposition.

Information management: The planning, budgeting, manipulating, and controlling of information throughout its life cycle

Information resources management: The process of managing information resources to accomplish agency missions. The term encompasses both information itself and the related resources, such as personnel, equipment, funds, and information technology.

Information system: A discrete set of information resources organized for the collection, processing, maintenance, transmission, and dissemination of information in accordance with defined procedures, whether automated or manual.

Information systems life cycle: The phases through which an information system passes, typically characterized as initiation, development, operation, and termination.

Information technology:

1. The hardware and software operated by a federal agency or by a contractor of a federal agency or other organization that processes information on behalf of the federal government to accomplish a federal function, regardless of the technology involved, whether computers, telecommunications, or other. It includes automatic data processing equipment as that term is defined in Section 111(a)(2) of the Federal Property and Administrative Services Act of 1949.

2. Any equipment or interconnected system or subsystem of equipment that is used in the automatic acquisition, storage, manipulation, management, movement, control, display, switching, interchange, transmission, or reception of data or information by the executive agency. IT

includes computers, ancillary equipment, software, firmware and similar procedures, services (including support services), and related resources, including National Security Systems (NSSs). It does not include any equipment that is acquired by a federal contractor incidental to a federal contract.

Limited rights: In technical data, refers to the rights to use, duplicate, or disclose technical data in whole or in part, by or for the government, with the express written permission of the party furnishing the technical data. Such data may be released or disclosed outside the government; used by the government for manufacture (or if software documentation, for preparing the same or similar software); or used by a party other than the government except under certain restricted circumstances.

Intellectual property: Includes inventions, trademarks, patents, industrial designs, copyrights, and technical information.

Mean time between failure (MTBF): For a particular interval, the total functional life of a population of an item divided by the total number of failures (requiring corrective maintenance actions) within the population. The definition holds for time, rounds, miles, events, or other measures of life unit. A basic technical measure of reliability recommended for use in the research and development contractual specification environment, where "time" and "failure" must be carefully defined for contractual compliance purposes.

Modular contracting: Intended to reduce program risk and incentivize contractor performance, while providing for the timely access to rapidly changing technology. Modular contracting consists of dividing the acquisition of a system of information technology into smaller acquisition increments.

National security system: Any telecommunications or information system operated by the U.S. government, the function, operation, or use of which

- Involves intelligence activities;

- Involves cryptologic activities related to national security;

- Involves command and control of military forces;

- Involves equipment that is an integral part of a weapon or weapons system; or

- Is critical to the direct fulfillment of military or intelligence missions. This does not include a system that is to be used for routine administrative and business applications, such as payroll, finance, logistics, and personnel management applications.

Network systems:

- **Federal:** Computer equipment or interconnected systems or subsystems of equipment used in the automatic acquisition, storage, manipulation, management, movement, control, display, switching interchange, transmission, or reception of data or information by a federal agency or under a contract with a federal agency. These systems include computers, servers, ancillary equipment, software, and related services.

- **Commercial:** Systems that transmit any combination of audio, video, and/or data between users. The network includes the network operating system in the client and server machines, the cables connecting them, and all the supporting hardware in between, such as bridges, routers, and switches. In wireless systems, antennas and towers are also port of the network. In general, the network is a col-

lection of terminals, computers, servers, and components that function in relation to each other to allow for the easy flow of data and use of resources among the interrelated entities.

Outsourcing: A version of the make-or-buy decision, commonly used for services, in which a firm elects to purchase an item/service that previously was made or performed in-house.

Telecommunications:

- **Federal:** Equipment used for such modes of transmission as telephone, data facsimile, video, radio, and audio, and such corollary items as switches, wire, cable, access arrangements, and communications security facilities and related services.

- **Commercial:** The branch of electrical engineering concerned with the technology of electronic communication at a distance. It includes systems of hardware and software use to carry audio, video, and/or data. Includes telephone wires, satellite signals, cellular links, coaxial cable, and so on, and related devices.

Unlimited rights: Rights to use, duplicate, release, or disclose technical data or computer software in whole or in part in any manner and for any purpose and to have or permit others to do so.

4.4 Major Systems

A combination of elements that function together to produce the capabilities required to fulfill a mission need, including hardware, equipment, software, or any combination of these, but excluding construction. Major systems are defined as those programs that, as determined by the agency head, are directed at and are critical to fulfilling an agency mission need; entail allocating relatively large resources for the particular agency; and warrant special management attention, including specific agency-head decisions.

Major systems acquisition policies are designed to ensure that agencies acquire major systems in the most effective, economical, and timely manner. The policies require agencies to promote innovation and full and open competition in the development of major system concepts by

- Expressing agency needs and program objectives in terms of the agency's mission and not in terms of specified systems to satisfy needs,

- Focusing agency resources and special management attention on activities conducted in the initial stage of major programs, and

- Sustaining effective competition between alternative system concepts and sources for as long as it is beneficial.

Major systems acquisition requires the direct involvement of senior agency management, including the agency head, in the planning, execution, and continuing evaluation of the status of the program.

LEXICON FOR MAJOR SYSTEMS:

Acquisition categories (ACAT): U.S. DOD ACAT 1 programs are Milestone Decision Authority Programs or programs designated ACAT 1 by the Milestone Decision Authority.

Acquisition policies and principal regulations:

- DoDD 5000.01: This DOD directive states the policies and principles that guide all defense acquisition programs. In addition, this directive identifies the DOD key acquisition officials and forums.

- DoDI 5000.02: This DOD instruction establishes a simplified and flexible management system for translating joint capability needs and technological opportunities into stable, affordable, and well-managed acquisition programs. It applies to all defense technology projects and acquisition programs, although some requirements where stated apply only to major defense acquisition programs (MDAPs) and major automated information systems (MAISs).

- *Defense Acquisition Guidebook*: This provides nonmandatory guidance on best practices, lessons learned, and expectations.

Balanced scorecard: A conceptual framework enabling an organization to clarify its vision and strategy, effectively translating them into action.

Best practice: A superior method or innovative practice that contributes to the improved performance of an organization, usually recognized as "best" by other peer organizations. It implies accumulating and applying knowledge about what is working and not working in different situations and contexts, including lessons learned and the continuing process of learning, feedback, reflection, and analysis (what works, how, and why).

Concept exploration contracts: Used to refine the proposed concept and to reduce the concept's technical uncertainties. The scope of work for this phase of the program shall be consistent with the government's planned budget for the phase. Follow-on contracts for such tasks in the exploration phase shall be awarded as long as the concept approach remains promising, the contractor's progress is acceptable, and it is economically practicable to do so.

Critical path: The sequence of activities that must be completed on schedule for an entire project to be completed on schedule. Each task on the critical path is called a critical task. If a critical task is delayed, then the entire project will be delayed by the same amount (unless another activity on the critical path can be accelerated). The critical path may change from time to time as activities are completed ahead of or behind schedule. There may be more than one critical path depending on durations and work flow logic.

Demonstration contracts: Provides for contractors to submit, by the end of the phase, priced proposals, totally funded by the government, for full-scale development. The contracting officer should provide contractors with operational test conditions, performance criteria, life cycle cost factors, and any other selection criteria necessary for the contractors to prepare their proposals.

Design to cost: A process that constrains design options to a fixed cost limit. The cost limit is usually what the buyer can pay or what the marketplace demands. An affordable product is obtained by treating target cost as an independent design parameter that needs to be achieved during the development.

Effective competition: A market condition that exists when two or more contractors, acting independently, actively contend for the government's business in a manner that ensures that the government will be offered the lowest cost or price alternative or best technical design meeting its minimum needs.

Full-scale development contracts: Provides for contractors to submit priced proposals for production that are based on the latest quantity, schedule, and logistics requirements and other considerations that will be used in making the production decision.

Full production: Contracts for full production of successfully tested major systems selected from the full-scale development phase may be awarded if the agency head

- Reaffirms the mission need and program objectives, and

- Grants approval to proceed with production.

Gantt chart: A diagrammatic representation of the timing and duration of the various sequential phases of a project. It is commonly used in project management and routinely available in many project management software packages.

Mean time between failure (MTBF): A measure of the theoretical times a component or device will operate without failing. It is expressed in hours. It comes initially from military standards but has been extended widely to other economic segments.

Milestone: A significant event in the project, usually completion of a major deliverable. A milestone has the duration of zero and no effort. Milestones are essential to manage and control a project, but there is no task associated with it (although preparing a milestone can involve significant work). Usually a milestone is used as a project checkpoint to validate how a project is progressing and revalidate the work.

Milestone decision authority (MDA): The designated individual with overall responsibility for a program. The MDA shall have the authority to approve entry of an acquisition program into the next phase of the acquisition process and shall be accountable for cost, schedule, and performance reporting to higher authority, including congressional reporting.

Program management: The process whereby a single leader and team are responsible for planning, organizing, coordinating, directing, and controlling the combined efforts of participation and assigned personnel and organizations in the accomplishment of program objectives. This special management approach provides centralized authority and responsibility for the management for a specific program.

Quality assurance (QA): A formal methodology designed to assess the quality of products or services provided. QA includes formal review of care, problem identification, corrective actions to remedy any deficiencies, and evaluation of actions taken. QA implies that necessary precautions have been taken so that the entire production of a product or service is within specifications under a wide conditions of operation. This usually requires that the production process is mastered and monitored using indicators.

Reliability: The probability that an item will continue to function at customer expectation levels at a measurement point, under specified environmental and duty cycle conditions.

Schedule: The project timeline, identifying the dates (absolute or relative to a start date) that project tasks will be started and completed, the resources that will be required, and which milestones will be reached.

System acquisition process (life cycle): The sequence of acquisition activities starting with the agency's reconciliation of its mission need with capabilities, priorities, and resources and extending through the introduction of a system into operational use or the otherwise successful achievement of program objectives.

Validation: The process of ensuring that a product or a process conforms to defined user needs, requirements, and/or specifications under defined operating conditions. Validation has numerous slightly different meanings depending on the company and the context. It normally implies that a quality assurance plan has been put in place so that a product or process cannot be wrong after it has been validated. It is closely related to quality testing, but is different in the sense that testing implies verification of each unit produced or a statistically relevant subset of samples, whereas validation proves that all of the production will be within specification.

Work breakdown structure: A hierarchical tree structure decomposing a project into activities and subactivities to help define and control the project and its elements of work.

4.5 Service Contracts

Contracts that directly engage the time and effort of a contractor whose primary purpose is to perform an identifiable task rather than furnish an end item of supply.

Many organizations have increased the number and scope of service contracts in recent years. Organizations, with increasing frequency, are contracting for a variety of services rather than performing the related functions with internal resources, especially when the functions are not part of the core mission or purpose of the organization. The increase in the use of service contracts, particularly in government contracting, brings with it the need for additional skills and knowledge.

As it relates to contracting for general services, the government's policy includes the following precepts:

- Performance-based acquisition is the preferred method for obtaining services.

- Government agencies shall generally rely on the private sector for commercial services.

- Agencies shall not award a contract to perform inherently governmental functions.

- Program officials are responsible for accurately describing the service contracting requirement in a manner that ensures full understanding and performance by contractors.

- Services should be obtained in the most cost-effective manner, without barriers to full and open competition, and free of any potential conflicts of interest.

Advisory and assistance services: Services acquired to support or improve agency policy development, decision making, management, and administration, or to support or improve the operation of management systems.

Some organizations use advisory and assistance services to help managers achieve maximum effectiveness or economy in their operations. Advisory and assistance service contracts can be used to:

- Obtain outside points of view to avoid limited judgment on critical issues;

- Obtain advice regarding developments in industry, university, or foundation research;

- Obtain the opinions, special knowledge, or skills of noted experts;

- Enhance the understanding of and develop alternative solutions to complex issues;

- Support and improve the operation of organizations; and

- Ensure the more efficient or effective operation of managerial or hardware systems.

Advisory and assistance service contracts may not be used to:

- Perform work of a policy, decision making, or managerial nature, which is the direct responsibility of agency officials;

- Bypass or undermine personnel ceilings, pay limitations, or competitive employment procedures;

- Contract for, on a preferential basis, former federal employees;

- Specifically aid in influencing or enacting legislation; and

- Obtain professional or other technical advice, which is readily available within the agency or another federal agency.

Consulting: The process of providing subject matter expertise to one who needs such knowledge. The knowledge may be provided in the form of either verbal or written advice. In addition, the consulting may provide the customer with some form of deliverable (e.g., reports that address the client's need). Consulting services may be paid for in a number of ways. Two common means for determining a consultant's fee are time and materials, and fixed fee.

Facilities contract: A contract under which government facilities are provided to a contractor or subcontractor by the government to perform one or more related contracts for supplies or services. It is used occasionally to provide special tooling or special test equipment. Facilities contracts are cost contracts and contractors receive no fee.

Inherently governmental: An activity that is so intimately related to the public interest that it mandates performance by federal employees. Activities that meet these criteria are not in competition with commercial sources, are not generally available from commercial sources, and are therefore not subject to OMB Circular A-76 or it supplement. Examples include directing and controlling federal employees; approving any contractual documents, to include documents defining requirements, incentive plans, and evaluation criteria; determining whether contract costs are reasonable, allocable, and allowable; and participating as a voting member on performance evaluation boards.

OMB Circular A-76: Establishes federal policy regarding the performance of commercial activities. It implements the statutory requirements of the federal activities Inventory Reform Act of 1998, *Public Law* 105-270.

Outsourcing: A specialized form of consulting. When a client elects to outsource, the client generally turns a specific task over to a consultant. In the computer industry, this task might be to run a data center. The client is concerned with *what* is outsourced (in this example, running a data center). The client is typically not concerned with *how* the operation occurs. The client is hiring the consultant to provide the service based on the consultant's expertise in the following areas' process, people, and technology to perform the outsourced task. This type of service is normally contracted for on a fixed-fee basis, in which the client pays a flat fee per month for a given service. Therefore, the vast majority of the financial risk is shifted from the client to the consultant. If the consultant can effectively and efficiently provide the service, the consultant will realize a profit. Conversely, if the consultant is either ineffective or inefficient , the consultant still has to deliver the contracted deliverable for service: however, the consultant will be doing so at his or her own loss.

Performance-based contracting: Intended to ensure that required outcome quality levels are achieved and that total payment is related to the degree that outcomes achieved meet contract standards. Performance-based contracts should

- Describe the requirements in terms of results required rather than the methods of performing the work,

- Use measurable performance standards and quality assurance plans,

- Specify procedures for reductions of fees or for reductions to the price of fixed-price contracts when services are not performed or do not meet certain specified requirements, and

- Include performance incentives where appropriate.

Performance work statement: The portion of a contract describing the actual work to be done in terms of desired performance results, often including specific measurable objectives.

Service contract: A contract that directly engages the time and effort of a contractor to perform an identifiable task, rather than to furnish an end item or good. Service contracts can be nonpersonal or personal, professional or nonprofessional.

- **Nonpersonal services contract**: A contract under which the personnel providing the services are not subject, either by the contract's terms or the manner in which it is administered, to the supervision and control usually prevailing in relationships between employers and employees.

- **Personal services contract**: A contract under which the personnel providing the services are subject, either by the contract's terms or the manner in which it is administered, to the supervision and control usually prevailing in relationships between employers and employees.

Service Contract Act of 1965: Provides for minimum wages and fringe benefits as well as other conditions of work under certain types of government service contracts. Contracting professionals need to be aware of the potential impact of this law on potential service contracts, such as the need to incorporate Service Contract Act wage determinations in contractual documents.

Statement of work: The portion of a contract describing the actual work to be done by means of specifications, or other minimum requirements, quantities, performance date, and a statement of the requisite quality.

Stop-work order: The instruction served on the seller by the buyer requiring that the seller cease to perform the contract and take alternate steps to limit the risk and liabilities of the parties.

Time and materials: One common way to pay for consulting services. When using this method of calculating payment, the consultant is paid for any time he devotes to the needs of a client. The consultant is typically paid for each hour he logs to a client's project. In addition, the consultants are generally paid for any expenses they incur on behalf of the client (i.e., travel, engagement-specific tools or materials, copy services). All of the aforementioned items may either be limited or expanded (i.e., authorization of air travel in first class versus coach) by the specific contract entered into between the consultant and the client. This form of consulting places virtually all the risk on the client (as opposed to the consultant). That is to say, the client typically has a budget for a specific task. The client is betting the consultant can complete the assigned work within that budget. However, the consultant is typically under no such obligation, and the bill for the consultant's time may well exceed the client's projected budget.

4.6 International Contracting

The policies and procedures that govern the acquisition and sale of goods and services with foreign nationals and governments.

Contracting domestically is sometimes a difficult process, as evidenced by the misunderstandings, lack of compliance with terms and conditions, late delivery, and payment issues that can develop. When contracting internationally, the potential for problems can expand almost exponentially. Whether functioning as a buyer or seller, contracting professionals who operate in the international market require an enhanced set of skills and knowledge to be effective. International contracting can sometimes result in lower costs and improved quality for buyers, and increased sales and profitability for sellers. However, there are many significant differences between operating in the domestic market and the international market.

International contracting presents many positive opportunities, but also presents many challenges that are not present in the domestic sector. Contracting professionals should ensure they have a complete understanding of this more dynamic and volatile environment, and use appropriate caution to avoid mistakes.

LEXICON FOR INTERNATIONAL CONTRACTING

Ad valorem: A customs duty usually charged on the value only of goods that are dutiable, irrespective of quality, weight, or any other considerations.

Agreements and restrictions: Agreements exist among the United States and its trading partners regarding international procurement. These include the General Agreement on Tariffs and Trade (GATT), the GATT Government Procurement Code, the North American Free Trade Agreement (NAFTA), as well as bilateral agreements that have been negotiated between the United States and other countries (such as the United States–Canada Free Trade Agreement). Congress has routinely included in appropriation acts restrictions on the procurement of certain foreign items, usually to protect domestic industries.

Bank acceptance: An instrument used in financing foreign trade, making possible the payment of cash to an exporter covering all or part of the amount of a shipment made by that exporter.

Counter-purchase: A form of countertrade that occurs when a firm agrees to purchase a specified dollar volume of materials from a country in return for a sale made to that country.

Counter-trade: A requirement imposed by a country on a foreign exporter or supplier to purchase materials in the receiving country as part of the original sales transaction. Payment is made partially or in full with goods instead of money.

Currency differences: Currency differences, and the constantly changing exchange rates, can have impacts on the business relationship and feasibility of doing business in certain countries.

Domestic end product:

- An unmanufactured end product mined or produced in the United States;

- An end product manufactured in the United States, if

  o The cost of its components mined, produced, or manufactured in the United States exceeds 50 percent of the cost of all its components. Components of foreign origin of the same class or kind as those that the agency

determines are not mined, produced, or manufactured in sufficient and reasonably available commercial quantities of a satisfactory quality are treated as domestic. Scrap generated, collected, and prepared for processing in the United States is considered domestic; or

  o The end product is a commercial off-the-shelf (COTS) item.

Domestic offer: An offer of a domestic end product. When the solicitation specifies that award will be made on a group of line items, a domestic offer means an offer where the proposed price of the domestic end products exceeds 50 percent of the total proposed price of the group.

Due bill: A bill levied by a government on the importation, exportation, or use and consumption of goods.

Eligible offer: An offer of an eligible product. When the solicitation specifies that award will be made on a group of line items, an eligible offer means a foreign offer where the combined proposed price of the eligible products and the domestic end products exceeds 50 percent of the total proposed price of the group.

Eligible product: A foreign end product, construction material, or service that, due to applicability of a trade agreement to a particular acquisition, is not subject to discriminatory treatment.

Exempt commodities: Goods that are not subject to import duties, or specific goods that can be transported exempt of regulation by the Interstate Commerce Commission.

Export Administration Regulations (EAR): Regulations administered by the Bureau of Industry and Security that, among other things, provide specific instructions on the use and types of export licenses required for certain commodities, software, and technology.

Export controls: The comprehensive set of controls that have been established to protect national security interests and to foster foreign policy initiatives. The Department of State monitors and controls the export and re-export of goods and services in accordance with the *International Traffic in Arms Regulations* (*ITAR*), and the Department of Commerce *Export Administration Regulation* (*EAR*) enforces the Export Administration Act.

Export-Import Bank: An independent U.S. government agency that provides loans, loan guarantees, and credit risk insurance coverage to U.S. exporters and foreign importers.

Export issues: Export is defined as the transfer of commodities, technical data, articles, or services from the United States to a foreign person, corporation, or other entity. The company may be required to obtain export permission from the Bureau of Export Administration within the Department of Commerce or the Office of Defense Trade Controls within the U.S. Department of State.

Foreign construction material: A construction material other than a domestic construction material.

Foreign contractor: A contractor or subcontractor organized or existing under the laws of a country other than the United States.

Foreign end product: An end product other than a domestic end product.

Foreign Military Sales (FMS): That portion of the U.S. security assistance authorized by the Foreign Assistance Act (1961), as amended, and the Arms Export Control Act, as amended, where the recipient provides reimbursement for defense articles and services transferred FMS includes Department of Defense (DOD) cast sales from stock; DOD guarantees covering financing by private or Federal Financing Bank sources for credit sales of defense articles and defense services, sales financed by appropriated direct credits, and sales funded by grants under the Military Assistance Program.

Foreign offer: Any offer other than a domestic offer.

Foreign trade zone: A site sanctioned by the Customs Services in which imported goods are exempted from customs duties until withdrawn for domestic sale or use. These sites are ideal for commercial warehouses or foreign production plants.

Free trade agreement: A treaty between two or more countries that do not impose tariffs for commerce conducted across their borders. This doesn't mean capital and labor moves freely between them, and tariffs are still imposed upon nonmember countries. The idea is to open markets and provide opportunities for businesses to compete globally.

Free trade agreement country: Australia, Bahrain, Canada, Chile, Costa Rica, Dominican Republic, El Salvador, Guatemala, Honduras, Mexico, Morocco, Nicaragua, Oman, Peru, or Singapore.

Free Trade Agreement country end product: An article that

- Is wholly the growth, product, or manufacture of a free trade agreement (FTA) country; or

- In the case of an article that consists in whole or in part of materials from another country, has been substantially transformed in an FTA country into a new and different article of commerce with a name, character, or use distinct from that of the article or articles from which it was transformed. The term refers to a product offered for purchase under a supply contract, but for purposes of calculating the value of the end product, includes services (except transportation services) incidental to the article, provided that the value of those incidental services does not exceed that of the article itself.

Global issues: A corporate framework for conducting international business, including evaluation of objectives, strengths, and weaknesses as well as development of strategies for product development and marketing.

Incoterms® (International Commercial Terms): The Incoterms® rules are an internationally recognized standard and are used worldwide in international and domestic contracts for the sale of goods. First published in 1936, Incoterms® rules provide internationally accepted definitions and rules of interpretation for most common commercial terms.

International Traffic in Arms Regulations (ITAR): U.S. State Department regulations that govern the export of restricted technology to foreign states other than Canada. The *ITAR* included restrictions on commercial encryption products until the end of 1996, when they were passed to the *Export Administration Regulations* (*EAR*) of the Department of Commerce.

Language: There are obvious potential issues when multiple languages are introduced into the contracting process. Some international firms have personnel who are multilingual. In other cases, the use of third-party interpreters may be appropriate. Regardless, the contracting professional needs to ensure that the sometimes subtle context and nuances inherent in one language are accurately reflected in the translation to a different language.

Least developed country: Any of the following countries: Afghanistan, Angola, Bangladesh, Benin, Bhutan, Burkina Faso, Burundi, Cambodia, Central African Republic, Chad, Comoros, Democratic Republic of Congo, Djibouti, East Timor, Equatorial Guinea, Eritrea, Ethiopia, Gambia, Guinea, Guinea-Bissau, Haiti, Kiribati, Laos, Lesotho, Liberia, Madagascar, Malawi, Maldives, Mali, Mauritania, Mozambique, Nepal, Niger, Rwanda, Samoa, Sao Tome and Principe, Senegal, Sierra Leone, Solomon Islands, Somalia, Tanzania, Togo, Tuvalu, Uganda, Vanuatu, Yemen, or Zambia.

Least developed country end product: An article that

- Is wholly the growth, product, or manufacture of a least developed country; or

- In the case of an article that consists in whole or in part of materials from another country, has been substantially transformed in a least developed country into a new and different article of commerce with a name, character, or use distinct from that of the article or articles from which it was transformed. The term refers to a product offered for purchase under a supply contract, but for purposes of calculating the value of the end product, includes services (except transportation services) incidental to the article, provided that the value of those incidental services does not exceed that of the article itself.

Noneligible offer: An offer of a noneligible product.

Noneligible product: A foreign end product that is not an eligible product.

Political climate: The political and social climate in many countries is sometimes subject to abrupt and significant change. Contracting professionals must have a thorough understanding of past, present, and future trends that may influence the degree to which business in a foreign country may be affected by changes in the political and social climate.

Social customs: Business, cultural, and social customs and norms, to the degree that they are different from one's experience and expectations, can present significant obstacles to the successful completion of business agreements.

Tax implications: The tax-cost implications of doing business in foreign countries can be tremendous. For example, the foreign country may have a right to assess its own income or value-added tax on the company's global earnings that have a connection to that country. There may be personal tax implications for company employees who are temporarily transferred to the country for contract performance.

Third-party involvement: Buying and selling internationally often requires the use of various third-party entities, such as trading companies, local representatives, foreign banks, freight forwarders, customs brokers, etc. Some foreign countries require an in-country firm on the company team.

United States: The 50 States, the District of Columbia, and outlying areas.

U.S.-made end product: An article that is mined, produced, or manufactured in the United States or that is substantially transformed in the United States into a new and different article of commerce with a name, character, or use distinct from that of the article or articles from which it was transformed.

World Trade Organization Government Procurement Agreement (WTO GPA) country: Any of the following countries: Aruba, Austria, Belgium, Bulgaria, Canada, Cyprus, Czech Republic, Denmark, Estonia, Finland, France, Germany, Greece, Hong Kong, Hungary, Iceland, Ireland, Israel, Italy, Japan, Korea (Republic of), Latvia, Liechtenstein, Lithuania, Luxembourg, Malta, Netherlands, Norway, Poland, Portugal, Romania, Singapore, Slovak Republic, Slovenia, Spain, Sweden, Switzerland, Taiwan, or United Kingdom.

4.7 State and Local Government

The policies and procedures that govern the acquisition and sale of goods and services at the state and local government levels. When viewed as a single entity, the purchasing power of state and local governments represents a huge and often untapped source of business for commercial contracting professionals. However, the unfortunate reality is that state and local government is not a homogenous market segment, but rather a somewhat artificial category that in fact is comprised of literally thousands of buying entities, often with their own unique processes, procedures, and challenges.

Advantages in pursuing business in the state and local government sector:

- State and local governments tend to be more commercially oriented than their federal counterparts. Many potentially new customers already exist for firms that deal in commercial goods and services.

- The local government can benefit from the close proximity of a company that can provide high quality goods and services at competitive prices, and that can be available for consultation and advice.

- The success of local businesses generates additional tax revenue for the state and local governments, which can be used to help provide additional government services and also to reinvest in the local business community and infrastructure to create more businesses and economic growth.

- Dealing locally tends to help both the buyer and the seller by developing personal, long-term relationships based on mutual need and mutual benefit.

Disadvantages in dealing with the state and local government segment:

- A lack of standardized processes, procedures, and regulatory guidance. Many state and local government entities have unique requirements, forms, and local ordinances that may increase the cost to the seller of doing business with multiple entities simultaneously.

- Many local governments seek out the best value, which may make some local businesses, particularly smaller ones, less competitive.

- Local and regional politics often influence purchasing decisions. Vendors should be aware that sometimes buying decisions are made based on facts or perceptions that have little or nothing to do with price, quality, or service.

LEXICON FOR STATE AND LOCAL GOVERNMENT:

(Though the following terms and definitions are used in state and local procurement, each entity may have its own definition or interpretation. For the purposes of this study guide and the CPCM examination, these terms and definitions are appropriate. Also, while many of the terms and definitions are similar to federal government and commercial contracting, in many cases there are subtle differences. This lexicon was formed to provide the reader with insight into the similarities and differences.)

Appeal: Action taken by a bidder, offeror (actual or prospective), or by a vendor to seek a hearing before a disinterested person or panel or in an appropriate circuit court challenging a decision.

Authority: The sources from which entities or people receive their empowerment to engage in procurement activities, and which set forth the framework and parameters and extend to their empowerment. Such authority includes state statutes; state and local regulations charters; local ordinances; and administrative resolutions, policies, or edicts.

Best value: The overall combination of quality, price, and various elements of required services that are in total optimal relative to a public body's needs. Public bodies are encouraged to consider best-value concepts when making procurement decisions involving goods and nonprofessional services, but not construction or professional services.

Bid: A competitively priced offer made by an intended seller, usually in reply to an invitation for bids. A price offer made at a public auction.

Bid bond: An insurance agreement in which a third party agrees to be liable to pay a certain amount of money in the event a selected bidder fails to accept the contract as bid.

Bidder: One who submits a competitively priced offer in response to an invitation for bids.

Blanket purchase agreement (BPA): An arrangement under which a purchaser contracts with a vendor to provide the purchaser's requirements for an item or service, on an as-required and over-the-counter basis. Properly prepared, such an arrangement sets a limit on the period of time it is valid and the maximum amount of money that may be spent at one time or within a specified period and specifically identifies these persons authorized to accept goods.

Competitive bidding: The offer of vendor bids by individuals or vendors competing for a contract, privilege, or right to supply specified services or goods.

Competitive sealed bid: A bid submitted in a sealed envelope to prevent disclosure of its contents before the deadline set for the receipt of all bids.

Competitive negotiation: A method for purchasing goods and services, usually of a highly complex and technical nature whereby qualified individuals or vendors are solicited by means of a request for proposals. Negotiations are conducted with selected offerors and the best proposal, as judged against criteria contained in the request for proposals, is accepted and an award issued.

Confirming purchase order: A purchase order issued after the fact by a procuring agency to a vendor for goods or services ordered orally or by some other informal means.

Consideration: Something of value given for a promise to make the promise binding. One of the essential elements of a legal contract.

Construction: Building, altering, repairing, improving, or demolishing any structure, building, or highway, and any draining, dredging, excavation, grading, or similar work upon real property.

Construction management contract: A contract in which a party is retained by the owner to coordinate and administer contracts for construction services for the benefit of the owner, and may also include, if provided in the contract, the furnishing of construction services to the owner.

Consulting services: Advice or assistance of a purely advisory nature provided for a predetermined fee to an agency by an outside individual, vendor, or organization under contract to that agency.

Contract: An agreement enforceable by law, between two or more competent parties, to do or not to do something not prohibited by law, for a consideration. Any type of agreement or order for the procurement of goods or services.

Contract administration: The management of all facets of a contract to ensure the vendor's total performance is in accordance with the contractual commitments and that the obligations of the vendor under the terms and conditions of the contract are fulfilled.

Contract, cost-plus-a-fixed-fee: A cost reimbursement type contract that provides for the payment of a fixed fee to the vendor. The fixed fee, once negotiated, does not vary with the actual cost but may be adjusted as a result of any subsequent changes in the scope of work or services to be performed under the contract.

Contract, cost-plus-a-percentage-of-cost: A form of contract that provides for a fee or profit at a specified percentage of the vendor's actual cost of accomplishing the work. Except in case of emergency affecting the public health, safety, or welfare, and for some insurance contracts, no public contract shall be awarded on the basis of cost plus a percentage of cost.

Contract, fixed-price: A contract that provides for a vendor price under which a vendor bears the full risk for profit or loss.

Contract, fixed-price with escalation/de-escalation: A fixed-price type of contract that provides for the upward and downward revision of the stated contract price upon the occurrence of certain contingencies (such as fluctuations in material costs and labor rates) specifically defined in the contract.

Contract, requirements-type (open-end contracts): A form of contract covering long-term requirements, used when the total quantity required cannot be definitely fixed, but can be stated as an estimate or within maximum and minimum limits, with deliveries on demand. Such contracts are usually one year or more in duration.

Contract, service: A contract for work to be performed by an independent vendor wherein the service rendered does not consist primarily of the acquisition of equipment or materials, or the rental of equipment, materials, and supplies.

Contract, time-and-material: A contract providing for the procurement of supplies or services on the basis of direct labor hours at specified fixed hourly rates (which include direct and indirect labor, overhead, and profit) and material at cost, or at some bid percentage discount from the manufacturer's catalog or list prices.

Contract officer, purchase officer, buyer: An employee of the institution whose primary assignment is purchasing goods or services.

Contractor: An individual or vendor which has entered into an agreement to provide goods or services.

Cooperative purchasing: A process whereby two or more communities, counties, or other governmental jurisdictions voluntarily agree to coordinate their purchases of one or more commodities to obtain the best unit price through volume buying.

Cure notice: A notice, either oral or in writing, that informs vendors that they are in default and states what the vendor has to do to correct the deficiency. If the notice is oral, it shall be confirmed in writing.

Debarment: An action taken to exclude individuals or vendors from contracting with institutions for particular goods or nonprofessional services for specified periods of time.

Default: Failure of a vendor to comply with the terms and conditions of a contract.

Design-build contract: A contract between an institution and another party in which the party contracting with the institution agrees to both design and build the structure, roadway, or other item specified in the contract.

Design specification: A purchase specification setting forth the essential physical characteristics that an item bid must possess to be considered for award.

Designated public area: An area that is available to the public during normal business hours and is the area designated by an agency for the posting of procurement solicitations and notices.

Evaluation of bids: The process of examining a bid after opening to determine the bidder's responsiveness to requirements, responsibility, and other characteristics of the bid relating to selection for award.

General terms and conditions: Standard clauses and requirements incorporated into all solicitations (IFB/RFP) and resulting contracts which are derived from laws or administrative procedures of the government agency.

Goods: Material, equipment, supplies, printing, and automated data processing hardware and software.

Intergovernmental relations: A range of cooperative activities among governments, including various forms of intergovernmental cooperative purchasing, joint or shared use of facilities and supplies, and procurements made by one government from another.

Liquidated damages: A sum stated in a contract to be paid as ascertained damages for failure to perform in accordance with the contract. The damage figure stipulated must be a reasonable estimate of the probable loss to the agency and not calculated simply to impose a penalty on the vendor.

Minor informality: A minor defect or variation of a bid or proposal from the exact requirements of the invitation for bids or the request for proposals, which does not affect the price, quality, quantity, or delivery schedule for the goods, services, or construction being procured.

Multiple award: The award of contracts to more than one bidder. When a solicitation in its terms and conditions so provides, awards may be made to more than one vendor. Appropriate in situations where the award of a single contract would be impractical and awards are limited to the least number of suppliers necessary to satisfy program requirements.

Noncompetitive negotiation: The process of arriving at an agreement through discussion and compromise when only one source is practically available.

Offeror: A person who makes an offer in response to a request for proposals.

Payment bond for labor and material: A bond required of a vendor to assure fulfillment of the vendor's obligation to pay all persons supplying labor or materials in the performance of the work provided for in the contract.

Performance bond: A contract of guarantee executed in the full sum of the contract amount subsequent to award by a successful bidder to protect the government from loss due to their inability to complete the contract in accordance with its terms and conditions.

Performance specification: A specification setting forth performance requirements that have been determined necessary for the item involved to perform and last as required.

Prebid or preproposal conference: Meeting held with prospective bidders or offerors before submitting bids or proposals to review, discuss, and clarify technical considerations, specifications, and standards relative to the proposed procurement.

Prequalification: A procedure to prequalify products or vendors and limit consideration of bids or proposals to only those products or vendors that have been prequalified.

Procurement: The procedures for obtaining goods or services, including all activities from the planning steps and preparing and processing a requisition, through receiving and accepting delivery and processing a final invoice for payment.

Professional services: Work performed by an independent vendor within the scope of the practice of accounting, actuarial services, architecture, land surveying, landscape architecture, law, dentistry, medicine, optometry, pharmacy, or professional engineering.

Proposal: An offer made by one party to another as a basis for negotiations for entering into a contract.

Proprietary specification: One that restricts the acceptable products or services to those of one manufacturer or vendor.

Protest: A written complaint about an administrative action or decision brought by a bidder or offeror to the appropriate administrative section with the intention of receiving a remedial result.

Public bid opening: The process of opening and reading bids at the time and place specified in the invitation for bids and in the presence of anyone who wishes to attend.

Public posting: The display of procurement notices in an area or on a board designated and regularly used for that purpose that is available to the public during normal working hours.

Purchase order: A document the institutions use to execute a purchase transaction with a vendor. It serves as notice to a vendor that an award has been made and that performance can be initiated under the terms and conditions of the contract.

Regular dealer: A person or vendor that owns, operates, or maintains a store, warehouse, or other establishment in which the materials, supplies, articles, or equipment of the general character described by the specifications and required under the contract are bought, kept in stock, and sold to the public in the usual course of business.

Responsive bidder: A person or vendor who has submitted a bid that conforms in all material respects to the invitation for bids.

Reverse auctioning: A procurement method wherein bidders are invited to bid on the opportunity to provide specified goods or nonprofessional services through real-time electronic bidding, with the award being made to the lowest responsive and responsible bidder. During the bidding process, bidders' prices are revealed and bidders shall have the opportunity to modify their bid prices for the duration of the time period established for bid opening. Reverse auctioning may be used to buy goods or nonprofessional services, but not construction or professional services.

Sealed bid: A bid that has been submitted in a sealed envelope to prevent its contents from being revealed or known before the deadline for the submission and opening of all bids.

Services: Any work performed by an independent vendor wherein the service rendered does not consist primarily of acquisition of equipment or materials, or the rental of equipment, materials, and supplies.

Sheltered workshops: A work-oriented rehabilitative facility with a controlled working environment and individual goals that utilizes work experience and related services for assisting the handicapped person to progress toward normal living and a productive vocational status.

Sole source: A product or service practicably available only from one source.

Solicitation: A method to obtain bids or proposals from potential vendors. It may include an invitation for bids (IFB) or a request for proposals (RFP), and could be done in writing or verbally through a telephone call; or any other document issued to obtain bids or proposals for the purpose of entering into a contract.

Special terms and conditions: Special clauses pertaining to a specific procurement that may supplement or, in some cases, supersede one or more general terms and conditions.

Spot purchase: A one-time purchase made in the open market.

Surplus property: Property in excess of what an agency needs and not required for any foreseeable needs. The property may be used or new, but has some usefulness for the purpose for which it was intended or for some other purpose. It includes scrap, which is material that is damaged, defective, or deteriorated to the extent that it has no value except for its basic material content.

Technical proposal: An unpriced proposal that sets forth in detail that which a vendor proposes to furnish in response to a solicitation.

Technical specifications: Specifications that establish the material and performance requirements of goods and services.

Term contract: Normally covers a 12-month period or may cite another specific time to complete the project or service.

Term contracting: A technique by which a source of supply is established for a specific period of time. Term contracts are established based on indefinite quantities to be ordered "as needed," although such contracts can specify definite quantities with deliveries extended over the contract period.

Termination for convenience: A purchasing office may terminate work done in whole or in part at its discretion. The purchasing office will settle the vendor's claims in accordance with appropriate policy and procedures.

Termination for default: Action taken by the purchasing office to order a vendor to cease work under the contract, in whole or in part, because of the vendor's failure to perform in accordance with the contract's terms and conditions.

Unsealed bid: An unsealed written offer conveyed by letter or any other viable means of delivery. The bids are normally opened and recorded when received.

Unsolicited proposal: Proposal received that is not in response to any institutionally initiated solicitation or program.

Used equipment: Equipment that has been previously owned and used and is offered "where is" and "as is." It does not include demonstration or factory rebuilt or re-manufactured equipment marketed through normal distribution outlets.

Vendor: One who sells goods or services.

4.8 Supply Chain Management

Supply chain management is the sum total of all functions, operations, and facilities that are involved in the procurement and delivery of goods to a customer. It includes manufacturers, warehouses, transportation, distribution centers, retail outlets, and inventory at stages from raw materials to finished package that flows between and among facilities.

The concept of supply chain management as a natural, evolutionary managerial advancement over the traditional purchasing function has become more prevalent and commonly accepted in recent years. Traditional supply chain management theory holds that an organization can reduce procurement costs, reduce procurement cycle time, and add value to the procurement process by taking actions such as

- **Reducing the number of suppliers used.** Many organizations have found that maintaining large numbers of suppliers for the same or similar products or services and attempting to manage that supplier base was more expensive than the savings potentially realized from extensive competition among the suppliers for orders. Having many suppliers also introduced quality and consistent performance issues that were more difficult to manage.

- **Negotiating long-term contracts with the few preferred suppliers.** Cost savings can be realized by making significant commitments to a few suppliers as opposed to making only short-term commitments to many suppliers.

- **Conducting more rigorous and detailed timelines and quality tracking of the preferred supplier base.** The significant purchase commitments made to a few suppliers are coupled with increased requirements for quality and performance.

- **Analyzing and seeking to improve every action and link in the supply chain**, from the end customer to the lowest level supplier, with involvement, input, and cooperation from all stakeholders.

Supply chain management concepts recognize that the acquisition function does not operate in a reactive vacuum, but rather is a component in a larger management system that provides value and profitability by merging customer needs and supplier capabilities with the value-added processes of the organization. Supply chain management also recognizes the inter-dependencies and inter-relationships between and among all members of the supply chain. It seeks to maximize the power and competitiveness of the entire supply chain through collaboration, cooperation, continuous improvement, and the maintenance of long-term relationships that benefit all members of the chain.

LEXICON FOR SUPPLY CHAIN MANAGEMENT:

Abandonment: The decision of a carrier to give up or to discontinue service over a route. Railroads must seek Interstate Commerce Commission permission to abandon routes.

Acceptance sampling: A statistical quality control method that tests samples of products at defined points as opposed to testing each product.

Anticipated inventory: A type of inventory created for a well-defined future need.

Back order: Occurs when items are ordered but cannot be shipped because of a stockout or some other reason.

Bar code: A pattern of lines and spaces representing numbers and other characters that are machine readable. Its use helps to reduce error rates and improve inventory accuracy. Also referred to as a Uniform Product Code (UPC).

Base-stock system: In its simplest form, this is an inventory system in which a replenishment order is issued each time a withdrawal is made, and the order quantity is equal to the amount of the withdrawal.

Break bulk: Splitting one consolidated or large-volume shipment into smaller ones for ultimate delivery to consignees.

Business-to-business (B2B): As opposed to business-to-consumer (B2C). Many companies are now focusing on this strategy, and their sites are aimed at businesses (such as wholesale). Only other businesses can access or buy products on the site. Internet analysts predict this will become the biggest sector on the web.

Business-to-consumer (B2C): The hundreds of e-commerce websites that sell goods directly to consumers are considered B2C. This distinction is important when comparing websites that are B2B, as the entire business model, strategy, execution, and fulfillment are different.

CAGE code: The Commercial and Government Entity code is a five-character alphanumeric code used to identify contractors doing business with the U.S. government.

Capacity: Work that can be done over a specified period of time. Can be calculated at the work center, work area, or plant level. It is usually stated in hours. Capacity = (number of machines) x (utilization) x (efficiency) per time period.

Consequential damages: These costs result from a particular cause. For example, a product's failure may mean that a purchaser not only has incurred the added cost necessary to replace the product, but also has lost income that would have resulted had the product not failed.

Constructive acceleration: This describes a requirement (based on the reasonable interpretation of the buyer's words, acts, or inaction) that a contractor complete its work by a date earlier than one that would reflect the time extensions to which it is entitled because of excusable delays.

Cost of goods sold: These are the direct costs of producing goods for sale.

Critical-value analysis: An analysis concept in which the subjective value of criticalness, as opposed to the actual dollar value, is assigned to each inventory item.

Cumulative discount: A variation of quantity discount that is based on the quantity purchased over a specific period of time, rather than computed on the size of a single order placed at one time.

Cycle count: This is a physical stock-checking system in which the inventory is divided into 52 equal groups, one of which is counted each week. Thus, the physical inventory operation goes on continuously without interrupting operations or storeroom activities.

Cycle stock: This is the active portion of an inventory.

Cycle time: In a purchasing context, this represents the period of time required to order and to make available the required stock.

Decoupling stock: This type of inventory is retained to make possible the independent control of two operations; sometimes referred to as line-balancing stock.

Demand curve: A chart that shows the relationship between price and quantity. The horizontal axis shows the quantity demanded of a product. The vertical axis shows the price.

Demurrage: Additional fees charged by a carrier when rail freight cars and ships are held beyond a agreed-upon time.

Dependent demand: This is derived or contingent upon the demand for a component or a finished product (i.e., the demand for axles used in the assembly of automobiles is dependent on the demand for the finished automobiles.)

Economies of scale: The most efficient operating level. The point where it costs less per unit to produce.

Fill rate: This is the proportion of all stock requisitions that are filled from stock that is present on the shelf.

Finished goods inventory: This is the cost of a manufacturer's completed product that is being held for sale.

Forecast: An estimation of the future demand for a product. It is usually stated as a quantity (or value) over a specific time period. There are a number of inputs into a forecast, such as historical data, market trends, marketing data, and sales force feedback.

Forecast error: A comparison between actual demand and forecasted demand. It is usually stated as a percentage.

Forward buying: This is the practice of buying materials in a quantity exceeding specified current requirements, but not beyond the actual foreseeable requirements.

Horizontal integration: This describes a firm that owns several plants and each plant does the same thing. For example, a company buying two retail stores in a mall is an example of horizontal integration.

Hub & spoke: A distribution model. Stock is held at the hub location and then sent out to the spoke locations (distribution centers) when needed. This model usually allows for reduced overall inventory because the safety stock is mostly held at the hub rather than at numerous spokes.

Idle time: The time interval during which the workman, the equipment, or both do not produce useful work.

Integrated supply: A special type of partnering arrangement usually developed between a buyer and a distributer on an intermediate or long-term basis. The objective is to minimize the labor and expense involved in the acquisition and possession of maintenance, repair, and operating (MRO) supplies, which are items that are repetitive, generic, high transaction, and have a low unit cost.

Inventoriable cost: The cost associated with units produced.

Load: The number of hours of work assigned to a facility or work area.

Logistics: Managing and controlling the flow of goods from the source of the production to the marketplace.

Logistics management: That part of supply chain management that plans, implements, and controls the efficient, effective forward and reverse flow and storage of goods, services, and related information between the point of origin and the point of consumption in order to meet customers' requirements. Logistics management activities typically include inbound and outbound transportation management, fleet management, warehousing, materials handling, order fulfillment, logistics network design, inventory management, supply/demand planning, and management of third-party logistics services providers. To varying degrees, the logistics function also includes sourcing and procurement, production planning and scheduling, packaging and assembly, and customer service. It is involved in all levels of planning and execution—strategic, operational, and tactical. Logistics management is an integrating function, which coordinates and optimizes all logistics activities, as well as integrates

logistics activities with other functions including marketing, sales manufacturing, finance, and information technology.

Machine-to-machine interface (M2M): A term describing the process whereby machines are remotely monitored for status; problems are reported and resolved automatically or maintenance is scheduled by the monitoring systems.

Obsolete inventory: Inventory for which there is no forecast demand expected. A condition of being out of date. A loss of value occasioned by new developments that place the older property at a competitive disadvantage.

Point of sale (POS) data: Data that shows the actual units sold. Usually tracked by bar code scanning.

Pull system: A system for replenishing distribution center inventories in which the inventory decisions are made at the distribution center and "pulled" from the manufacturing plant. This is decentralized decision making.

Push system: A system for replenishing distribution center inventories where the inventory decisions are made at the manufacturing location. The stock is then "pushed" out to the distribution centers. This is centralized decision making.

Quantity discount: A price reduction given to a buyer for purchasing increasingly larger quantities of materials. A quantity discount is normally offered (1) for purchasing a specific quantity of items at one time, (2) for purchasing a specified dollar total at one time, or (3) for purchasing a specified dollar total over an agreed-upon time period (also known as a cumulative discount).

Reorder point (ROP): A pre-determined number usually calculated based on a number of factors. Once the inventory drops below the ROP, a replenishment order is created.

Rough cut capacity planning (RCCP): A type of capacity planning. It compares requirements to the available capacity at key work centers or critical bottlenecks. It attempts to balance workloads broadly and often takes into account the areas of labor, machinery, storage space, and supplier capacity.

Safety stock: Stock held at a distribution center that is in excess of what the organization expects to sell. The purpose of safety stock is to act as buffer inventory to account for unexpected customer orders, longer than expected manufacturing, or transportation time.

Sales cycle time: Measures the time required for a product to sell out completely from the store/shelf (i.e., beginning from the day it enters the floor).

Sell in: Units which are sold to retail stores by the manufacturer or distributor for resale to consumers. The period of time in a product life cycle in which the manufacturer works with its resellers to market and build inventory for sale.

Sell through: Units sold from retail stores to customers. The point in a product life cycle in which initial consumption rates are developed and demand established.

Takt time: The maximum time per unit allowed to produce a product in order to meet demand. It is derived from the German word *taktzeit* which translates to *cycle time*. Takt time sets the pace for industrial manufacturing lines. The formula is Takt Time = Available Time/Sold Units. So if 42 units are produced in 840 minutes, then it takes 20 minutes to produce one unit (840 minutes/42 units = 20 minutes per unit).

Vertical integration: This describes firms that own several plants with each one owning a different stage in the production process. For example, a food manufacturer buying a chain of supermarkets would be vertical integration.

4.9 Performance-based Acquisition

Commercial contracting has used performance-based acquisition as a standard practice, but is relatively new in the federal sector. For government contracting, however, these methods have been more difficult to adopt. Performance-based acquisition ensures that the required outcome quality levels are achieved and that total payment is related to the degree that outcomes achieved meet contract standards. Performance-based acquisition relies on a performance work statement that is expressed in terms of desired performance results, often including specific measurable objectives. Performance-based contracts should

- Describe the requirements in terms of results required rather than the methods of performing the work,

- Use measurable performance standards and quality assurance plans,

- Specify procedures for reductions of fees or for reductions to the price of fixed-price contracts when services are not performed or do not meet certain specified requirements, and

- Include performance incentives where appropriate.

Performance-based contracts are frequently incentive contract types (award or incentive fee). Performance incentives must correspond to the performance standards set forth in the contract.

Award-fee board: The team of individuals identified in the award-fee plan who have been designated to assist the fee-determining official in making award-fee determinations.

Cost incentives:

- Most incentive contracts include only cost incentives, which take the form of a profit or fee adjustment formula and are intended to motivate the contractor to effectively manage costs. No incentive contract may provide for other incentives without also providing a cost incentive (or constraint).

- Except for award-fee contracts, incentive contracts include a target cost, a target profit or fee, and a profit or fee adjustment formula that (within the constraints of a price ceiling or minimum and maximum fee) provides that

  o Actual cost that meets the target will result in the target profit or fee,

  o Actual cost that exceeds the target will result in downward adjustment of target profit or fee, and

  o Actual cost that is below the target will result in upward adjustment of target profit or fee.

Delivery incentives: Should be considered when improvement from a required delivery schedule is a significant government objective. It is important to determine the government's primary objectives in a given contract (e.g., earliest possible delivery or earliest quantity production).

Fee-determining official (FDO): The designated agency official who reviews the recommendations of the Award-Fee Board in determining the amount of award fee to be earned by the contractor for each evaluation period.

Incentive: Motivating the contractor in calculable monetary terms to turn out a product that meets significantly advanced performance goals, to improve on the contract schedule up to and including final delivery, to substantially reduce work costs, or to complete the project under a weighted combination of some or all of these objectives.

Incentive arrangement: A negotiated pricing arrangement that structures a series of relationships designed to motivate and reward the contractor for performance in accordance with the contract specifications; involves target costs, fees, and/or profits. In the case of award-fee arrangements, it involves the payment of a fee tied to negotiated incentive criteria.

Performance incentives: May be considered in connection with specific product characteristics (e.g., a missile range, an aircraft speed, an engine thrust, or vehicle maneuverability) or other specific elements of the contractor's performance. These incentives should be designed to relate profit or fee to results achieved by the contractor, compared with specified targets.

Performance work statement (PWS): (1) A performance work statement is a statement of the technical, functional, and performance characteristics of the work to be performed. It determines performance factors, including the location of the work, the units of work, the quantity of work units, and the quality and timeliness of the work units. It serves as the scope of work and is the basis for all costs entered on the cost comparison form. (2) A statement of work expressed in terms of desired performance results, often including specific measurable objectives.

Quality assurance surveillance: Used to supervise in-house or contract performance to ensure that the standards of the PWS are met within the costs bid.

Rollover of unearned award fee: The process of transferring unearned award fee, which the contractor had an opportunity to earn, from one evaluation period to a subsequent evaluation period, thus allowing the contractor an additional opportunity to earn that previously unearned award fee.

Statement of objectives: The portion of the contract that establishes a broad description of the buyer's required performance objectives.

Target cost: Final agreed-upon cost that serves as a basis for computing cost savings in incentive-type contracts.

4.10 Government Property

When the U.S. government contracts for supplies and services, the contractor is generally required to provide all necessary resources to successfully meet the terms and conditions of such a contract. These "resources" also include all property necessary to perform the work required under government contracts. Re-utilization of government property promotes cost savings and efficiency for the government. The federal government also has a responsibility to protect the public trust and serves as the guardian of the property with public funds.

LEXICON FOR GOVERNMENT PROPERTY:

(See Competency 3.5, Property Administration, for additional information.)

Contractor-acquired property: Property acquired or otherwise provided by the contractor for performing a contract and to which the government has title.

Contractor inventory:

- Any property acquired by and in the possession of a contractor or subcontractor under a contract for which title is vested in the government and that exceeds the amounts needed to complete full performance under the entire contract;

- Any property that the government is obligated or has the option to take over under any type of contract (e.g., as a result either of any changes in the specifications or plans), or of the termination of the contract (or subcontract), before completion of the work, for the convenience or at the option of the government; and

- Government-furnished property that exceeds the amounts needed to complete full performance under the entire contract.

Equipment: A tangible item that is functionally complete for its intended purpose, durable, nonexpendable, and needed for the performance of a contract. Equipment is not intended for sale, and does not ordinarily lose its identity or become a component part of another article when put into use. Equipment does not include material, real property, special test equipment, or special tooling.

Facilities: The property category that refers to property used in production, maintenance, research, development, or testing.

Government-furnished property: Property in the possession of or directly acquired by the government and subsequently made available to the contractor.

Government property: All property owned by or leased to the government or acquired by the government under the terms of the contract. It includes both government-furnished property and contractor-acquired property.

Material: Property that may be incorporated into or attached to a deliverable end item or that may be consumed or expended in performing a contract. It includes assemblies, components, parts, raw and processed materials, and small tools and supplies that may be consumed in normal use in performing a contract.

Nonseverable: Property that cannot be removed after construction or installation without substantial loss of value or damage to the installed property or to the premises where installed.

Precious metals: Silver, gold, platinum, palladium, iridium, osmium, rhodium, and ruthenium.

Property: All tangible property, both real and personal.

Real property: In English Common Law, real property, real estate, realty, or immovable property is any subset of land that has been legally defined and the improvements to it made by human efforts: ny buildings, machinery, wells, dams, ponds, mines, canals, roads, various property rights, and so forth.

Sensitive property: Property potentially dangerous to the public safety or security if stolen, lost, or misplaced, or that shall be subject to exceptional physical security, protection, control, and accountability. Examples include weapons, ammunition, explosives, controlled substances, radioactive materials, hazardous materials or wastes, or precious metals.

Surplus property: Excess personal property not required by any federal agency as determined by the administrator of the General Services Administration (GSA).

4.11 Other Specialized Areas

As contracting becomes more complex, there are many more areas that contracting professionals need to be familiar with. While they may not have in-depth knowledge of these specialties (they are often managed by other offices), contracting professionals need to have a working knowledge of the basic concepts as far as they may "touch" their duties.

LEXICON FOR OTHER SPECIALIZED AREAS:

Contingency contracting: Contracting in an emergency, involving military forces, caused by natural disasters, terrorists, subversives, or required military operations. Due to the uncertainty of the situation, contingencies require plans, rapid response, and special procedures to ensure the safety and readiness of personnel, installations, and equipment.

Contractor System Reviews:

- **Contractor Purchasing System Review (CPSR):** The objective is to evaluate the efficiency and effectiveness with which the contractor spends government funds and complies with government policy when subcontracting. The review provides the administrative contracting officer a basis for granting, withholding, or withdrawing approval of the contractor's purchasing system.

- **Earned Value Management System (EVMS):** A project management technique for measuring project performance and progress in an objective manner. EVMS has the ability to combine measurements of scope, schedule, and cost in a single integrated system. It is notable for its ability to provide accurate forecasts of project performance problems.

Environmental contracting: A broad category that covers contracts for analysis, investigation, and studies in support of compliance, pollution prevention, conservation, recycling, and remediation to comply with all federal, state, and local environmental laws and regulations. Environmental contracting can be an extremely complex undertaking, especially in the case of site cleanup where scope, technical requirements, site characterization, impacts on health and the environment, timelines, and regulatory community oversight are difficult to accommodate in a scope of work, and difficult to accomplish without the built-in flexibility of contingency plans and options.

Foreign Military Sales: The portion of U.S. security assistance authorized by the Foreign Assistance Act of 1961, as amended, and the Arms Export Control Act of 1976, as amended. This assistance differs from the Military Assistance Program and the International Military Education and Training Program in that the recipient provides reimbursement for defense articles and services transferred.

Interagency contracting: Commonly conducted through indefinite-delivery contracts, such as task- and delivery-order contracts. The indefinite-delivery contracts used most frequently to support interagency acquisitions are Federal Supply Schedules (FSS), government-wide acquisition contracts (GWACs), and multi-agency contracts (MACs)

Spend analysis: The process of collecting, cleansing, classifying, and analyzing expenditure data with the purpose of reducing procurement costs, improving efficiency and monitoring compliance. It can also be leveraged in other areas of business such as inventory management, budgeting and planning, and product development. There are three core areas of spend analysis: visibility, analysis, and process. Spend analysis is often viewed as part of a larger domain known as spend management, which incorporates spend analysis, commodity management, and strategic sourcing.

1. If government-furnished property is delivered late or not suitable for its intended use, the contractor could

    a. submit a claim for equitable adjustment in accordance with the changes clause.
    b. supply the required property and charge the government for the additional cost.
    c. file a claim with the government accountability office charging the government with breach of contract.
    d. continue performance and wait for the government-furnished property to be delivered.

2. Using one or more contracts to acquire information technology systems in successive, interoperable increments is called

    a. incremental contracting.
    b. modular contracting.
    c. successive system contracting.
    d. bundling.

3. When publicizing requirements for government research and development contracts, agencies must obtain a broad base of the best contractor sources from the scientific and industrial community. How do agencies accomplish this objective?

    a. Follow the requirements of FAR Part 5, "Publicizing Contract Actions."
    b. Follow the requirements of FAR Part 5, "Publicizing Contract Actions" AND use research and development pools.
    c. Conduct market research.
    d. Specify needs to promote full and open competition.

4. The seller is responsible for risk of loss or damage occurring before delivery to the carrier in which of the following?

    a. Report of shipment (REPSHIP)
    b. Government transportation system (GTS)
    c. Free on board destination
    d. Free on board origin

5. The maximum number of offerors normally selected to submit phase-two proposals in a two-phase architect and engineer contract is

    a. 5
    b. 10
    c. 3
    d. unlimited

The following scenario and associated follow-on questions is a new, additional style of CPCM question you can expect to see beginning with the 2012 exam. The questions appear after the scenario.

Use the information provided in the following scenario to answer questions 6–10. The questions ask you to apply your knowledge of contract management to the given scenario. These questions require candidates to understand the concepts and terminology and apply that knowledge to answer the question correctly.

Scenario

The contractor shall manage the total work effort associated with the custodial and maintenance services required herein to ensure adequate and timely completion of these services. The contractor shall manage the work including, but not limited to, planning, scheduling, and quality control. The contractor shall provide an adequate staff to ensure the work is performed in accordance with the contract.

General Office Space Cleaning:

1. *Floors*: Once per day, clean the floors and entrance mats. They shall be free of

litter, soil, stains, and embedded foreign matter and grit. Chairs, wastebaskets, and garbage cans shall be moved to clean underneath. Lift entrance mats to remove soil underneath and return to original location. Vacuum all carpeted floors, including carpet underneath furniture.

2. *Furniture and Fixtures*: Once per week, clean desks, tables, filing cabinets, partitions, chairs, fixtures, and doors. They shall be free of dust, dirt, cobwebs, and spots.

3. *Trash Removal*: Once per day, empty garbage and the wastebaskets. They shall be free of dirt, spots, debris, and other encrustations. Both the interiors and exteriors of wastebaskets and garbage containers shall be free of debris. All trash shall be tied in garbage bags before being placed in the dumpsters.

Performance Evaluation Process: An evaluation worksheet is used for each inspection to record the satisfactory or unsatisfactory work. The work will be evaluated for each building level: basement, first floor, and second floor. If two-thirds of the building is unacceptable, the entire building is unacceptable. The evaluation worksheet will also be used to summarize the results of those inspections on a monthly basis and to recommend if there are to be any monthly deductions. At the end of the month, the project inspector will summarize the results of the month's inspections and calculate recommended payroll deductions on a monthly payment analysis form.

Examples of Unacceptable Work: Dirt in corners; mop splashes on baseboards and walls; dust build-up on surfaces; dirt, debris, etc. under wastebaskets, garbage cans and chairs; accumulated filth in cracks, joints, stair treads, etc.; failure to remove trash such as cups, paper clips, staples from floor; and other manifestations of lack of concern or capability of producing top-quality work.

Deduction Provisions: Assessments of unsatisfactory work shall be made by withholding payment as would ordinarily be paid under the terms of the contract for properly performing the item in question. The assessment is determined by applying the unit time for the item to the standard hourly rate paid by the contractor. Assessment shall also be made for additional cost of government inspection when items reported as complete by the contractor are not ready for inspection. All deductions are subtracted monthly from the total amount due under the contract.

6. The inspectors issued several daily deficiency reports with multiple deficient work items listed. The contracting officer should use the deficiency reports to

    a. determine deductions assessed for unsatisfactory performance as authorized by the contract.

    b. initiate a cure notice before terminating the contract for default for failure to perform the contract.

    c. document the contractor's past-performance assessment for lack of customer satisfaction.

    d. modify the contract and change the inspection standards so daily deficiency reports aren't required.

7. The inspector did not give credit for a partially clean building. If any dirt was found on the floor, the entire building was marked as unsatisfactory. What should the contractor do in this situation?

    a. Document the cleanliness of the area with photographs and include them with the monthly invoice.

    b. Provide a rebuttal response to the past-performance assessment that the work was actually completed to standards of good workmanship.

c. Notify the contracting officer that the inspections are not being done in accordance with contract requirements.
d. Ask the contracting officer to assign a different inspector to conduct the performance evaluations.

8. How did the agency describe its needs in this scenario?

   a. performance work statement
   b. purchase description
   c. design specification
   d. statement of work

9. How does the government establish a performance level required to meet the contract's requirements?

   a. "protection of government building" clause
   b. higher-level contract quality requirements
   c. contractor responsibility standards
   d. performance standards

10. The subcontractor performing the trash removal part of the contract lost some of the staff assigned to this contract. What should the subcontractor do in this situation?

    a. Request a contract change from the contracting officer to empty the trash weekly rather than daily.
    b. Locate another subcontractor to perform the work in a timely manner.
    c. Request that the prime contractor use its own staff to complete the work.
    d. Reassign staff from another contract to do the work.

1. If government-furnished property is delivered late or not suitable for its intended use, the contractor could

   a. **(Correct) submit a claim for equitable adjustment in accordance with the changes clause.**
   b. supply the required property and charge the government for the additional cost.
   c. file a claim with the government accountability office charging the government with breach of contract.
   d. continue performance and wait for the government furnished property to be delivered.

   (Source: FAR 52.245)

2. Using one or more contracts to acquire information technology systems in successive, interoperable increments is called

   a. incremental contracting. *Not a recognized term.*
   b. **(Correct) modular contracting.**
   c. successive system contracting. *Not a recognized term.*
   d. bundling. *Contract bundling is the practice of combining requirements into one "umbrella" solicitation, with the end result that the offeror must be able to perform increasingly larger contracts covering multiple and diverse elements of performance.*

   (Source: FAR 39.002)

3. When publicizing requirements for government research and development contracts, agencies must obtain a broad base of the best contractor sources from the scientific and industrial community. How do agencies accomplish this objective?

   a. Follow the requirements of FAR Part 5, "Publicizing Contract Actions." *Complying with the requirements of FAR Part 5 is not exclusive to R&D contracts for scientific and industrial sources.*
   b. **(Correct) Follow the requirements of FAR Part 5, "Publicizing Contract Actions" AND use research and development pools.**
   c. Conduct market research. *Agencies should always conduct market research to comply with FAR Part 10.*
   d. Specify needs to promote full and open competition. *This is required by the Competition in Contracting Act.*

   (Source: FAR 35.004)

4. The seller is responsible for risk of loss or damage occurring before delivery to the carrier in which of the following?

   a. Report of shipment (REPSHIP) *is advance notification of shipment to facilitate transportation control.*
   b. Government transportation system (GTS). *Not a recognized term.*
   c. **(Correct) Free on board (F.O.B.) destination.**
   d. Free on board (F.O.B.) origin. *The buyer is responsible for the cost of shipping and risk of loss.*

   (Source: FAR 47.303-1)

5. The maximum number of offerors normally selected to submit phase-two proposals in a two-phase architect and engineer contract is

   a. **(Correct) 5**
   b. 10
   c. 3
   d. unlimited

   (Source FAR 36.303-1)

6. The inspectors issued several daily deficiency reports with multiple deficient work items listed. The contracting officer should use the deficiency reports to

   a. (Correct) determine deductions assessed for unsatisfactory performance as authorized by the contract.
   b. initiate a cure notice before terminating the contract for default for failure to perform the contract.
   c. document the contractor's past-performance assessment for lack of customer satisfaction.
   d. modify the contract and change the inspection standards so daily deficiency reports aren't required.

7. The inspector did not give credit for a partially clean building. If any dirt was found on the floor, the entire building was marked as unsatisfactory. What should the contractor do in this situation?

   a. Document the cleanliness of the area with photographs and include them with the monthly invoice.
   b. Provide a rebuttal response to the past-performance assessment that the work was actually completed to standards of good workmanship.
   c. (Correct) Notify the contracting officer that the inspections are not being done in accordance with contract requirements.
   d. Ask the contracting officer to assign a different inspector to conduct the performance evaluations.

8. How did the agency describe its needs in this scenario?

   a. (Correct) performance work statement
   b. purchase description
   c. design specification
   d. statement of work

9. How does the government establish a performance level required to meet the contract's requirements?

   a. Protection of Government Building clause
   b. Higher level contract quality requirements
   c. Contractor responsibility standards
   d. (Correct) Performance standards

10. The subcontractor performing the trash removal part of the contract lost some of the staff assigned to this contract. What should the subcontractor do in this situation?

    a. Request contract change from the contracting officer to empty the trash weekly rather than daily.
    b. Locate another subcontractor to perform the work in a timely manner.
    c. Request that the prime contractor use its own staff to complete the work.
    d. (Correct) Reassign staff from another contract to do the work.

Use the full text of the scenario case to better understand the correct answer choices.

ASBCA No. 22784, Clarkies, Inc. Under Contract No. N62472-73-B-4882, August 13, 1981

Clarkies signed a contract for janitorial services in federal government office buildings. The period of performance was August 1 through July 31 and the government had an option to extend the period of performance for an additional 12 months subject to the same terms and conditions as set forth in the basic contract.

The contract included the following special provisions pertinent to this case:

2.3 Inspection. Each cleaning task is subject to Government inspection during the contractor's operations and after completion of the tasks. Unsatisfactory work shall be corrected promptly. The Government reserves the right to charge to the contractor any additional cost of Government inspection when maintenance tasks are not ready at the time such inspection is requested by the contractor.

2.5 Workmanship. The work shall be thorough and neat in all respects. Hasty and careless performance of the work will not be tolerated. Evidence given of such practices by dirt in corners, mop splashes on baseboards, and work that is otherwise sloppy and unsatisfactory will be called to the attention of the Contractor with the request to clean up the areas in question and take steps to improve on the work assuring satisfactory results.

2.21 Working hours. All work shall be performed between the hours of 4:30 p.m. and 12:30 a.m. except for a deficiency crew which will be required to remain on the Center between the hours of 12:30 a.m. and 2:00 a.m.

5.2 Daily work accomplishment report. The Contractor shall submit a daily report of the work performed on that day at the completion of each days work. The report will be submitted on a Government furnished form all will include the information outlined above. This report along with reports by Government inspector will be the basis for computing deductions for nonperformance of work.

5.3 Contractor inspection report. The Contractor will submit a Contractor Inspection Report at 8:30 p.m. and 11:30 p.m. daily reporting the work completed prior to the time of submission. The Contractor will be responsible for making a preliminary inspection of all work and insuring its satisfactory completion before reporting its accomplishment. The work will be reported on a Government furnished form and will include the information outlined above.

5.4 Inspection.

5.4.1 Representatives of the Officer in Charge will make a daily inspection of each building and area serviced. The contractor shall make his representative available to accompany the inspector to insure that any deficiencies found are promptly corrected.

5.4.2 Any deficiencies found by the inspector will be recorded on a Deficiency Report Form and a copy furnished promptly to the contractor's representative, who will acknowledge receipt in writing of the report of deficiencies on the original form.

5.4.3 Failure of the contractor to have his representative accompany the inspector shall constitute acceptance of the deficiencies as noted by the inspector.

5.4.4 The contractor's representative shall arrange to have all deficiencies of daily work found by the inspector corrected on the same day the work was performed.

5.4.5 Deficiencies in non-daily work shall be corrected within one working day from the date when the work had been performed improperly or was not performed when due.

5.4.6 The contractor shall have sufficient personnel available to correct any deficiencies. The contractor will be given one opportunity to correct all deficiencies of work. On re-inspection, acceptance or further rejection of work shall be so noted on the form citing the original deficiency. If still found unsatisfactory on reinspection, the deficiencies shall constitute grounds for deduction.

5.4.7 The Officer in Charge or his authorized representative shall be the final authority with respect to whether a building or area has not been cleaned or has been cleaned improperly.

5.4.8 If the contractor fails to promptly correct the deficiencies as herein provided or if in the opinion of the Officer in Charge the work contracted for is not being performed or not being performed properly, the Government may, in addition to deducting for such failure to perform or properly perform the services, terminate the contract for default.

5.5 Deficiency crew. The Contractor will provide at least two janitors between the hours of 12:30 a.m. and 2:00 a.m. only for the correction of deficiencies noted by Government inspectors. The janitors will not be engaged in scheduled work items except in correcting unsatisfactory work on previously reported items and will be available to receive reports of improperly performed work from Government inspectors.

5.6 Deduction provisions. Assessments for failure to satisfactorily perform work as required by this contract shall be made by withholding such payment as would ordinarily be paid under the terms of the contract for proper performance of the item in question. The amount of the assessment will be determined by applying the unit time for the item in question to the standard hourly rate paid by the Contractor in performance of this contract. The unit time shall be man-hour value as determined by Agency regulations and Government inspector's reports. In addition, assessment shall be made for additional cost of Government inspection when items reported as complete by the Contractor are not ready for inspection. All deductions assessed hereunder will be subtracted monthly from the total amount due under the contract.

Clarkie's bid for subject contract was approximately $45,000 lower than the next low bid received and some $113,000 lower than the Government's estimate for the contract work. In view of this price differential, Clarkie's was requested to verify the accuracy of its low bid and did so.

In performing the contract, Clarkie's realized it had seriously underbid the work requirement and requested that the price of the contract be increased to $272,815. The Government refused to increase the contract price but agreed not to exercise its option to extend the contract for a second year.

Clarkie's performance of subject contract was characterized as poor by the Government's Chief Inspector. The Government's inspectors issued approximately 1850 daily deficiency reports with multiple items of deficient work items listed thereon during the contract performance period. These reports were the basis for the deductions assessed for unsatisfactory performance as authorized by special provision 5.6 of the contract. These reports were either handed to Clarkie's on site supervisor or placed in his assigned office space. Clarkie's admits that a deficiency correction crew was not always on hand to receive the daily deficiency report as required by special provision 5.5

The daily deficiency reports and the deductions taken from the contract payments based thereon were summarized in monthly letters addressed to the Clarkie's by the contracting officer. A total of $38,069 was withheld from the contract payments based upon the Government's daily deficiency reports.

Three of the four Government inspectors assigned to inspect the Clarkie's work applied identical inspection standards in evaluating the Clarkie's performance. They either rejected the work entirely or accepted it entirely. No credit was given for that part of an area which had been satisfactorily cleaned. If any part of an area was found to be dirty, the entire area was marked as an area of non-performance. Inspector Geissler testified that he always attempted to ascribe a clean percentage to a work area but preferred to work on a 100 per cent basis. His inspection reports did not identify a great percentage of cleaning credit to Clarkie's work and he operated on the principle that if dirt was found in a room he considered the entire room to be an area of non-performance. Inspector Brittingham testified that he gave no percentage of cleaning credit to an assigned area. In his opinion it was either all clean or all dirty. Chief Inspector Wayne testified that he also gave no credit for percentages of clean.

The method of Government inspection is the cause of Clarkie's complaint. Clarkie's seeks to recover the sum of $38,069 withheld under subject contract as assessments for failure to perform satisfactorily the work requirements of the contract.

DECISION

We think it to be indisputable that since the Government reduced the contract price it had the burden of proof with respect to establishing that the price deduction taken reasonably represented the reduced value of the Clarkie's services. We do not think this burden has been sustained.

The proper inspection procedure, according to the contracting officer, required that Clarkie's be credited *pro rata* for satisfactory work performed. It is clear from the sworn testimony of the Government inspectors that, in the main, no credit was accorded the Clarkie's for a partial performance of satisfactory work. In the opinion of the contracting officer this was an improper inspection and an unfair 'gigging' of the Clarkie's. The Government's belated recognition of *pro rata* inspection with respect to restroom areas is a tacit recognition of improper inspection previously performed. The record does not inform us as to why the recognition was limited to restrooms.

The 'all or none' inspection procedure employed by the Government was improper under the circumstances and an unfair and unreasonable payment penalty to impose on the Clarkie's.

The failure of the Government to credit the Clarkie's with the percentage of custodial services properly performed militates against a finding that the price deductions taken were reasonable. This is true even as to the twenty-two deficiency reports indicating that deficient work was not corrected, since there is no indication that the Government ever gave credit for partial performance. In the absence of such a showing, the Government may not retain the contract payment deductions taken.

Accordingly, this appeal is sustained.

SOW & QSP From Bureau of Land Mgmt Solicitation: L11PS00465 Requisition Number 0040005409 BLM WY-Rawlins Field Ofc (WYD03) Rawlins WY 82301

These readings can be found in NCMA's online Research Articles Database. To access the database, you must be an NCMA member. If you are not an NCMA member, you may be able to obtain equivalent readings by inserting relevant keywords into your web browser's search engine.

From NCMA's *Contract Management* magazine

Borchardt, John K., *Contracts and the Gulf of Mexico Oil Spill*, September 2010.
The massive well blowout in the Gulf of Mexico has resulted in extensive efforts to prevent further environmental damage and repair the damage already done. All these efforts have resulted in hundreds of contracts being written.

Dobriansky, John, *Major Systems Acquisitions: A Paradigm for Success*, July 2010.
A review of major systems acquisitions, outlining their scope, illustrating common risk areas with high-profile examples, and presenting a framework of critical success factors.

Dobriansky, John, *Major Systems Acquisitions: Managing for Success*, October 2010.
A framework of contracting strategy, requirements, program management, and funding needs that are critical to success in the management of major systems acquisitions.

Felber, Bryan, *Contractor Purchasing System Reviews—A Tale of Two Companies*, August 2011.
Passing a CPSR is necessary to avoid the potentially significant adverse impacts felt by Company A and Company B in this article.

Frye, Jan, *The New Class: A Holistic Approach to Training VA Acquisition Interns*, August 2011.
The Department of Veterans Affairs Acquisition Academy is pioneering a new approach to training the next generation of trusted business advisors.

Garrett, Gregory A., *U.S. Government Services Contracting, Part 1: Buying and Selling Lifecycle*, April 2011.
A structured approach to understand how professional services are acquired by, sold to, and delivered/performed for the U.S. government.

Garrett, Gregory A. and Thomas Reid, *U.S. Government Services Contracting, Part 2: Requirements Determination*, May 2011.
A discussion of the nature of government services contracting requirements determination.

Jacobs, Daniel M., *Contract Management in the War Zone--Mission-Focused and Succeeding*, September 2010.
There's a new and dynamic team on today's battlefield--the warfighter, the civil servant, and the contractor.

Jain, Rajeshwar L. and Prodosh K. Mitra, *Engineering, Procurement, and Construction Contracting in the Kuwait Oil and Gas Industry: Constraints and Improvement Efforts*, April 2011.
Valuable information on the prevalent contracting practices of the oil and gas industry in Kuwait, a sector expected to invest hugely in projects in the coming years.

Knauer, Robert, and Steve Sorett, *The Transitional Benefits Corporation Process*, February 2011.
A new model for state and local governments with reduced tax revenue.

Lassekert, Kristine and C. Bradford Jorgensen, *Software Maintenance Payments: Don't Let Them Come Back to Bite You*, December 2010.
As contracting officials face increasingly complex questions regarding how the U.S. government may pay for software maintenance, contracting professionals may look to the GSA Schedules as a guide.

Livingstone, Stan, *A New Approach to Performance-Based Acquisition: Three Phases to Success*, May 2010.
Several factors that can influence a PBA's outcome will help agencies move in the right direction in implementing PBA.

Miller, John "Johnny" E., *115 Issues In Commercial Services Agreements for the Service Provider*, June 2011.
A hand checklist for use as a contractual risk prevention tool for commercial services agreements.

Muench, Marilyn L., *Are You Headed for a Merger with a Foreign Company? A National Security Review May Be in Your Future*, May 2010.
An analysis of the process by which the Committee on Foreign Investment in the United States reviews proposed transactions involving the foreign acquisition of U.S. contractors.

Pennington, Richard, *The Anatomy of Change: Georgia's State Procurement Transformation*, April 2011.
The State of Georgia underwent a procurement transformation from 2004 through 2010, and this article highlights key elements of managed change in this major procurement transformation initiative.

Prentice, Rowena, *Performance-Based Acquisition: Acquiring the Right Outcomes*, July 2010.

Many agencies believe that contracts must be firm-fixed-price and performance-based and nothing else. However, one size most certainly does not fit all.

Post, Robert H., *Don't be Caught Short in Meeting Evolving Security Requirements*, July 2011.
An examination of the legal and regulatory frameworks driving new security requirements for unclassified systems, how these requirements are being implemented by federal clients, and how to successfully meet these provisions.

Rector, Richard P., and C. Bradford Jorgensen, *New DOD Rule Authorizes Withholding of Payments for Deficiencies in Business Systems*, August 2011.
A summary of the key provisions of the new rule with practical insight to help contractors identify and avoid the competitive and cash-flow risks presented by the rule.

Sica, Albert L., *Supply Chain Risk: Hidden Exposures for your Company*, June 2011.
How to develop a formal process to identify risks at each level of your supply chain, their likelihood to occur, the harm each would present, and how to identify strategies to deal with them.

Vincent, Lenn, "Moore" *Money: How the Department of Homeland Security Captures Big Savings from Falling IT Prices*, July 2010.
Defense Acquisition University Industry Chair Lenn Vincent examines the steps taken by Soraya Correa at the Department of Homeland Security Office of Procurement Operations to ensure ongoing best value on IT purchases.

Waeber, Kim, *Get Caught In Web 2.0*, April 2011.
Most companies, to some degree, struggle with information sharing. Web 2.0

tools help facilitate information sharing and are inexpensive and effective ways for employees to communicate, regardless of location.

From NCMA's *Journal of Contract Management*

Apte, Aruna, Uday M. Apte, and Rene G. Rendon, *Contracting for Services in the U.S. Army: An Empirical Study of Current Management Practices*, September 2010, Volume 8, Issue 1.
An analysis of the implications of different deficiencies of services acquisitions in the U.S. Army, as well as the effectiveness of current contract management processes and recommendations for improvement.

Grant, Mark, *Performance-Based Service Acquisition: Cornerstone of Government Contract Reform or Stepping Stone to More Refined Methods of Procurement and Contract Management?*, September 2010, Volume 8, Issue 1.
PBSA could be improved by revising it into two levels: 1) transactional and 2) transformational (specification versus objective-oriented).

Wyatt III, John B., *Has Torncello's Change of Circumstances Rule Been Reinvigorated?*, September 2010, Volume 8, Issue 1.
Although severely limited in application by federal courts, Torncello's "change of circumstances" rule has been enthusiastically adopted by various state courts to limit governmental termination for convenience power.

Competency

5.0:

Business

The duties and responsibilities of a contracting professional extend well beyond the specialized set of knowledge and experience unique to the profession. Current business and government organizational models are rapidly and continuously changing in pursuit of increased efficiency and decreased cost. Given the current environment of rightsizing, outsourcing, lean management, six sigma, continuous process improvement, balanced scorecards, transformation, and reinvention—just to name a few—it's easy to see that the people who work in this environment have to change as well.

Contracting professionals, as well as other professionals in business and government, can no longer perform effectively in the neatly insulated isolation of specialized knowledge and experience. Most organizations rely, to greater or lesser degrees, on various forms of matrix-managed functions, project or program teams, permanent or temporary process improvement groups, and similar types of collaborative entities. These structures exist primarily to bring more attention to the idea that each segment of an organization, whether public or private, needs to make a positive contribution to the business's objectives or the agency's mission.

The team approach to operating a business and government often results in a smaller and necessarily more proficient and agile staff. The knowledge required to be an effective contracting professional today extends beyond the complex and dynamic contracting environment. A contracting professional must also (and some would argue first) be a business professional. One must have a clear understanding of the business's and government's general functions and how those functions combine with and complement each other to achieve organizational goals.

The following descriptions discuss some of the key general business competencies that contracting professionals might reasonably be expected to possess. While no one person will be an expert in all of these areas, a seasoned contracting professional should at least have a basic understanding of each business competency.

5.1 Management

The ability to manage is essential for successful contract management because it determines the contract's success or failure. Management consists of the processes used to accomplish a contract organization's goals. The size of an organization and the complexity of its business normally dictates the size of the contract management staff. A small business may have only one person in charge of all contract organization management activities. A large corporation or government agency may have hundreds, or even thousands of managers, with each being responsible for some segment of the organization's contracting activities. Regardless of the entity's size and business purpose, and at all levels within the contract management organization team, the four key functions of management noted here are essential.

The basic and commonly accepted functions of contract management include planning, organizing, staffing, leading/directing, and controlling/monitoring.

- **Planning**: Deciding what needs to happen in the future (the next day, week, month, year, five years, etc.) and generating plans of action.

- **Organizing**: Implementation; making optimum use of the resources required to successfully carry out plans.

- **Staffing**: Analyzing the job, then recruiting and hiring individuals for appropriate jobs.

- **Leading/Directing**: Determining what needs to be done in a situation and getting people to do it.

- **Controlling/Monitoring**: Checking progress against plans.

In addition to the five basic functions of management, there are a number of other direct and indirect skills that are most valuable in ensuring managerial effectiveness:

- **Technical skills**: Although it may seem intuitively obvious, the need for managers to be technically competent cannot be overemphasized. It is imperative that managers possess the knowledge required to perform the work they require of their subordinates. Though it is likely that a manager will be less proficient than his or her subordinates in actually performing the work on a day-to-day basis, the ability to manage well has a direct relationship to the manager's level of technical knowledge.

- **Communication skills**: The ability to effectively communicate is an essential skill for effective management. Effective communication is a two-way street and has multiple facets, including the ability to speak clearly and concisely to individuals, small groups and large groups; the ability to listen and understand others at all levels within an organization; the ability to plan, conduct, and control formal and informal meetings; and the ability to convey information in written form in a format and at the intended recipient's level.

- **Human relations skills**: Effective managers must be able to work with a wide variety of other individuals and groups, with differing social, educational, and experiential backgrounds, and with varying capabilities to ensure that goals are accomplished. These human relations skills, often more art than science, are of increasing importance as most organizations' workforces continue to become more and more diverse.

- **Time management skills**: Most managers wish they had more time. The ability to structure one's time in a hierarchical manner; to know what is important now and what can be deferred; to recognize "time wasting" activity masquerading as productive effort; to be accessible when needed and alone when required; to organize, plan, and execute how to use time; and to know when to modify the plans are all vital to a manager's ability to succeed.

- **Technology skills**: The continuing advancements in information technology and communications technology provide significant opportunities for managers to increase their effectiveness. It is important that all managers—particularly those who were educated and began their careers before such technology was widely available—become familiar with and appropriately use technological advances.

LEXICON FOR MANAGEMENT:

Balanced scorecard: A measurement-based strategic management system that provides a method of aligning business activities to the strategy and monitoring accomplishment of strategic goals over time.

Baseline: Data on the current process that provides the metrics against which to compare improvements and to use in benchmarking.

Benchmarking: The process of comparing one set of measurements of a process, product, or service to those of another organization. The objective of benchmarking is to set appropriate reliability and quality metrics for your organization based on metrics for similar processes in other organizations.

Business case: A structured proposal for business improvement that functions as a decision package for organizational decision-makers. A business case includes analyzing business process performance and associated needs or problems, proposing alternative solutions, assumptions, constraints, and conducting a risk-adjusted cost-benefit analysis.

Customer: In the private sector, those who pay or exchange value for products or services. In government, customers consist of the taxpayers, taxpayer representatives in Congress, the sponsors of the agency, the managers of an agency program, and the recipients of the agency's products and services. There may be several more categories of "customers" who should be carefully segmented for maximum strategic benefit.

Gap analysis: Gap analysis naturally flows from benchmarking or other assessments. Once the general expectation of performance is understood, comparing that with current capabilities becomes the gap analysis.

Goal: A specific, intended result of a strategy. A goal's characteristics include the starting point, the desired end point, and when the organization will reach the desired end point (i.e., from x to y by when).

Governance: The systems and processes in place for ensuring proper accountability and openness to conduct an organization's business. An organization's board of directors has ultimate responsibility for the organization's governance.

Improvement: An activity undertaken based on strategic objectives, such as reduced cycle time, reduced cost, and customer satisfaction. This includes improvements in mission activities (production, design, testing, etc.) and/or in support of activities for the mission.

Indicator: A simple metric that is intended to be easy to measure. Its intent is to obtain general information about performance trends by means of surveys, telephone interviews, and the like.

Key performance indicators (KPI): A short list of metrics that an organization's managers have identified as the most important variables reflecting operational or organizational performance.

Knowledge management (KM): A process in which an organization consciously and comprehensively gathers, organizes, shares, and analyzes its knowledge in terms of resources, documents, and people skills. KM efforts typically focus on organizational objectives such as improved performance, competitive advantage, innovation, the sharing of lessons learned, integration, and continuous improvement of the organization. KM efforts overlap with organizational learning, and may be distinguished from that by a greater focus on the management of knowledge as a strategic asset and a focus on encouraging the sharing of knowledge.

Measurement: An observation that reduces the amount of uncertainty about the value of a quantity. In the balanced scorecard, measurements are collected for feedback. The measurement system gathers information about all the significant activities of a company. Measurements are the data resulting from the measurement effort. Measurement also implies a methodology, analysis, and other activities involved with *how* particular measurements are collected and managed. There may be many ways of measuring the same thing.

Metrics: Often used interchangeably with measurements. However, it may be helpful to separate these definitions. Metrics are the various parameters or ways of looking at a process that is to be measured. Metrics define *what* is to be measured. Some metrics are specialized, so they can't be directly benchmarked or interpreted outside a mission-specific business unit. Other metrics will be generic, and they can be aggregated across business units, (e.g. cycle time, customer satisfaction, and financial results).

Mission activities: Things that an agency does for its customers. For private companies, profit or value creation is an overarching mission. For nonprofit organizations, the mission itself takes priority, although cost reduction is still usually a high-priority activity.

Mission effectiveness: Degree to which mission activities achieve mission outcomes or results.

Mission statement: A brief description of a company's fundamental purpose. A mission statement answers the question, "Why do we exist?" The mission statement articulates the company's purpose both for those in the organization and for the public.

Objective: An aim or intended result of a strategy.

Organization: The command, control, and feedback relationships among a group of people and information systems. Examples: a private company or government agency.

Performance goal: A target level of performance expressed as a tangible, measurable objective against which actual achievement can be compared, including a goal expressed as a quantitative standard, value, or rate.

Performance indicator: A particular value or characteristic used to measure output or outcome.

Performance measurement: The process of developing measurable indicators that can be systematically tracked to assess progress made in achieving predetermined goals and using such indicators to assess progress in achieving these goals.

Plan: A prescribed, written sequence of actions to achieve a goal, usually ordered in phases or steps with a schedule and measureable targets; defines who is responsible for achievement, who will do the work, and links to other related plans and goals.

Primary customer: The customer group that must be satisfied if the overall mission of the organization is to succeed. Generally, this is the end user or direct recipient of an organization's products or services, and has the capabilities to report satisfaction and give feedback. In a commercial organization, it is the group that is the main source of income.

Profit: Financial gain or revenues minus expenses. Profit is the overarching mission of private-sector companies. Nonprofit or governmental organizations either operate at a loss or attempt to achieve a zero profit; for them, the overarching mission is a charter for a service, or a goal to be achieved. Therefore, there is a basic distinction in measures of strategic success between profit and non-profit or governmental organizations.

Project management: A set of well-defined methods and techniques for managing a team of people to accomplish a series of work tasks within a well-defined schedule and budget. The techniques may include work breakdown structure, workflow, earned value management (EVM), total quality management (TQM), statistical process control (SPC), quality function deployment (QFD), design of experiments, concurrent engineering, Six Sigma etc. Tools include flowcharts, PERT charts, GANTT charts (e.g., Microsoft Project), control charts, cause-and-effect (tree or wishbone) diagrams, Pareto diagrams, etc. (The balanced scorecard is a strategic management, *not* a project management technique.)

Return on investment (ROI): In the private sector, the annual financial benefit after an investment minus the cost of the investment. In the public sector, cost reduction or cost avoidance obtained after an improvement in processes or systems, minus the cost of the improvement.

Risk analysis: A technique to identify and assess factors that may jeopardize the success of a project or achieving a goal. This technique also helps define preventive measures to reduce the probability of these factors from occurring and identify countermeasures to successfully deal with these constraints when they develop.

Stakeholder: An individual or group with an interest in the success of an organization in delivering intended results and maintaining the viability of the organization's products and services. Stakeholders influence programs, products, and services. Examples include congressional members and staff of relevant appropriations, authorizing, and oversight committees; representatives of central management and oversight entities, such as OMB and GAO; and representatives of key interest groups, including those groups that represent the organization's customers and interested members of the public.

Strategic plan: A document used by an organization to align its organization and budget structure with organizational priorities, missions, and objectives.

Strategy: (1) Hypotheses or educated guesses that propose the direction an organization should go to fulfill its vision and maximize the possibility of its future success. (2) Unique and sustainable ways by which organizations create value. It answers the question, "Are we doing the right things?"

Sunk cost: A cost incurred in the past that will not be affected by any present or future decision. Sunk costs should be ignored in determining whether a new investment is worthwhile.

SWOT analysis: An assessment tool for identifying the overall strategic situation in an organization by listing its Strengths, Weaknesses, (external) Opportunities, and Threats. Sometimes the word "challenges" is substituted for "threats."

Target: The numerical value of a performance metric that is to be achieved by a given date. Both the metric and the schedule need to be specified for targets. A stretch target is the same thing, but its numerical value is higher, demanding breakthrough performance to achieve.

Threshold: A specified numerical value of a performance metric. Thresholds are often used to indicate changes from red to yellow to green (or other colors) in displays of performance data.

Unit: (1) A functional or business component of an agency, generally with a specified mission or support activity. (2) A standard basis for quantitative measurements.

Unit cost: A financial metric in which cost is based on the unit of delivery or consumption of a product or service, such as number of requests processed per day.

Vision statement: Sometimes called a picture of the organization in the future. The vision statement is the organization's inspiration, the framework for all of its strategic planning. A vision statement may apply to an entire organization or to a single division. Whether for all or part of an organization, the vision statement answers the question, "Where do we want to go?"

5.2 Marketing

The business process that develops, prices, places, and promotes goods, ideas, or services to enhance exchanges between buyers and sellers. The process of planning and executing the conception, pricing, promotion, and distribution of ideas, goods, and services to create exchanges that satisfy individual and organizational goals.

The contracting professional may interact with marketing professionals during the acquisition planning and pre-award phases of the contract life cycle. Marketing professionals are identifying business opportunities during these phases. It is important for the contracting professional to give equal treatment to each vendor during these acquisition planning and pre-award phases to ensure the integrity of the procurement process.

LEXICON FOR MARKETING:

Acculturation: The process by which people in one culture or subculture learn to understand and adapt to the norms, values, life styles, and behaviors of people in another culture or subcultures.

Acquisition value: The users' perception of the relative worth of a product or service to them. Formally defined as the subjectively weighted difference between the most a buyer would be willing to pay for the product or service, less the actual price of the item.

Adopter categories: People or agencies who adopt an innovation are often classified into five groups according to the sequence of their adoption of it.

1. Innovators (first 2–5%),

2. Early adopters (10–15%),

3. Early majority (next 35%),

4. Late majority (next 35%), and

5. Laggards (final 5–10%).

This is important when considering how long it may take for the general public to "adopt" a product or service.

Advertising: Placing and purchasing announcements and persuasive messages in time or space in various mass media outlets by business firms or nonprofit organizations.

Aggregation: A concept of market segmentation that assumes that most consumers are alike.

Aging: The length of time merchandise has been in stock.

Attitudes: Enduring systems of positive or negative evaluations, emotional feelings, and action tendencies with respect to an object. The consumers' overall liking or preference for an object.

Audience: The number and/or characteristics of the persons or households who are exposed to a particular type of advertising media or media vehicle.

Balanced stock: The composition of merchandise inventory in the colors, sizes, styles, and other assortment characteristics that will satisfy user wants.

Body language: The nonverbal signals communicated in interactions through facial expressions, arms, legs, and hands—or nonverbal communication. This can be positive (a smile) or negative (a frown.)

Brand: A name, term, design, symbol, or any other feature that identifies one seller's good or service as distinct from those of other sellers. The legal term for brand is "trademark." A brand may identify one item, a family of items, or all items of that seller. If used for the firm as a whole, the preferred term is "trade name." "Library" could be considered a trade name.

Channel of distribution: An organized network of agencies and institutions that in combination perform all the functions required to link producers with end customers to accomplish the marketing task.

Competition: The rivalry among sellers trying to achieve such goals as increasing profits, market share, and sales volume by varying the elements of the marketing mix: price, product, distribution, and promotion.

Consumer: The ultimate user of goods, ideas, or services. Also, the buyer or decision maker.

Consumer behavior: The behavior of the consumer or decision maker in the marketplace of products and services.

Consumer satisfaction: The degree to which a consumer's expectations are fulfilled or surpassed by a product.

Convenience product: A consumer good and/or service (such as soap, candy bar, and shoe shine) that is bought frequently, often on impulse, with little time effort spent on the buying process. A convenience product is usually low-priced and widely available.

Customer: The actual or prospective purchaser of products or services.

Demand: The number of units of a product sold in a market over a period of time. For example, 6,000 library books were circulated in Branch X's market area last year.

De-marketing: The process of reducing the demand for a product or decreasing consumption.

Demographics: Objective characteristics of consumers such as age, income, education, sex, or occupation.

Direct marketing: Marketing efforts directed toward a specific, targeted group (including direct selling, direct mail, catalog, or cable) for eliciting a response from a customer.

Distribution: The marketing and carrying of products to customers.

Growth stage of product life cycle: Second stage during which sales/use are increasing.

Market: The set of actual of potential users/customers.

Market demand: The total volume of a product or service bought/used by a specific group of customers/users in a specified market area during a specified period.

Market development: Expanding the total market served by entering new segments, converting nonusers, and increasing use by present users.

Market positioning: Positioning refers to the user's perceptions of the place that a product or brand occupies in a market segment.

Market segmentation: The process of subdividing a market into distinct subsets of users that behave in the same way or have similar needs.

Market share: A proportion of the total sales/use in a market obtained by a given facility or chain.

Marketing channel: A set of institutions necessary to transfer the title to goods and to move goods from the point of consumption.

Marketing mix: The mix of controllable variables that the firm/library uses to reach desired use/sales level in target market, including price, product, place, and promotion (the 4 Ps).

Maturity stage of product life cycle: Initial rapid growth is over and use/sales level off.

Microenvironment: The set of forces close to an organization that have direct impact on its ability to serve its customers, including channel member organizations, competitors, user markets, publics, and the capabilities of the organization.

Motivation: The positive or negative needs, goals, desires, and forces that impel an individual toward or away from certain actions, activities, objects, or conditions. The inner needs and wants of an individual—what affects behavior.

Norms: The rules of behavior that are part of the ideology of the group. Norms tend to reflect the values of the group and specify those actions that are proper and those that are inappropriate, as well as rewards for adherence and punishment for conformity.

Penetrated market: Actual set of users actually consuming the product/service.

Perception: Perception is the cognitive impression that is formed of "reality," which in turn influences the individual's actions and behavior toward that object.

Potential market: Set of users who profess some level of interest in a designed market offer.

Price: The formal ratio that indicates the quantities of money goods or services needed to acquire a given quantity of goods or services.

Product: A bundle of attributes, features, functions, benefits, and uses capable of exchange, usually in tangible or intangible forms.

Product life cycle: The four stages products go through from birth to death: introduction, growth, maturity, and decline.

Public relations: The relationship that exists between an organization and its several publics; efforts to influence this relationship by obtaining favorable publicity.

Publicity: Corporate or product promotion that is obtained free of charge.

Publics: The various groups in a society that can influence or bring pressure to bear upon a firm's decision making and have an impact on its marketing performance; these groups include the financial public, media public, government public, citizen action public, local public, general public, and international public.

Puffing: The legitimate practice of making obviously exaggerated claims in advertising (e.g., "cleaner than clean.")

Pull strategy: Promotion to end-users (mainly by means of advertising, sales promotion, and publicity) rather than to members of the marketing channel (mainly by personal selling) to facilitate the flow of a good or service from producer to final consumer. (See "push strategy," "push-pull strategy.")

Pulsing: Scheduling advertising campaigns in fairly regular bursts followed by periods of relative or complete inactivity.

Puppy dog close: A closing technique in which a salesperson urges an indecisive prospect to "take it home, play with it overnight," believing that once the product is in the customer's keeping, he or she will be unwilling to part with it.

Purchase probability scale: A tool used in marketing research surveys of buying intentions. Respondents are asked to rate the likelihood of their purchase of a particular product on a scale ranging, for example, from "definitely not" to "certain to buy."

Pure competition: A marketing situation in which there are a large number of sellers of a product that cannot be differentiated and, thus, no one firm has a significant influence on price. Other prevailing conditions are ease of entry of new firms into the market and perfect market information. Also referred to as "perfect competition."

Pure monopoly: A marketing situation in which there is only one seller of a product.

Push strategy: Promotion to members of the marketing channel (mainly by means of personal selling) rather than promotion to end-users (mainly by means of advertising, sales promotion, and publicity) to facilitate the flow of a good or service from producer to final consumer. (See "pull strategy," "push-pull strategy.")

Push-pull strategy: Promotion of a good or service both to end-users and members of the marketing channel to facilitate its flow from producer to final consumer. (See "pull strategy," "push strategy.")

Sale: The exchange of goods or services for an amount of money or its equivalent; the act of selling.

Sale advertising: Advertising, common in retailing, which announces the sale of products at temporarily or permanently reduced prices.

Sale of goods acts: Legislation in various states aimed at safeguarding consumers by ensuring that goods offered for sale are of reasonable quality and fit for their intended purpose.

Sales: Activities involved in selling goods or services; also, gross receipts.

Sales administration-to-sales ratio: A marketing control measure used to determine whether the amount spent on sales administration in a given period was excessive; total expenditure on sales administration is expressed as a percentage of total sales revenue for the same period.

Sales analysis: The breakdown of sales figures by region, product, customer, market, etc., for a given period as a control measure.

Sales branch: A manufacturer's office established simply to facilitate sales; no manufacturing is done at this location.

Sales calls: The visits salespeople make to a buyer's premises in order to sell their companies' products.

Sales contests: Sales promotions aimed at members of a company's sales force. Sales contests are competitions designed to boost sales and lift performance by offering awards or prizes to top-achievers in a sales team in a given period.

Sales effect of advertising: The effectiveness of an advertisement or advertising campaign in boosting sales of a product; generally hard to measure as sales may be influenced by factors other than advertising, such as the product's price, its other features, its availability, and the actions of competitors.

Sales effect research: Marketing research to assess the effect an advertisement or some other promotional activity is having or has had on sales of the product being advertised.

Sales force composite: A method of forecasting future demand for a product by adding together what each member of the sales force expects to be able to sell in his or her territory.

Sales forecast: An estimation of the likely volume of sales, measured in dollars and units, for a future planning period. Typically, sales forecasting is done on the basis of past trends, sales force estimations, survey of consumer buying intentions, managerial judgment, or quantitative models.

Sales leads: Telephone inquiries, letters, responses to advertising, or direct mail, etc., that direct a salesperson to a prospective customer.

Sales management: The process of planning, organizing, controlling, and evaluating the activities of the sales force.

Sales planning: The assessment of the current situation in a sales region, the setting of objectives, the formulation of strategies and tactics, and the establishment of control and evaluation procedures.

Sales potential: An organization's expected sales of a product in a given market for a specified period; the share of the total market that a firm can reasonably expect to attain in a given time.

Sales promotion: A form of promotion that encourages customers to buy products by offering incentives, such as contests, coupons, sweepstakes, samples, free gifts, and so on; one of the four major elements (with advertising, personal selling, and publicity) of the promotion mix.

Sales promotion-to-sales ratio: A marketing control measure used to determine whether the amount spent on sales promotion was excessive. Total expenditure on sales promotion in a given period is expressed as a percentage of total sales revenue for the same period.

Sales quota: A sales assignment, goal, or target set for a salesperson in a given accounting period; commonly used types of sales quotas are dollar volume quotas, unit volume quotas, gross margin quotas, net profit quotas, and activity quotas.

Sales report: A salesperson's detailed record of sales calls and results for a given period. Typically, a sales report will include information such as the sales volume per product or product line, the number of existing and new accounts called upon, and the expenses incurred in making the calls.

Sales representative: A salesperson; an individual employed to sell goods on behalf of a producer or some other member of a marketing channel by contacting prospective customers and developing in them an interest in the company's products.

Sales resistance: Anything the prospective buyer says or does to prevent or delay the salesperson from closing the sale.

Sales tactics: The planned day-to-day activities of the sales team when implementing the strategies it hopes will achieve its objectives.

Sales tasks: The job activities carried out by salespeople. These may include direct selling tasks (e.g., making product presentations to prospective buyers); indirect selling tasks (e.g., mailing sales literature to new and prospective accounts); and non-selling tasks (e.g., attending sales meetings, writing call reports).

Sales territory: The specific region or group of customers for which a salesperson has direct responsibility.

Sales territory performance modeling: A method of evaluating sales territory performance using a model depicting the environmental factors that may have had an impact on the territory and on the salesperson assigned to it. The model assists a sales supervisor to better understand the quality of the performance.

Sales volume: The total revenue produced or the total number of units of a product sold in a given period.

Sales volume analysis: A detailed study of an organization's sales, in terms of units or revenue, for a specified period; the analysis of sales volume (by sales region or territory, industry, customer type) is commonly used as an aid in determining the effectiveness of the selling effort.

Sales wave experiment: A technique used to test consumer reaction to new products prior to full-scale commercialization. New products are placed in consumer homes to determine the reaction to them, and the rate at which the products are repurchased is tracked.

Sales-response function: A measure of the likely level of sales in a given period at different levels of expenditure on any of the major marketing mix variables.

Target market: The particular segment of a total population on which the retailer focuses its merchandising expertise to satisfy that submarket in order to accomplish its profit objectives.

Wants: People's wishes, needs, cravings, demands, or desires.

Word-of-mouth (WOM) communication: This occurs when people share information about products or promotions with friends. Research indicates that WOM is more likely to be negative than positive.

5.3 Operations Management

Operations Management is a subset of management activity that is primarily concerned with actions related to the directing and controlling functions of management. Operations management is attuned to ensuring that

- The function has the correct quantity of necessary inputs, such as materials or labor, required to perform the desired tasks;

- The transformation process, the way or system in which inputs are changed into something of desired value (e.g., an accounting report), is valid and efficient;

- Outputs are what were in fact initially desired and that they conform to the quality and quantity originally planned for; and

- Appropriate feedback occurs, whether it is:

   o Informational feedback, a two-way exchange between management and workers to seek clarification, discuss improvements, and share status;

∘ Corrective feedback, an exchange from the manager to workers to point out mistakes and redirect effort toward improvement; or

∘ Reinforcing feedback, an exchange from the manager that includes praise for a job well done or for exceeding standards, to promote continued improvements.

LEXICON FOR OPERATIONS MANAGEMENT:

Business process improvement: A methodology for focused change in a business process achieved by analyzing the "as-is" process using flowcharts and other tools, then developing a streamlined "to be" process in which automation may be added to result in a process that is better, faster, and cheaper. BPI aims at cost reductions of 10–40 percent with moderate risk.

Contingency planning: Developing plans to provide alternative plans to the main plan. This is proactive management that deals with events considered unlikely to occur.

Core competency: A distinctive area of expertise of an organization that is critical to its long-term success. These are built up over time and cannot be imitated easily.

Core product: The central benefit or purpose for which a consumer buys a product or service. The core product varies from purchaser to purchaser.

Cost-benefit analysis: A technique used to compare the various costs associated with an investment with the benefits that it proposes to return. Both tangible and intangible factors should be addressed and accounted for.

Design: Turning a concept or idea into a configuration, drawing, model, mould, pattern, plan, or specification (on which the actual or commercial production of an item is based) and that helps achieve the item's designated objective.

Effectiveness: Degree to which an activity or initiative is successful in achieving a specified goal; degree to which activities of a unit achieve the unit's mission or goal.

Efficiency: (1) Degree of capability or productivity of a process, such as the number of contracts awarded or contracts won per year; (2) tasks accomplished per unit cost.

Feedback: Information obtained from the results of a process that is used in guiding the way that process is done. There should be feedback loops around all important activities. Strategic feedback (for each strategic activity) validates effectiveness of the strategy by measuring outcomes (long-term). Diagnostic feedback tracks efficiency of internal business processes (usually generic across all mission activities). Metrics feedback allows for refining the selection of metrics to be measured. Measurement feedback allows for the improvement of measurement techniques and frequency.

Input: Resources (funds, labor, time, equipment, space, technology) used to produce outputs and outcomes.

Logistics: Inventory management, transportation and traffic, and distribution supporting the product/service mission of the organization.

Mission value: (1) Mission outcome benefits per unit cost; a key metric for nonprofit and governmental organizations. (2) For a collection of missions within an organization, the relative value contributed by each mission. (3) The combination of strategic significance and results produced by a mission.

Non-value-added work: Work activities that add no value to the mission of the organization. Such activities may or may not be necessary; necessary ones may include utilities, supplies, travel, and maintenance; unnecessary ones may include searching for information, duplicating work, rework, time not working, etc.

Outcome: A description of the intended result, effect, or consequence that will occur from carrying out a program or activity. The end result that is sought. (For example, in the private sector, financial profitability; in the public sector, cleaner air or reduced incidence of disease)

Outcome measure: A long-term, ultimate measure of success or strategic effectiveness. An event, occurrence, or condition that is outside the activity or program itself and is of direct importance to customers or the public.

Output: Products and services delivered. Outputs are the immediate products of internal activity: the amount of work done within the organization or by its contractors (such as miles of road repaired or number of calls answered).

Procurement: Acquiring the goods and services supporting the missions of the organization, including developing and maintaining relationships with suppliers and internal customers.

Production/R&D/services: Operational strategies, system design, capacity planning, scheduling, and quality.

Value: The power of any good to command other goods in peaceful and voluntary exchange.

Value-added: Those activities or steps that add to or change a product or service as it goes through a process; these are the activities or steps that customers view as important and necessary.

Value chain: The sequential set of primary and support activities that an enterprise performs to turn inputs into value-added outputs for its external customers.

Value proposition: The unique added value an organization offers customers through their operations.

5.4 Financial Analysis

Financial analysis is an aspect of the overall business finance function that involves examining historical data to gain information about the current and future financial health of a company. Financial analysis can be applied in a wide variety of situations to give business managers the information they need to make critical decisions. Business goals and objectives are set in financial terms and their outcomes are measured in financial terms. Finance involves analyzing the data contained in financial statements to provide valuable information for management decisions.

LEXICON FOR FINANCIAL ANALYSIS:

Break-even analysis: A means of determining the number of goods or services that must be sold at a given price to generate sufficient revenue to cover costs.

Capital budgeting: Planning and financing long-term investment proposals, taking into account the time value of money.

Cash budgeting: A schedule of expected cash receipts and disbursements for a designated period. The primary reason for a cash budget is to forecast a company's future financing needs. A cash budget is also used to avoid either unnecessary idle cash or possible cash shortages. In case of cash shortage, it indicates whether the shortage is temporary or permanent (i.e., whether short-term or long-term borrowing is needed).

169

Corporate: Concepts and techniques of asset financing, capital investment, taxes, investor relations, risk and return, cost of capital, and cash management.

Cost as an independent variable (CAIV): An acquisition strategy focusing on cost-performance trade-offs in setting program goals. The goal of trade-offs is to achieve an affordable balance among cost, performance, and schedule. CAIV engages the end user, the developer, and the supporter to facilitate meaningful trade-offs.

Earned value: A management technique that relates resource planning to schedules and to technical cost and schedule requirements. All work is planned, budgeted, and scheduled in time-phase "planned value" increments constituting a cost and schedule measurement baseline. There are two major objectives of an earned-value system: (1) to encourage contractors to use the effective internal cost and schedule management control systems, and (2) to enable the customer to rely on timely data produced by those systems for determining product-oriented contract status.

Export financing: Financing international transactions in the exporting or importing of products and services. Addresses factors such as transit times, customs regulations, banking rules and regulations, buyer and seller credit, exchange rates, and political risk.

Finance: Corporate or business financial analysis relates to the methodology employed to allocate financial resources with a financial value that optimizes their benefits to the organization or agency. Contracting professionals need to have a basic understanding of how finance interacts with the other business competencies in their organization.

Financial reporting: Includes financial statements, sales forecasting, planning, and control.

Forecasting: An estimate of financial position, results of operations, and changes in cash flows for one or more future periods based on a set of assumptions representing the most probable outcomes. If the assumptions are not necessarily the most likely outcomes, the estimate is called a "projection."

General and administrative (G&A): A subcategory of overhead; includes costs necessary for overall management and operations but not directly associated with a specific cost objective or business segment. Typical G&A costs include sales staff salaries, insurance, executive compensation, and central office expenses.

Lease: A rental agreement in which the lessor conveys to the lessee the right to use the lessor's personal or real property, usually in exchange for a payment of money.

Overhead: Indirect costs other than those related to general and administrative expense and selling expenses; a general term often used to identify an indirect cost.

Revenue recognition: The process of formally recording or incorporating a revenue item in the accounts and financial statements of an organization. The revenue recognition principle provides that revenue is recognized when (1) it is realized or realizable and (2) it is earned. Revenues are realized when goods and services are exchanged for cash or claims to cash (receivables). Revenues are realizable when assets received in exchange are readily convertible to known amounts of cash or claims to cash. Revenues are earned when the entity has substantially accomplished what it must do to be entitled to the benefits represented by the revenues—that is, when the earnings process is complete or virtually complete.

Working capital: The excess of current assets over current liabilities that represents a company's financial liquid resources to meet demands of the operating cycle.

A body of principles and conventions as well as an established process for capturing financial information related to an organization's resources and using that information to meet the organization's goals. Contract professionals need to consider the accounting function very early in the acquisition planning process. Understanding the pricing structure of a contract, its payment terms and conditions, as well as how overhead rates are established, are all key accounting issues that have a direct impact on successful contract performance.

LEXICON FOR ACCOUNTING:

Accounting equation: Assets = liabilities + owner's equity. The accounting equation is the basis for the financial statement called the balance sheet.

Accounts payable (A/P): The bills a business owes to its suppliers.

Accounts receivable (A/R): The amounts owed to a business by its customers.

Accrual method of accounting: With the accrual method, a business records income when the sale occurs, not necessarily when the business receives payment. The business records an expense when it receives goods or services, even though it may not pay for them until later.

Adjusting entries: Special accounting entries that must be made when you close the books at the end of an accounting period. Adjusting entries are necessary to update your accounts for items that are not recorded in your daily transactions.

Aging Report: An aging report is a list of customers' accounts receivable amounts and their due dates. It alerts you to any slow-paying customers. You can also prepare an aging report for your accounts payable, which will help you manage your outstanding bills.

Allowance for bad debts: Also called reserve for bad debts, it is an estimate of uncollectable customer accounts. It is known as a contra account because it is listed with the assets, but it will have a credit balance instead of a debit balance. For balance sheet purposes, it is a reduction of accounts receivable.

Assets: Things of value held by the business. Assets are balance sheet accounts. Examples of assets include cash, accounts receivable, and furniture and fixtures.

Balance sheet: Also called a statement of financial position, it is a financial snapshot of your business at a given date in time. It lists your assets, your liabilities, and the difference between the two, which is your equity, or net worth.

Budgeting: The process of generating a quantitative plan of operations that identifies the resources needed to accomplish the organization's goals and objectives. It can include both financial and nonfinancial aspects.

Capital: Money invested in the business by the owners; also called equity.

Cash method of accounting: If a business uses the cash method, it records income only when it receives cash from its customers. The business records an expense only when it writes the check to the vendor.

Chart of accounts: The list of account titles you use to keep your accounting records.

Closing: "Closing the books" refers to procedures that take place at the end of an accounting period. Adjusting entries are made, and then the income and expense accounts are "closed." The net profit that results from the closing of the income and expense accounts is transferred to an equity account such as retained earnings.

Corporation: A legal entity that a state forms by issuing a charter. A corporation is owned by one or more stockholders.

Cost of goods sold: Cost of inventory items sold to your customers. It may consist of several cost components, such as merchandise purchase costs, freight, and manufacturing costs.

Credit memo: Writing off all or part of a customer's account balance. A credit memo would be required, for example, when a customer who bought merchandise on account returned some merchandise, or overpaid on their account.

Credits: At least one component of every accounting transaction (journal entry) is a credit. Credits increase liabilities and equity, and decrease assets.

Current assets: Assets in the form of cash or that will generally be converted to cash or used up within one year. Examples are accounts receivable and inventory.

Current liabilities: Liabilities payable within one year. Examples are accounts payable and payroll taxes payable.

Debit memo: Billing a customer again. A debit memo would be required, for example, when a customer has made a payment on their account by check, but the check bounced.

Debits: At least one component of every accounting transaction (journal entry) is a debit. Debits increase assets and decrease liabilities and equity.

Depreciation: An annual write-off of a portion of the cost of fixed assets, such as

vehicles and equipment. Depreciation is listed among the expenses on the income statement.

Double-entry accounting: In double-entry accounting, every transaction has two journal entries: a debit and a credit. Debits must always equal credits. Double-entry accounting is the basis of a true accounting system.

Drawing account: A general ledger account used by some sole proprietorships and partnerships to keep track of amounts drawn out of the business by an owner.

Equity: The net worth of your company. Also called owner's equity or capital. Equity comes from the owners' investment in the business, plus the business' accumulated net profits that have not been paid out to the owners. Equity accounts are balance sheet accounts.

Expense accounts: The accounts a business uses to keep track of the costs of doing business—where its money goes. Examples are advertising, payroll taxes, and wages. Expenses are income statement accounts.

Fixed assets: Assets that are generally not converted to cash within one year. Examples are equipment and vehicles.

Foot: To total the amounts in a column, such as a column in a journal or a ledger.

General ledger: A general ledger is the collection of all balance sheet, income, and expense accounts used to keep the accounting records of a business.

Income accounts: The accounts a business uses to keep track of its sources of income. Examples are merchandise sales, consulting revenue, and interest income.

Income statement: Also called a profit and loss statement (P&L). It lists income, expenses, and net profit (or loss). The net profit (or loss) is equal to the income minus expenses.

Inventory: Goods held for sale to customers. Inventory can be merchandise bought for resale, or it can be merchandise manufactured or processed, selling the end product to the customer.

Journal: The chronological, day-to-day transactions of a business are recorded in sales, cash receipts, and cash disbursements journals. A general journal is used to enter period end adjusting and closing entries and other special transactions not entered in the other journals. In a traditional, manual accounting system, each of these journals is a collection of multicolumn spreadsheets usually contained in a hardcover binder.

Liabilities: What a business owes creditors. Liabilities are balance sheet accounts. Examples are accounts payable, payroll taxes payable, and loans payable.

Long-term liabilities: Liabilities that are not due within one year. An example would be a mortgage payable.

Merchandise inventory: Goods held for sale to customers.

Net income: Also called profit or net profit, it is equal to income minus expenses. Net income is the bottom line of the income statement (also called the profit and loss statement).

Partnership: An unincorporated business with two or more owners.

Post: To summarize all journal entries and transfer them to the general ledger accounts. This is done at the end of an accounting period.

Prepaid expenses: Amounts a business has paid in advance to a vendor or creditor for goods or services. A prepaid expense is actually an asset because the vendor or supplier owes the business the goods or services. An example would be the unexpired portion of an annual insurance premium.

Prepaid income: Also called unearned revenue, it represents money a business has received in advance of providing a service to its customer. Prepaid income is actually a liability of the business because the business still owes the service to the customer. An example would be an advance payment to a business for some consulting services the business will be performing in the future.

Profit and loss statement (P&L): Also called an income statement , it lists a business's income, expenses, and net profit (or loss). The net profit (or loss) is equal to the income minus the expenses.

Proprietorship: An unincorporated business with only one owner.

Reserve for bad debts: Also called allowance for bad debts, it is an estimate of uncollectable customer accounts. It is known as a contra account because it is listed with the assets, but it will have a credit balance instead of a debit balance. For balance sheet purposes, it is a reduction of accounts receivable.

Retained earnings: Profits of the business that have not been paid to the owners; profits that have been "retained" in the business. Retained earnings is an "equity" account that is presented on the balance sheet and on the statement of changes in owners' equity.

Trial balance: A trial balance is prepared at the end of an accounting period by adding up all the account balances in your general ledger. The debit balances should equal the credit balances.

Unearned revenue: Also called prepaid income, it represents money a business has received in advance of providing a service to its customer. It is actually a liability of the business because the business still owes the service to the customer. An example would be an advance payment for consulting services the business will be performing in the future.

5.6 Economics

The social science that studies how a society solves the human issues of unlimited wants and limited resources. Economics makes distinctions between needs, those things that are required; and wants, those things that are desired but in excess of a need. Economics also recognizes that resources are scarce to the extent that there are never enough resources to completely satisfy all wants. The issue of scarce resources forces individuals, organizations, governments, and society-at-large to study the relationships between needs, wants, and resources; to prioritize how needs and wants might be satisfied; and to make economic trade-offs and choices to maximize the utilization of scarce resources.

LEXICON FOR ECONOMICS:

Antitrust: Government policy for dealing with monopoly. Antitrust laws aim to stop abuses of market power by big companies and sometimes aim to prevent corporate mergers and acquisitions that would create or strengthen a monopolist.

Arbitrage: Buying an asset in one market and simultaneously selling an identical asset in another market at a higher price.

Balance of payments: The total of all money coming into a country from abroad less all of the money going out of the country during the same period. This is usually broken down into the current account and the capital account.

Balanced budget: When total public-sector spending equals total government income during the same period from taxes and charges for public services.

Barrier to entry: An institutional, government, technological, or economic restriction on the entry of firms into a market or industry. The four primary barriers to entry are resource ownership, patents and copyrights, government restrictions, and start-up costs. For example, the federal government's cost accounting and auditing rules are considered a barrier.

Barter: A method of trading goods, commodities, or services directly for one another without the use of money. In a barter exchange, one good is traded directly for another.

Business cycle: The recurring expansions and contractions of the national economy (usually measured by real gross domestic product). A complete cycle typically lasts from three to five years, but could last 10 years or more. It is divided into four phases: expansion, peak, contraction, and trough.

Cartel: A formal agreement between businesses in the same industry, usually on an international scale, to get market control, raise the market price, and otherwise act like a monopoly.

Ceteris paribus: A Latin term meaning that all other factors are held unchanged. The *ceteris paribus* assumption is used to isolate the effect one economic factor has on another. Without this assumption, it would be difficult to determine cause and effect in the economy.

Competition: In general, the actions of two or more rivals in pursuit of the same objective. In the context of markets, the specific objective is either selling goods to buyers or alternatively buying goods from sellers.

Competition tends to come in two varieties— (1) competition among the few, which is a market with a small number of sellers (or buyers), such that each seller (or buyer) has some degree of market control; and (2) competition among the many, which is a market with so many buyers and sellers that none is able to influence the market price or quantity exchanged. With increased competition, firms are more likely to be efficient and prices low.

Competitive forces: Forces in the marketing environment that are based on competition among customers and competition with other firms. As the organization looks out at its business environment, competition is a critical factor.

Corporation: One of the three basic forms of business organization (the other two are proprietorship and partnership). A corporation is a business established through ownership shares (termed corporate stock). A corporation is considered a distinct legal person, that can be sued, pay taxes, etc., just like an individual person. Unlike proprietorships and partnerships, a corporate business exists separately from its owners. As such, the owners have limited liability. Owners cannot be held personally responsible for corporate debts. The owners can only lose the value of their ownership shares, but no more.

Demand: The willingness and ability to buy a range of quantities of a good at a range of prices, during a given time period. Demand is one half of the market exchange process; the other is supply. This demand side of the market draws inspiration from the unlimited wants and needs dimension of the scarcity problem. People desire the goods and services that satisfy wants and needs. This is the ultimate source of demand.

Demand curve: A graphical representation of the relationship between the demand price and quantity demanded (that is, the law of

demand), holding all *ceteris paribus* dem determinants constant.

Economic analysis: The process of investigating economic phenomena in a systematic manner. In one sense, this is the heart and soul of the economic discipline. While economists spend ample time identifying economic concepts, the end result of this discovery process is usually aimed at combining these concepts in such a way as to evaluate or analyze alternative consequences.

Economic forces: Forces in the marketing environment that include decisions made by consumers and business organizations. The economy tends to follow business cycles of prosperity, recession, depression, and recovery—all which impact decisions made by an organization. It is critical for a business to correctly assess the current and near-term trends in the business cycle. Incorrect decisions of inventory buildup, expansion, contraction, etc., can seriously impact a firm's market position and subsequent survivability.

Economies of scale: Declining long-run average cost that occurs as a firm increases all inputs and expands its scale of production. This is graphically illustrated by a negatively sloped long-run average cost curve and typically occurs for relatively small levels of production. Economies of scale are then overwhelmed by diseconomies of scale for relatively large production levels. Together, economies of scale and diseconomies of scale cause the long-run average cost curve to be U-shaped.

Economies of scope: A production process in which it is cheaper to produce two (or more) products together rather than separately. This property is also termed "joint production." For example, the production of beef also results in the production of leather, and the production of lumber also results in the production of sawdust. Economies of scope can be beneficial, that is, giving a producer multiple products to sell. But it can also be problematic when one of the joint products is undesirable, such as pollution or waste residual.

Elastic demand: Relatively small changes in demand price cause relatively larger changes in quantity demanded. Elastic demand means that changes in the quantity demanded are relatively responsive to changes in the demand price.

Elastic supply: Relatively small changes in supply price cause relatively larger changes in quantity supplied. Elastic supply means that changes in the quantity supplied are relatively responsive to changes in the supply price.

Elasticity: The relative response of one variable to changes in another variable. The phrase "relative response" is best interpreted as the percentage change. For example, the price elasticity of demand, one of the more important applications of this concept in economics, is the percentage change in quantity demanded measured against the percentage change in price.

Equilibrium: The state that exists when opposing forces exactly offset each other and there is no inherent tendency for change. Once achieved, an equilibrium persists unless or until it is disrupted by an outside force.

Excess capacity: A condition that exists when monopolistic competition achieves long-run equilibrium such that production by each firm is less than minimum efficient scale. The implication of this condition is that each firm is not producing up to its fullest capacity, as would be the case under perfect competition, and thus more firms are need to produce total market output compared to perfect competition. Excess capacity results because market control means a monopolistically

competitive firm faces a negatively sloped demand curve. Long-run equilibrium is thus achieved by the tangency of the negatively sloped demand curve and the long-run average cost curve, which results in economies to scale.

Free enterprise: A term often used, erroneously, in reference to capitalism. In principle, free enterprise is an economy in which businesses and consumers are "free" to engage their resources in any desired production, consumption, or exchange without government restriction, regulation, or control.

Homogeneous goods: Goods that are either physically identical or at least viewed as identical by buyers. In particular, the producer of a good cannot be identified from the good itself. This is a key assumption underlying the perfect competition market structure. Examples include agricultural products, metals, and energy goods.

Imperfect competition: Any markets or industries that do not match the criteria for perfect competition. The key characteristics of perfect competition are (1) a large number of small firms, (2) identical products sold by all firms, (3) freedom of entry into and exit out of the industry, and (4) perfect knowledge of prices and technology. These four characteristics are essentially impossible to match.

Inelastic: In general, if changes in variable A cause changes in variable B, then the relative change in B is less than the relative change in A. In other words, large changes in variable A cause relatively smaller changes in variable B. An inelastic relationship between two variables is not a very responsive, or stretchable, relationship.

Joint venture: An activity undertaken by two or more entities in which each entity has some degree of control. Joint ventures are commonly undertaken by two or more business firms, allowing each firm to participate in the benefits of the venture without the loss of control that would come from a formal merger of the firms.

Law of demand: The inverse relationship between demand price and the quantity demanded, *ceteris paribus*. This fundamental economic principle indicates that as the price of a commodity decreases, the quantity of the commodity that buyers are able and willing to purchase in a given period of time, if other factors are held constant, increases.

Law of supply: The direct relationship between supply price and the quantity supplied, *ceteris paribus*. This fundamental economic principle indicates that as the price of a commodity increases, then the quantity of the commodity that sellers are able and willing to sell in a given period of time, if other factors are held constant, also increases.

Macroeconomics: The branch of economics that studies the entire economy, especially such topics as aggregate production, unemployment, inflation, and business cycles.

Market: The organized exchange of commodities (goods, services, or resources) between buyers and sellers within a specific geographic area and during a given period of time. Markets are the exchange between buyers who want a good—the demand side of the market; and the sellers who have it—the supply-side of the market. In essence, a buyer gives up money and gets a good, while a seller gives up a good and gets money. From a marketing context, to be a market, the following conditions must exist. The target consumers must have the ability to purchase the goods or services. They must have a need or desire to purchase. The target group must be willing to exchange something of value for the product. Finally, they must have the authority to make the purchase. If all these variables are present, a market exits.

Microeconomics: The branch of economics that studies the parts of the economy, especially such topics as markets, prices, industries, demand, and supply.

Monopolistic competition: A market structure characterized by a large number of small firms, similar but not identical products sold by all firms, relative freedom of entry into and exit out of the industry, and extensive knowledge of prices and technology. This is one of four basic market structures. The other three are perfect competition, monopoly, and oligopoly. Monopolistic competition approximates most of the characteristics of perfect competition, but falls short of reaching the ideal benchmark that is perfect competition.

Monopoly: A market structure characterized by a single seller of a unique product with no close substitutes. This is one of four basic market structures; the other three are perfect competition, oligopoly, and monopolistic competition. As the single seller of a unique good with no close substitutes, a monopoly firm essentially has no competition. The demand for a monopoly firm's output is *the* market demand. This gives the firm extensive market control—the ability to control the price and/or quantity of the good sold—making a monopoly firm a price maker. However, while a monopoly can control the market price, it cannot charge more than the maximum demand price that buyers are willing to pay.

Oligopoly: A market dominated by a small number of participants who are able to collectively exert control over supply and market prices.

Partnership: One of the three basic forms of business organization (the other two are corporation and proprietorship). A partnership is a business owned and operated more or less equally by two or more people. The owners and the business are legally considered one and the same. As such, each owner has unlimited liability, which means that an owner is held personally responsible for any and all of the business's debts, including those made by a partner.

Perfect competition: An ideal market structure characterized by a large number of small firms, identical products sold by all firms, freedom of entry into and exit out of the industry, and perfect knowledge of prices and technology. This is one of four basic market structures; the other three are monopoly, oligopoly, and monopolistic competition. Perfect competition is an idealized market structure that does not exist in the real world. For example, perfect competition efficiently allocates resources. While unrealistic, it does provide an excellent benchmark that can be used to analyze real world market structures.

Proprietorship: One of the three basic forms of business organization (the other two corporation and partnership). It is a business owned and operated by one person. The owner and the business are legally considered one and the same. As such, the owner gets any and all profit and has what is termed as unlimited liability. The owner is held personally responsible for any and all of the business's debts. The owner can lose personal property over and above the amount invested in the business itself. The majority of businesses in our economy are proprietorships, but because their size is limited by the resources of a single person, they tend to be relatively small.

S Corporation: A legal firm type that is officially structured as a corporation, especially with limited liability of the owners, but is able to avoid the double taxation of profits through the use of a special section of the Internal Revenue Service tax code (Chapter S). The profit of an S corporation is considered the income of its owners and is thus taxable only as individual income.

Scarcity: A pervasive condition of human existence that exists because society has unlimited wants and needs, but limited resources to be used for their satisfaction.

Supply: The willingness and ability to sell a range of quantities of a good at a range of prices during a given time period. Supply is one half of the market exchange process; the other is demand. This supply side of the market is directly connected to the limited resources dimension of the scarcity problem. Those who have ownership and control over resources (labor, capital, land, and entrepreneurship) use them to produce the goods and services that satisfy others' wants and needs. Ownership and control of resources is the ultimate source of supply.

Supply curve: A graphical representation of the relationship between the supply price and quantity supplied (that is, the law of supply), holding all *ceteris paribus* supply determinants constant.

Surplus: A condition of the market in which the quantity supplied is greater than the quantity demanded at the existing price. A surplus occasionally goes by the terms "excess supply" and "buyers' market." A surplus causes a decrease in the equilibrium price.

5.7 Information Science or Information Technology

The study, design, development, implementation, support, or management of computer-based information systems, particularly software applications and computer hardware.

LEXICON FOR INFORMATION SCIENCE OR INFORMATION TECHNOLOGY:

Access point: A transceiver in a wireless local area network that connects a wired local area network to wireless devices or that connects wireless devices to each other.

Compliance certificate: An official statement that something has passed all the necessary tests for the regulations.

Content management: The act of using a database system that allows large amounts of content to be entered, accessed, edited, and stored.

Cookie: A computer file containing information about a user that is sent to the central computer with each request. The server uses this information to customize data sent back to the user and to log the user's requests.

Database: A compendium of information on current and prospective users that usually includes demographic data as well as use data, volume, and content. For example, past-performance data can be kept in a database.

Database management: Includes data modeling, query languages database design, and transaction processing.

Decision support system (DSS): A decision support system is a systematic collection of data, techniques, and supporting software and hardware by which an organization gathers and interprets relevant information from business and the environment, and turns it into a basis for making management decisions. A DSS differs from a management information system in that it is designed to answer precise questions and "what if" questions.

Delphi technique: A frequently used method in futures research to gain consensus opinion among experts about likely future events through a series of questionnaires.

Deterministic models: These models include linear programming and geometric programming.

File shredders: Special computer programs used to destroy computer files beyond retrieval.

Firewall: Specialized software used to protect privacy and security of users of network connected computers by controlling inbound and outbound data traffic.

Forecasting models: In forecasting sales or other objectives, a variety of statistical models are used and available, offering insights otherwise difficult to obtain.

Information science: The technical, managerial, and policy issues associated with computer-based information systems in modern organization.

Information management: The applications of information science to the practical aspects of specifying, designing, implementing, and managing information systems.

Local area network (LAN): A system linking computers, terminals, and printers, within a restricted geographical area, which share the same stored information in the network memory.

Management information system: A system for gathering the financial, production, and other information that managers need to operate a business, especially a system that is computerized.

Network: A large number of people, organizations, or computers that work together as a system.

Observation: A method of data collection in which observers watch a particular situation and record the relevant facts, actions, and behaviors.

Programming: The data structures and algorithms supplied in programming solutions to problems.

Statistics: Tools including descriptive statistics, probability theory, probability and sampling distribution, inference estimation, and hypothesis testing.

Trojan horse: A special kind of malicious software (malware) that can carry out many unwanted actions after infecting a computer.

User group: A group of people who use a service or facility and come together to discuss how it can be improved.

Utility program: A computer program that performs routine activities such as searching, copying, and replacing files.

Wide area network (WAN): A network of terminals with links outside the local area by radio, satellite, and cable.

5.8 Leadership Skills

There are several ways to define leadership. Essentially, leadership inspires its followers to want to accomplish high goals in an honorable manner. Leadership qualities are typically not inborn but can be developed gradually through education, self-study, and experience—it is a continuous learning process.

As professionals, contract managers are expected to work together in teams of all sizes. If you are a team leader, you are expected to keep your team members engaged and focused. However, there will be many times when you will not be appointed as the formal team leader, but you are still expected to display leadership skills and contribute in a positive manner to influence the team in achieving its goals.

Many people make no distinction between management and leadership, and often confuse the characteristics of the terms. The following comparison presents some differences between the two competencies.

Management	Leadership
Doing things right	Doing the right things
Efficiency	Effectiveness
Speed	Direction
Bottom line (profits)	Top line (gross sales or revenue)
Methods	Purposes
Practices	Principles

Leadership and management are complementary skills. An organization will thrive with a balance of strong leadership and strong management. However, an imbalance of either skill can lead to misaligned systems and resources, thus producing suboptimal results.

LEXICON FOR LEADERSHIP SKILLS:

Business acumen: This is a keen understanding of what it takes for an organization to achieve its goals. It is the combination of business education, experience, on-the-job training, and expert mentoring across a diverse range of business topics including:

- Marketing and sales,

- Accounting and finance,

- Strategic planning and economic forecasting,

- Purchasing and supply chain management,

- Operations and project management, and

- Business law and contract management.

When the business acumen of leaders increases, they think more strategically and act within the bigger picture context of organizational success.

Coaching: This usually deals with enhancing specific skills and tactics. Coaching takes many forms. In a basic sense, it is a method of training, directing, or instructing a person or group of people to do a specific task, achieve a goal, or develop certain skills. The apprentices or protégés are supposed to come out looking like the master.

Communication: One of the most important skill areas one must master to achieve consistent success is communication. By successfully getting your message across, you convey your thoughts and ideas effectively. When not successful, the thoughts and ideas you convey do not necessarily reflect your own, causing a communications breakdown and creating roadblocks that stand in the way of your goals—both personally and professionally. Communication is only successful when both the sender and the receiver understand the same information as a result of the communication.

Decision-making: This is an essential leadership skill. If you can learn how to make timely, well-considered decisions, then you can lead your team to well-deserved success. If, however, you make consistently make poor decisions, your time as a leader will be brutally short.

Integrity: This is more than just honesty and living within the rules. Integrity includes congruence, humility, and courage.

- **Congruence:** To live in harmony with your deepest values and beliefs—you walk the talk.

- **Humility:** To stand firmly for principles, especially in the face of opposition. You are more concerned with what is right than being right.

- **Courage:** To act according to principles. You do the right thing, especially when it's hard to do.

Interpersonal relations: An association between two or more people that may range from fleeting to enduring. In a business context, this association is typically based on solidarity or regular business interactions to achieve a specific task or goal. Interpersonal relationships usually involve some level of interdependence. People in a relationship tend to influence each other, share their thoughts and feelings, and engage in activities together. Because of this interdependence, most things that change or impact one member of the relationship will have some level of impact on the other member.

Emotional intelligence (EI): The ability to understand and manage both your own emotions and those of the people around you. People with a high degree of emotional intelligence usually know what they're feeling, what it means, and how their emotions can affect other people. For leaders, having EI is essential for success. According to Daniel Goleman, an American psychologist who helped make the idea of EI popular, there are five main elements of emotional intelligence:

- Self-awareness,

- Self-regulation,

- Motivation,

- Empathy, and

- Social skills.

The more you, as a leader, manage each of these areas, the higher your emotional intelligence.

Ethical leadership: Ethical living—and leading—takes courage and conviction. It means doing the right thing, even when the right thing isn't popular or easy. But when you make decisions based on your core values, then you tell the world that you can't be bought—and you lead your team by example. Once you identify your organization's core values as well as your own, you can start to set the tone with your team and your organization. Actions always speak louder than words, so make sure you do as you would wish others to do. Ask yourself these questions:

- What standards of behavior are really important to my organization?

- What specific values do I admire in certain leaders? Do I identify with those values?

- Would I still live by those values, even if they put me at a competitive disadvantage?

Goal-setting: This is a powerful way of motivating people and of motivating yourself. Goal-setting theory is generally accepted as among the most valid and useful motivation theories in industrial and organizational psychology, human resource management, and organizational behavior. A useful way of making goals more powerful is to use the SMART mnemonic:

- Specific,

- Measurable,

- Attainable,

- Relevant, and

- Time-bound.

Mentoring: A developmental partnership through which one person shares knowledge, skills, information, and perspective to foster the personal and professional growth of someone else. An effective mentoring relationship occurs when both participants prosper.

Power: Leadership and power are closely linked. People tend to follow those who are powerful, and because others follow, the person with power leads. One of the most notable studies on power was conducted by social psychologists John French and Bertram Raven in 1959. They identified five bases of power:

- **Legitimate**: This comes from the belief that a person has the right to make demands, and expect compliance and obedience from others.

- **Reward**: This results from one person's ability to compensate another for compliance.

- **Expert**: This is based on a person's superior skill and knowledge.

- **Referent**: This is the result of a person's perceived attractiveness, worthiness, and right to respect from others.

- **Coercive**: This comes from the belief that a person can punish others for non-compliance.

Prioritization: This is the essential skill you need to make the very best use of your own efforts and those of your team. It's also a skill that you need to create calmness and space in your life so that you can focus your energy and attention on the things that really matter. It is particularly important when time is limited and demands are seemingly unlimited. It helps you to allocate your time where it is most needed and most wisely spent, freeing up you and your team from less important tasks that can be attended to later or be quietly dropped. With good prioritization (and careful management of deprioritized tasks) you can bring order to chaos, massively reduce stress, and move toward a successful conclusion. Without it, you'll flounder around, drowning in competing demands.

Problem-solving: Problem-solving is a key skill, and it's one that can make a huge difference to your career. At work, problems are at the center of what many people do every day. You're either solving a problem for a client (internal or external), supporting those who are solving problems, or discovering new problems to solve.

Team-building: The two most important factors in building and maintaining a successful, high-performing team are clear team goals and diversity. Leaders must have clear goals and expectations for the work groups before building the team. Having goals in place will improve communication within the group, increase commitment, and create harmony and a shared sense of responsibility. To accomplish these goals most effectively, a work team must have diverse personalities and skills. Different personality types balance the group dynamic and help with brainstorming. Some group members' strengths will compensate for other members' weaknesses. If these two factors are met, group synergy, which is the purpose of team-building, will be created. Group synergy occurs when the collective group effort is greater than the sum of the individual efforts.

Trust: The confidence born of the character and competence of a person or an organization. Successful leaders know how to build, extend, and restore trust. The opposite of trust is suspicion.

1. What is the systematic practice of identifying and reducing the threats that exist in the project?

   a. strategic management
   b. threat management
   c. quality management
   d. risk management

2. Most managerial functions can be described as planning, organizing, leading, and controlling. Which of the following statements describes the controlling function?

   a. Monitoring the progress of the project against the plan.
   b. Developing a detailed work breakdown structure
   c. Estimating the tasks to determine the required skills, effort, and equipment to do the job.
   d. Preparing contracts for vendors.

3. The work breakdown structure (WBS) breaks all the work of a project into separate tasks (or activities). There are two kinds of tasks on a WBS: summary tasks and work packages. Which of the following statements is true?

   a. By performing the summary tasks, you complete a work package.
   b. Both work packages and summary tasks are executed.
   c. By performing the work package tasks, you accomplish a summary task.
   d. Neither work packages nor summary tasks are executed.

4. The foundation of earned value analysis is a good work breakdown structure and a valid baseline. What does earned value analysis measure?

   a. the monetary value of work performed
   b. the actual cost of work scheduled
   c. the company's estimate for completion
   d. the performance measurement baseline

5. Schedule and budget development are required for day-to-day management. This statement is an example of which managerial function?

   a. organizing
   b. planning
   c. leading
   d. controlling

6. Maintaining a contingency and/or reserve in the project budget is known as

   a. risk management.
   b. budget management.
   c. strategic management.
   d. fiscal management.

7. The relationship between cost, schedule, and quality is also called the "triple constraint." When a manager decides to cut schedule and cost, what is the most likely result?

   a. risk increases
   b. sales increase
   c. cost decreases
   d. schedule improves

8. Delegating responsibility and authority by creating an environment where decision-making is at the lowest level possible defines which of the following leadership attributes?

   a. teamwork
   b. empowerment
   c. innovation
   d. respect

9. These are the fundamental, unchanging rules of conduct that govern all of your leadership actions.

a. values
b. standards
c. goals
d. objectives

10. Goals define success for the organization.
Goals that are well-defined should be
SMART. The acronym SMART stands for

a. Specific, Measurable, Attainable,
Relevant, and Timely
b. Serious, Metrics, Ambitious, Realistic,
and True
c. Simple, Manageable, Appropriate,
Resonant, and Tangible
d. Stretch, Meaningful, Agreeable,
Realistic, and Trackable

Answers and Explanations

1. What is the systematic practice of identifying and reducing the threats that exist in the project?

   a. strategic management
   b. threat management
   c. quality management
   d. (Correct) **risk management**

(Source: Verzuh, Eric. *The Portable MBA in Project Management.* © 2003. John Wiley & Sons.)

2. Most managerial functions can be described as planning, organizing, leading, and controlling. Which of the following statements describes the controlling function?

   a. (Correct) **Monitoring the progress of the project against the plan.**
   b. Developing a detailed work breakdown structure
   c. Estimating the tasks to determine the required skills, effort, and equipment to do the job.
   d. Preparing contracts for vendors.

(Source: Verzuh, Eric. *The Portable MBA in Project Management.* © 2003. John Wiley & Sons.)

3. The work breakdown structure (WBS) breaks all the work of a project into separate tasks (or activities). There are two kinds of tasks on a WBS: summary tasks and work packages. Which of the following statements is true?

   a. By performing the summary tasks, you complete a work package.
   b. Both work packages and summary tasks are executed.
   c. (Correct) **By performing the work package tasks, you accomplish a summary task.**
   d. Neither work packages nor summary tasks are executed.

(Source: Verzuh, Eric. *The Portable MBA in Project Management.* © 2003. John Wiley & Sons.)

4. The foundation of earned value analysis is a good work breakdown structure and a valid baseline. What does earned value analysis measure?

   a. (Correct) **the monetary value of work performed**
   b. the actual cost of work scheduled
   c. the company's estimate for completion
   d. the performance measurement baseline

(Source: Verzuh, Eric. *The Portable MBA in Project Management.* © 2003. John Wiley & Sons.)

5. Schedule and budget development are required for day-to-day management. This statement is an example of which managerial function?

   a. organizing
   b. (Correct) **planning**
   c. leading
   d. controlling

(Source: Verzuh, Eric. *The Portable MBA in Project Management.* © 2003. John Wiley & Sons.)

6. Maintaining a contingency and/or reserve in the project budget is known as

   a. (Correct) **risk management.**
   b. budget management.
   c. strategic management.
   d. fiscal management.

(Source: Verzuh, Eric. *The Portable MBA in Project Management.* © 2003. John Wiley & Sons.)

7. The relationship between cost, schedule, and quality is also called the "triple constraint." When a manager decides to cut schedule and cost, what is the most likely result?

a. (Correct) risk increases
b. sales increase
c. cost decreases
d. schedule improves

(Source: Verzuh, Eric. *The Portable MBA in Project Management.* © 2003. John Wiley & Sons.)

8. Delegating responsibility and authority by creating an environment where decision-making is at the lowest level possible defines which of the following leadership attributes?

    a. teamwork
    b. (Correct) empowerment
    c. innovation
    d. respect

(Source: Jacobs, Daniel M. *The Art of the Possible: Create an Organization with No Limitations.* (Federal Market Group: 2009)

9. These are the fundamental, unchanging rules of conduct that will govern all of your leadership actions.

    a. (Correct) values
    b. standards. *Standards are rules or principles that are used as a basis for judgment.*
    c. goals. *Goals and objectives are interchangeable and can be defined as results necessary to achieve your organization's mission. Goals define success for the organization.*
    d. objectives. *Goals and objectives are interchangeable and can be defined as results necessary to achieve your organization's mission. Goals define success for the organization.*

(Source: Jacobs, Daniel M. *The Art of the Possible: Create an Organization with No Limitations.* (Federal Market Group: 2009)

10. Goals define success for the organization. Goals that are well-defined should be SMART. The acronym SMART stands for:

    a. (Correct) Specific, Measurable, Attainable, Relevant, and Timely
    b. Serious, Metrics, Ambitious, Realistic, and True
    c. Simple, Manageable, Appropriate, Resonant, and Tangible
    d. Stretch, Meaningful, Agreeable, Realistic, and Trackable

(Source: Jacobs, Daniel M. *The Art of the Possible: Create an Organization with No Limitations.* (Federal Market Group: 2009)

These readings can be found in NCMA's online Research Articles Database. To access the database you must be an NCMA member. If you are not an NCMA member, you may be able to obtain equivalent readings by inserting relevant keywords into your web browser's search engine.

From NCMA's *Contract Management* magazine

Anderson, Kiel, *The Weapons School Approach: Preparing the Next Generation of Contract Management Professionals for "Battle"*, November 2010.
An unconventional strategy to improve DOD's contract management capability.

Anzelone, Rick and Jay McCulloc, *The 10 Worst Leadership Mistakes*, September 2010.
This list will show leaders how they can identify opportunities to improve their organizations and help them avoid fundamental business mistakes which could cost businesses huge lost profits.

Barber, Terry, *The Inspiration Factor: How to Revitalize Your Company Culture*, June 2010.
Many managers and organizations attempt to motivate their employees, rather than inspire them. While these terms are similar, their application in the workplace produces far different results.

Borchardt, John K., *Overcoming Barriers to Effective Decision-Making*, June 2010.
An examination of cognitive biases that cause us to make poor decisions.

Brown, Sara Elizabeth, *Where's Your Motivation? Stop Waiting and Go Get It Yourself*, December 2010.
Looking inward may be the key to unlocking the motivation essential to success in today's contracting environment.

Dodds, Michael A., *Professionalism in Contracting*, October 2010.
The Department of Defense has declared contracting as a professional career field, which is the right thing to do, but we as a contracting community must define those attributes that all of us should strive for and obtain if we are really going to be accepted as true professionals.

Hamilton, Carol-Ann, *The Power of Passionate Productivity*, October 2010.
Productivity is the direct result of passion in the workplace. Passion is the "special sauce" that turns the ingredients of an otherwise identical meal into a taste sensation!

Obermeyer, Andrew C., *Addressing the Shortage of Contract Specialists: Too Little, Too Late for Success?*, November 2010.
While the nation's political and executive leadership now recognize that sustained growth of the contracting workforce is necessary, it may be too little, too late given the pending retirement wave and the lack of attention to adequately measuring the size of the workforce necessary to conduct the nation's business.

Passwaters, Stacey, *When The Going Gets Tough...*, February 2011.
Making the most of challenges and growing our leadership skills in times of crisis.

Powell, Jonathan, *Leadership by Walking Around: 21st Century People Solutions for Software Problems*, May 2011.
"People solutions" to software problems is a misnomer. People are the only solution to software problems. A qualified team built on trust and engagement optimizes organizational productivity and can solve any software issue.

Reid, Tom, *Tactical and Strategic Contract Management*, August 2010.
Tactically, you manage the contract. Strategically, you manage the customer/supplier

relationship. Professionally, you manage yourself to balance the tactical and strategic aspects of contract management.

Sitler, Nicki, *Going the Distance: Taking the Lead amid Muddled Middle Management*, January 2011.
In a race, the first-place finisher isn't the only leader. Every "middle leader" carries the same powerful potential to shift and shape the experience and successes of those around them, provided they're willing to step up to the starting line and make a strong finish.

From NCMA's *Journal of Contract Management*

Jurich, James, *The Multisector Workforce Comes Full Circle*, September 2010, Volume 8, Issue 1.
This article examines the consequences of government policies on the multisector workforce and what this means for government procurement.

Nackman, Mark J., *The Aftermath of the Decision to Reduce the Defense Acquisition Workforce: Impacts, Difficulties Ahead, and Fixes*, September 2010, Volume 8, Issue 1.
The defense acquisition workforce reductions of the 1990s drove several unintended repercussions, spawning the next decade's series of acquisition policy reform issues. Now, as DOD stands poised to rebuild its acquisition workforce, it can find examples from the private sector to address recruiting and retention challenges.

Tonsil, Pauline V., *Human Capital Management: Succession Planning in the Federal Acquisition Workforce*, September 2010, Volume 8, Issue 1.
Succession planning will help develop future leaders in the acquisition workforce to effectively take over when the time comes for current leaders to exit their positions. Succession planning requires a sharp focus on the current and future workforce in order to develop initiatives to address the areas of recruitment, retention, and leadership development.

BIBLIOGRAPHY

Black, Henry Campbell, and Bryan A. Garner, *Black's Law Dictionary, Pocket Edition*, Fourth Edition. (West 2011).

Bova, Regina Mickells (revised by Margaret G. Rumbaugh). *Desktop Guide for Basic Contracting Terms, Sixth Edition* (NCMA 2006).

Cibinic, John, Jr., and Ralph C. Nash, Jr., *Formation of Government Contracts, Third Edition* (Wolters Kluwer 1998).

Cibinic, John, Jr., and Ralph C. Nash, Jr., *Administration of Government Contracts, Fourth Edition* (Wolters Kluwer 2006).

Federal Acquisition Regulation (FAR), U.S. Government Website. **http://farsite.hill. af.mil/**.

Fisher, Roger, William Ury, and Bruce Patton, *Getting to Yes, Second Edition* (Penguin Group 2011)

Jacobs, Daniel M., *The Art of the Possible: Create an Organization with No Limitations* (Federal Market Group 2009).

Keyes, W. Noel, and Steven W. Feldman, *Government Contracts in a Nutshell, Fifth Edition* (West 2011)

Norby, Marlis, Emmalyn Smith, and Ronald Smith. *Guide to the Contract Management Body of Knowledge (CMBOK), Second Edition* (NCMA 2004).

O'Connor, Terrence M., *Federal Procurement Ethics: The Complete Legal Guide* (Management Concepts 2009).

Remley, Catherine Z., and Robert A. Ludvik. *Annotated Guide to the Contract Management Body of Knowledge (CMBOK), Second Edition* (NCMA 2004).

Remley, Catherine Z. and Robert A. Ludvik, *Guide to the Contract Management Body of Knowledge (CMBOK), Third Edition* (NCMA 2011).

Rumbaugh, Margaret G., *Understanding Government Contract Source Selection* (Management Concepts 2010).

Uniform Commercial Code (UCC), Cornell University Law School Website, **www.law.cornell.edu/ucc.**

Verzuh, Eric., *The Portable MBA in Project Management* (John Wiley & Sons 2003).

INDEX

A